Languages and Publics

The Making of Authority

Edited by

Susan Gal and Kathryn A. Woolard

Routledge
Taylor & Francis Group

LONDON AND NEW YORK

First published 2001 by St. Jerome Publishing

Published 2014 by Routledge
2 Park Square, Milton Park, Abingdon, Oxon OX14 4RN
711 Third Avenue, New York, NY 10017, USA

*Routledge is an imprint of the Taylor & Francis Group,
an informa business*

ISBN 13: 978-1-900650-42-7 (pbk)
         978-1-900650-43-4 (hbk)

Cover design by
Steve Fieldhouse, Oldham, UK

Typeset by
Delta Typesetters, Cairo, Egypt

British Library Cataloguing in Publication Data
A catalogue record of this book is available from the British Library

Library of Congress Cataloging in Publication Data
Gal, Susan and Kathryn A Woolard.
Languages and Publics: The Making of Authority/Susan Gal and Kathryn
A. Woolard.
p. cm. (Encounters, ISSN 1471-0277)
Includes bibliographical references and index.
ISBN 1-900650-43-6 (hardback: alk. paper) –ISBN 1-900650-42-8 (pbk):
alk. paper)
1. Courtesy. 2. Sociolinguistics. I. Title. II. Encounters
(Manchester, England)
BJ1533.C9 E45 2001
177'.1–dc21
2001000426

Encounters

A new series on language and diversity
Edited by Jan Blommaert & Chris Bulcaen

Diversity has come to be recognized as one of the central concerns in our thinking about society, culture and politics. At the same time, it has proved one of the most difficult issues to deal with on the basis of established theories and methods, particularly in the social sciences. Studying diversity not only challenges widespread views of who we are and what we do in social life; it also challenges the theories, models and methods by means of which we proceed in studying diversity. Diversity exposes the boundaries and limitations of our theoretical models, in the same way it exposes our social and political organizations.

Encounters sets out to explore diversity *in* language, diversity *through* language and diversity *about* language. Diversity *in* language covers topics such as intercultural, gender, class or age-based variations in language and linguistic behaviour. Diversity *through* language refers to the way in which language and linguistic behaviour can contribute to the construction or negotiation of such sociocultural and political differences. And diversity *about* language has to do with the various ways in which language and diversity are being perceived, conceptualized and treated, in professional as well as in lay knowledge – thus including the reflexive and critical study of scientific approaches alongside the study of language politics and language ideologies. In all this, mixedness, creolization, crossover phenomena and heterogeneity are privileged areas of study. The series title, *Encounters*, is intended to encourage a relatively neutral but interested stance towards diversity, moving away from the all too obvious 'cultures-collide' perspective that is dominant within the social sciences. The target public of *Encounters* includes scholars and advanced students of linguistics, communication studies, anthropology, cultural studies, sociology, as well as students and scholars in neighbouring disciplines such as translation studies, gender studies, gay and lesbian studies, postcolonial studies.

Jan Blommaert is former Research Director of the IPrA Research Centre of the University of Antwerp and currently Professor of African linguistics at the University of Ghent. His publications include *Debating Diversity* (co-author, 1998), the *Handbook of Pragmatics* (co-editor, 1995-2003), *The Pragmatics of Intercultural and International Communication* (co-editor, 1991), and *Language Ideological Debates* (editor, 1999).

Chris Bulcaen studied African Philology and History (University of Ghent) and Cultural Studies (University of Lancaster), and has worked for the IPrA Research Centre in Antwerp, where he mainly did ethnographic and discourse-analytic research in the field of social work and immigration. He currently works for the Department of English at the University of Ghent and is co-editor of the *Handbook of Pragmatics* (1994-2003).

Contents

Foreword   *vii*

Susan GAL and Kathryn A. WOOLARD
1. Constructing Languages and Publics   1
    Authority and representation

Judith T. IRVINE
2. The Family Romance of Colonial Linguistics   13
    Gender and family in nineteenth-century
    representations of African languages

Susan GAL
3. Linguistic Theories and National Images in   30
    Nineteenth-century Hungary

Richard BAUMAN
4. Representing Native American Oral Narrative   46
    The textual practices of Henry Rowe Schoolcraft

Michael SILVERSTEIN
5. From the Meaning of Meaning to the Empires   69
    of the Mind
    Ogden's Orthological English

Jane H. HILL
6. Mock Spanish, Covert Racism and the (Leaky)   83
    Boundary between Public and Private Spheres

Joseph ERRINGTON
7. State Speech for Peripheral Publics in Java   103

Bambi B. SCHIEFFELIN
8. Creating Evidence   119
    Making sense of written words in Bosavi

Jacqueline URLA
9. Outlaw Language   141
    Creating alternative public spheres in Basque free radio

Benjamin LEE
10. Circulating the People   164

Notes on Contributors   182

Index   184

Foreword

This volume is based on a special issue of the journal *Pragmatics* on 'Constructing Languages and Publics' (Vol. 5, No. 2, 1995). All the articles have been updated, and in a few cases revised extensively, but the arguments they present have not changed fundamentally.

The history of this collection's development reaches even further back. The papers on which these chapters are based were first presented at the 92nd annual meeting of the American Anthropological Association (AAA), held in Washington D.C. in November 1993. Those presentations themselves had grown out of discussions in a working group sponsored by the Center for Transcultural Studies in Chicago. In turn, the working group had developed from the 1992 special issue of *Pragmatics* on 'Language Ideologies', which recently appeared in revised form as *Language Ideologies: Practice and Theory* (Schieffelin, Woolard and Kroskrity, OUP:1998).

The AAA sessions and *Pragmatics* issue on language ideologies also led in April 1994 to an Advanced Seminar on Language Ideology sponsored by the School of American Research (SAR) and organized by Paul Kroskrity, who also edited the resulting volume, *Regimes of Language* (Kroskrity (ed.), SAR:2000). As with the representation of languages, a branching tree image would not capture the development of these related intellectual efforts. Membership and discussions in the SAR seminar overlapped significantly with those of the working group at the Center for Transcultural Studies, and with the present volume.

This book is a product of these many intertwining conversations across years and places. Moreover, this entire web of interconnected activities developed from the interest in the relationships among language, political economy, and ideology that emerged in an earlier series of AAA sessions in the late 1980s. We owe many intellectual and personal debts to the colleagues who participated in these events over more than a decade, and we are only sorry that we cannot name them all here. We deeply appreciate the myriad ways in which they have influenced our thinking, advanced this enquiry, and contributed to the discussion represented in this volume.

We particularly thank the institutions that have supported these efforts to develop a new agenda for linguistic anthropology: the American Anthropological Association, the journal *Pragmatics* of the International Pragmatics Association, the Center for Transcultural Studies, and the School of American Research. We are grateful to the editors of this 'Encounters' series, Jan Blommaert and Chris Bulcaen, for their conviction that this work should reach a wider audience. Finally, many thanks to Kari Robinson for her assistance with earlier phases of the editorial work, and Andrew Gilbert for his help in this latest phase.

Susan Gal
Kit Woolard
December 2000

1. Constructing Languages and Publics
Authority and Representation

SUSAN GAL AND KATHRYN A. WOOLARD

1. Introduction

Cultural categories of communication, such as named languages, dialects, standards, speech communities and genres, are constructed out of the messy variability of spoken interaction. Such bounded and naturalized representations are the products of experts and expert knowledge as well as of more widely shared linguistic ideologies. These representations are enacted and reproduced in familiar linguistic practices: translation, the writing of grammars and dictionaries, the policing of correctness in national standards, the creation of linguistic and folklore collections or academies. The work of linguistic representation produces not only individualized speakers and hearers as the agents of communication, but also larger, imagined social groupings, including our focus here, publics. Such representational processes are crucial aspects of power, figuring among the means for establishing inequality, imposing social hierarchy, and mobilizing political action.

The essays in this collection investigate the public construction of languages, the linguistic construction of publics, and the relationship between these two processes. Using both historical and ethnographic approaches, they examine empirical cases ranging from small-scale societies to multiethnic empires, from Europe to Oceania to the Americas.

The immediate point of departure for these essays on the historical construction of languages and publics is the larger project of understanding language ideologies and the ways that they mediate between social structure and linguistic practices (Woolard 1998:3). In the simplest formulation, language ideologies are cultural conceptions of the nature, form, and purpose of language, and of communicative behaviour as an enactment of a collective order (Silverstein 1987; Rumsey 1990; Irvine 1989). These are phenomena that, under a variety of labels, linguistic

---

[1] We acknowledge in our own representational practice a contemporary obsession with language and power that may look as exotic, partial, and particular from another view as, say, the ubiquitous linkage made in the nineteenth century between religion and language (Olender 1992) now looks to us.

anthropologists and scholars in related fields have long studied. The recent reformulation of these as language ideology emphasizes the social positioning, partiality, and contestability of practical and discursive ideologies, as well as the way they reflexively (re)shape linguistic and social structures. (See Woolard and Schieffelin 1994; Gal and Irvine 1995; Schieffelin, Woolard and Kroskrity 1998; Blommaert 1999; Kroskrity 2000.)

The chapters gathered here explore two related questions: first, how different images of linguistic phenomena gain social credibility and political influence, both within the academic disciplines of language and in larger social fields; and second, the role of linguistic ideologies and practices in the making of political authority. We will take up these two themes in turn in this introduction, aiming to make explicit some of the questions, critiques, and arguments that underlie these concerns.

2. Authoritative representations of language

An ongoing project in the field of sociolinguistics is the critique of the concepts on which its growth in the 1960s was founded. For instance, the notion of speech community has come under scrutiny. Useful in theorizing the functional diversity of codes within linguistic repertoires, it has also directed attention to consensus and shared interpretations within a bounded social unit. Such a focus neglects processes of conflict, competition, exclusion, boundary-making, differentiation, and transgression, which are at the centre of current social scientific investigations of identity formation (Rickford 1986; Irvine 1987; Irvine and Gal 2000).

In the present collection, several chapters contribute to this critique of the analytical categories, sociolinguistic and more general, with which we work. They explore expert notions such as oral literature (Bauman) and genealogical relationship (Irvine) by locating their historical sources in discursive fields and particular social and political processes.

In examining the scholarly production of basic units of analysis such as the language family and folklore or oral literature, these chapters do for linguistic anthropology the reflexive task that has become familiar in the humanities and social sciences. Inspired in part by Foucault, but also by the history and sociology of science, scholars ask how – through what practices – their disciplines have constituted themselves and invented (not discovered) their objects of study. We follow this tradition by using 'representation' and 'constructing' in our title to signal a commitment to understanding scholarly categories less as aspects of some objective world than as ideologically loaded parts of culture and social life.

Not content to note that the categories of a discipline might work as cultural capital for its practitioners, these articles describe in detail the relationship between linguistic ideas and other cultural conceptions, e.g. about the individual, the psyche, sexuality, national provenance, or Christian morality. They attempt to specify, as well, the social location and historical context of the social actors who propose the different linguistic views. As Silverstein notes, however, the aim is not thereby to discredit such concepts, but rather to get a better sense of the way in which linguistic ideologies have real historical effects.[2] Thus, when Bauman shows the textual strategies and assumptions through which Henry Rowe Schoolcraft created a body of Chippewa folklore out of a series of oral interactions, he is not dismissing Schoolcraft. Rather, he sheds light on practices of entextualization that create an apparently unified *object* of study. These entextualizing practices are aspects of Schoolcraft's legacy that are still often taken for granted. Or, when Irvine shows that some nineteenth-century philological categorizations of African languages were entangled with assumptions about sexuality and family relations, she is not simply debunking the theory of genealogical relationships among languages. Rather, she shows how that theory, like all scholarly discourse, is comprehensible as a principled product of a historical moment. Similarly, Silverstein is not interested in presenting Ogden and Richards' project of Basic English as crackpot science. Instead, he wants to show how the popularity of the movement was made possible by the political structuring of applied science and language, not in the academy so much as in the public sphere.

The historical chapters in this volume share a number of other general strategies. Rather than a single conceptual schema characterizing an epoch, they each find within their historical period competing images of the aspects of language treated as focal. In other words, they attend to debates and discursive battles that reveal not only shared assumptions or presuppositions of the participants but also alternative commitments. Often, as in the chapters by Gal and Silverstein, the fights are between professionalizing students of language and those who will later be defined as amateurs. Thus, part of the battle has to do with the definition of legitimate enquiry. The chapters suggest that images of linguistic phenomena gain credibility when they create ties with other arguments about aspects of aesthetic or moral life. And, as Silverstein in particular argues,

---

[2] For a useful set of arguments showing that a constructivist stance towards knowledge does not necessarily imply a denial of reality, nor an embrace of relativism, see Levine (ed.) 1993.

representations of language phenomena gain social authority – in fact may only be thinkable – from the institutional locations from which their proponents speak.

Frequently, one position in such debates is subsequently established as natural, obvious, *objective*. That is, one characterization of language comes to be seen as emanating not from any particular social position but rather from the phenomenon itself. A careful recuperation and contextualization of such debates allows us to dislodge these later assumptions of naturalness. Showing the earlier positioning of a regime of representation that now seems simply to let nature speak for itself is especially important when, as often happens, the establishment of a natural phenomenon not only warrants a scholarly discipline but also authorizes political programmes.

We can illustrate with a brief, familiar example. By the end of the eighteenth century, and in contrast to well-established earlier views, languages were conceived in Western European thought as natural entities, out there to be discovered, the product of human nature, to be sure, but independent of individual voluntary acts, and therefore not the creation of any self-conscious human will or intervention (Taylor 1990). Exactly because they were understood to be prior to intentional human political activity, they could be called on to justify and legitimate political actions, such as the formation of nation-states. The Victorian linguist Max Müller commented that, "the science of language has been called in to settle some of the most perplexing social and political questions", acting "in favor of nations and languages against dynasties and treaties" (cited in Crowley 1989:67; see also Irvine, this volume).

As Daston and Galison (1992) have argued, our current notion of objectivity comprises a number of distinct ways in which what is seen as personal is systematically censored, denied, or extirpated from the project of scientific observation and analysis. The definition of a phenomenon as independent of human will, as in the example above, creates one kind of objectivity. Another kind depends on the attempt to escape from an individual or socially locatable perspective; it invokes a view from nowhere (Nagel 1986). This aperspectival objectivity, discussed in several of our chapters, is interestingly related to the category of the public.

3. Publics

We are interested in the category of the public as a language-based form of political legitimation. Discussion of publics has been reinvigorated in American social theory by the translation and republication of Habermas'

early work, *The Structural Transformation of the Public Sphere* ([1962]1989). Our aim here is not to add to the large literature of explication and criticism around this text (see, e.g. Landes 1988; Robbins 1990; Calhoun 1992). We note instead that very little of this commentary has been sociolinguistically or semiotically informed. How might a language-oriented perspective clarify ongoing debates, and how could we rework the notion of 'public' to advance our own understanding of linguistic ideologies?

In the present context, the category of public is perhaps best thought of as just one in a spectrum of forms of sociolinguistically created authority. One of the best-known forms is that described by Bourdieu for standard French, whose speakers' power is misrecognized insofar as it is perceived to be legitimately rooted in, rather than merely indexed by, their control of linguistic structures. Another is exemplary Javanese usage, which Errington reports here to be misrecognized as a quasi-natural attribute of elitehood. While these and many other examples of language ideology link socio-political systems to the formal structural properties of a communication code, Habermas' notion of public sphere valorizes a communication process. The Habermasian public is in part a form of verbal interaction; groups of private individuals gather to discuss matters of common political concern, bearing on state authority. Their debates are decided on the basis of reason rather than the relative status of the interactants. This is what Kant characterized approvingly as the "conversation of mixed companies, consisting not merely of scholars and subtle reasoners but also of business people or women [who have] besides storytelling and jesting [...] another entertainment, namely arguing" (cited in Calhoun 1992:2). The public opinion produced by such critical talk has authority by virtue of being construed as ruled by reason, openness, and political equality. It was conceived to be as free from the private status-given interests of the participants as from the coercive powers of the state and the economy.

Habermas presents this as a historically specific phenomenon, emerging not just as an ideology, but also as a set of institutions and everyday practices in the western Europe of the seventeenth and eighteenth centuries. For him, the category of the public is explicitly a product of an emerging bourgeois, urban society, based on an increased traffic in commodities and news, and spurred by early capitalist long-distance trade. The institutions that supported it included not only newspapers and the increasing use of print, but also coffeehouses, salons, and voluntary associations of innumerable kinds that provided the fora for reasoned debate. Clearly this is a different sense of public than that characteristic of the

ancient world or of feudal Europe, and it required a reconceptualization
of the private as the sphere for the formation of individuals. State and
society were understood as discrete entities set against each other, just as
private interest was set against the public opinion of a new category of
bourgeois citizens who did not fit into the feudal orders.

This portrait of the early bourgeois public sphere has been criticized
on numerous grounds. Not just a historical study, it is at least as much an
idealized and nostalgic image with which Habermas aims to criticize what
he considers a debasement of twentieth-century public discourse, overly
dependent on mass media and the culture industry. And there has been
much controversy since the work's initial publication about the actual historical processes involved. The institutional and ideological changes were
quite different in England, France, Germany, and the US, and the dating,
location, and even definition of the processes continue to be matters of
controversy. Many question whether egalitarian, politically significant,
public fora based on the rule of debate and reason ever existed anywhere.
Feminists have pointed out that eighteenth- and nineteenth-century public
fora were means of exclusion rather than of universal openness, and that
the discursive construction of the public – private split was enabled by its
association with a gender dichotomy that restricted women by definition
(Landes 1988; Fraser 1990). Finally, many scholars have suggested that
there have been, since as early as the seventeenth century, multiple
publics – proletarian, regional, religious – often in competition, contesting each other as well as the state.

But for our more modest purposes here, these criticisms only add to
the potential interest of the concept. Indeed, all the articles in this collection that deal with the construction of publics implicitly take one or another
of these critiques as their starting point.

First, many of them (see especially Gal, Lee, Hill, and Errington) observe a negative logic by which the public, as an ideological construct,
works to legitimate political action. One theme that has been developed in
Habermasian studies is that publics derive their authority from being in a
sense anonymous (most notably Warner 1990). They supposedly or potentially include everyone but abstract from each person's interest-bearing
and privately defined characteristics. By this reasoning, publics can represent everyone because they are no-one-in-particular. This disinterested,
disembodied public, a form of aperspectival objectivity, was constructed
against the personified and embodied legitimacy of the absolutist mon-
arch, whose authority was often enacted exactly through spectacle and
self-display.

However, many of the chapters here identify and explore an authority of authenticity (Hill, Errington, Gal, Bauman, Urla) that exists simultaneously with this authority of anonymity in the public sphere.[3] Although the projection of authenticity (in the sincere individual or the particularistic community) can oppose anonymity as a form of legitimation, it does not necessarily do so. The relationship is often far more complex. Strategic glimpses of authenticity may actually serve the authority of the impersonal, clinching the force of public discourse (see especially Hill and Errington for illustrations). Or, the voice-from-nowhere may be constructed as the most authentic of voices competing for recognition as the embodiment of a particular community (see Gal and Urla; cf. Bauman for a related process in the construction of oral literature).

Further, these articles assume that a public need not be a countable, face-to-face group. The critique of sociolinguistics discussed earlier has recognized the limitations and distortions that result from taking face-to-face communication as the prototype of all communication. To be sure, if we unpack central concepts such as speaker, hearer, and audience, recognizing their internal complexity, a focus on face-to-face interaction provides a subtle understanding of interpersonal power dynamics (see, e.g. Goffman 1979). But analyses based on the face-to-face model have had much less to say about the ways in which linguistic practices contribute to the reproduction and legitimation of hierarchy in larger social institutions, or about linkages between speech communities and broader political and economic organizations (see Gal 1989 for a review). Similarly, within this framework it has been difficult to analyze adequately the forms of mass-mediated communication that often connect disparate communities and that are increasingly of interest in social theory.

The chapters in this collection attempt to extend the notion of public in order to address some of these questions. Habermas himself attributed the disintegration of the public sphere to the advent of a mass-mediated culture industry, and he has been accused of mistakenly basing his later theory of communicative action on the face-to-face model of interaction. But we can follow Habermas's lead beyond his own confines, and examine versions of the public as folk notions about groupness, interest, and communication. Public at this level is a mobile concept, as is demonstrated by the different foci of the chapters here: for instance, a proto-public

---

[3] Bill Hanks highlighted this point in comments on the AAA session in which the papers on which this collection is based were first discussed. See also Fliegelman 1993 and Cmiel 1990 on this relationship in American history.

as a realm of discursive practices constituted by the state for communication with citizens (Errington); a leaky zone of discourse distinguished from the private, with little reference to the state (Hill); a reading public or audience as market (Bauman). This broader approach to publicity enables analyses of mass-mediated communication and encourages a re-thinking of speech community. The notion of public need not even rely on the idea of a concrete readership or spectatorship, but rather on the projection or imagination of groups or subjectivities in print or other mass media.

The process by which such projection occurs seems closely related to a very general semiotic property of language that is present as much in face-to-face as in other communication: the possibility of decontextualization and strategic recontextualization. Recontextualization of linguistic voices and genres can create images of continuity (and discontinuity) with times, places, and people not present in the immediate interaction. Goffman's (1979) notion of footing, Gumperz's (1982) contextualization cues, and Bakhtin's (1981) voicing all address this property. As Briggs and Bauman (1992) have pointed out, the gap between an earlier context and a recontextualization can be denied or highlighted, with different effects. Strategies that minimize intertextual gaps can contribute to constructions of history, authenticity, and community.

The impersonality, projection, and intertextuality discussed above are widely implicated in political authority and in the authoritative models of the language disciplines as well. For instance, Warner (1990) argues that the legitimacy of eighteenth-century American republicanism was based on the notion of disinterested individuals who could claim to represent the people because the decontextualized anonymity of print allowed them to be no-one-in-particular (routinely publishing unsigned or patently pseudonymous articles). In this volume, Benjamin Lee further develops this line of argument, semiotically analyzing a number of documents – including the American Declaration of Independence and Constitution – so as to draw out the implications of such an analysis for understanding new forms of subjectivity and new forms of legitimation. Other chapters show parallels in the ideology of language standardization. The standard language, usually best instantiated in print, defines (and legitimates) a political territory, sometimes precisely because it is not spoken by any actual group (Gal), and (as in the case of Indonesian) is "devoid of ethnic inflection" (Errington).

As another example, Anderson's ([1983]1991) notion of the nation as an imagined community plays on this same logic of non-face-to-face social groups defined through simultaneous readings as 'all of us'. The idea of the *Volk* originating in German philosophy and folklore studies

accomplishes the same thing: collections of tales whose authors were deliberately eliminated to produce the authentic folk who are everyone because no one. Indeed, as Hacking (1992) has argued, it was in the same late eighteenth-century German philosophy that language 'went public'. Hacking intends public not in the strictly Habermasian sense, but rather as part of the related belief that language is primarily for interpersonal communication, secondarily for internal thought, rather than vice versa. We might see Ogden's Orthological English, examined in Silverstein's paper, as an attempt to cure the pathologies of language (and thus of thought and social life) believed to derive from this primacy of social communication over thought in linguistic development.

Finally, the chapters allow us to consider the generalizability of a concept of a public.[4] Habermas located the emergence of an idea of a public in a particular period and set of conditions of European history. A public is not simply a collection of social structural features that result from a circumstance such as the introduction of print. Rather, it is in part an idea, a framing of such structures and practices that, while moveable, malleable, and borrowable, is hardly inevitable. This collection considers the dynamics that played a part in the production of publics under particular historical conditions, the extent to which they may be identifiable in other circumstances, and what their effects might be in such other settings. If we are to understand the ways in which the ideology of publics creates political authority, it is necessary to locate the phenomenon more precisely in institutions and histories.

As Schieffelin shows, the Kaluli cannot be said to think in terms of publics, in any of the forms discussed here. Yet they have experienced significant changes in forms of sociolinguistic authority, and the emergence of a new impersonal source of authoritative evidence, the book. (Schieffelin's paper is one of the few in this collection to examine closely the reflexive effect of linguistic ideologies of authority on formal linguistic structures.) Errington examines another public arena of discourse that is decidedly not Habermas's bourgeois public sphere, but rather a zone of state-to-citizen communication under construction by a post-colonial state. State-sponsored Indonesian linguistic strategies of objectivity reminiscent of the classic public are syncretically entwined with more traditional Javanese ways of indexing authority sociolinguistically.

Two chapters consider the possibility of alternative public spheres.

---

[4] Again, Bill Hanks raised this question of whether the production of publics can be detached from European historical conditions.

Although Irvine focuses on the construction of languages rather than of publics, she offers a passing glimpse of another possible version of the latter idea in Enlightenment France. In his quest for a universal society based on the ability to converse with fellow citizens of other continents, the early French anthropologist Degérando sketched a very different and more egalitarian basis for imagined community than the one that came to dominate. Degérando's vision nonetheless shared some key features of the public with the nation-based, state-bounded, exclusionary, and hierarchizing version that triumphed. Such an observation hints at interesting links between alternate constructions of the public and the alternative visions of family underpinning the varying models of African languages Irvine analyzes. A contemporary case of multiple publics is provided by Urla in her chapter on the Basque country. She identifies the linguistic strategies used by young people involved in alternative radio broadcasting, which is a self-conscious attempt to construct an alternative public sphere.

4. Conclusion

The chapters in this collection deploy two strategies to examine the links between the ideological construction of languages and the construction of publics. The first strategy focuses on the different social sources of authority for diverse definitions of language phenomena. The second strategy analyzes the ways in which particular linguistic practices and beliefs about languages buttress the legitimacy of specific political arrangements. Needless to say, the two are often related, and this recognition suggests a useful analytical technique that has been put to work here. Ideologies that present themselves as concerning language can be read as displacements or coded stories about political, religious, or scientific systems. In turn, ideologies that seem to be about religion, political theory, human subjectivity, or science can be reinterpreted as implicit entailments of language ideologies, or the precipitates of widespread linguistic practices (Lee 1993; Silverstein 2000). But in either of these analytic moves – to understand the creation of publics or the definition of languages – the phenomena under study must be located precisely in time, space, and everyday practice. The chapters gathered here contribute to that effort by examining in pragmatic detail some contrasting and limiting as well as exemplary cases of the construction of authority.

5. References

Anderson, Benedict ([1983]1991) *Imagined Communities: Reflections on the origin and spread of nationalism*, London: Verso.

Bakhtin, M.M. (1981) *The Dialogic Imagination*, Trans. Caryl Emerson and Michael Holquist. Austin: University of Texas Press.

Blommaert, Jan (ed) (1999) *Language Ideological Debates*, Berlin: Mouton de Gruyter.

Briggs, C.L. and R. Bauman (1992) 'Genre, Intertextuality and Social Power', *Journal of Linguistic Anthropology* 2(2):131-172.

Calhoun, Craig (ed) (1992) *Habermas and the Public Sphere*, Cambridge MA: MIT Press.

Cmiel, Kenneth (1990) *Democratic Eloquence: The fight over popular speech in nineteenth-century America*, Berkeley: University of California Press.

Crowley, Tony (1989) *Standard English and the Politics of Language*, Urbana: University of Illinois Press.

Daston, L. and P. Galison (1992) 'The Image of Objectivity', *Representations* 40:81-128.

Fraser, Nancy (1990) 'Rethinking the Public Sphere: A contribution to the critique of actually existing democracy', *Social Text* 2:56-80.

Fliegelman, Jay (1993) *Declaring Independence: Jefferson, natural language, and the culture of performance*, Stanford: Stanford University Press.

Gal, Susan (1989) 'Language and Political Economy', *Annual Review of Anthropology* 18:345-367.

Gal, Susan and J.T. Irvine (1995) 'The Boundaries of Languages and Disciplines: How ideologies construct difference', *Social Research* 62(4): 967-1002.

Goffman, Erving (1979) 'Footing', *Semiotica* 5:1-29.

Gumperz, John J. (1982) *Discourse Strategies*, Cambridge: Cambridge University Press.

Habermas, Jürgen ([1962]1989) *The Structural Transformation of the Public Sphere*, trans. Thomas Burger. Cambridge, MA: MIT Press.

Hacking, Ian (1992) 'How, Why, When, and Where did Language go Public?', *Common Knowledge* 1(2):74-91.

Irvine, Judith T. (1989) 'When Talk isn't Cheap', *American Ethnologist* 16(2):248-267.

------ (1987) 'Domains of Description in the Ethnography of Speaking: A retrospective on the speech community' in R. Bauman, J.T. Irvine and S.U. Philips (eds) *Performance, Speech Community and Genre*, Chicago: Center for Psychosocial Studies, 13-24.

Irvine, J.T. and S. Gal (2000) 'Language Ideology and Linguistic Differentiation' in Paul Kroskrity (ed) *Regimes of Language: Ideologies, polities, and iden-tities*, Santa Fe: School of American Research Press, 35-84.

Kroskrity, Paul (ed) (2000) *Regimes of Language: Ideologies, polities, and identities*, Sante Fe: School of American Research Press.

Landes, Joan (1988) *Women and the Public Sphere in the Age of the French Revolution*, Ithaca: Cornell University Press.

Lee, Benjamin (1993) 'Metalanguages and Subjectivities', in J. Lucy (ed) *Reflexive Language: Reported speech and metapragmatics*, Cambridge: Cambridge University Press, 365-392.

Levine, George (ed) (1993) *Realism and Representation: Essays on the problem of realism in relation to science, literature and culture*, Madison: University of Wisconsin Press.

Nagel, Thomas (1986) *The View from Nowhere*, New York: Oxford University Press.

Olender, Maurice (1992) *The Languages of Paradise: Race, religion and philology in the nineteenth century*, Cambridge MA: Harvard University Press.

Rickford, John (1986) 'The Need for New Approaches to Social Class Analysis in Sociolinguistics', *Language in Communication* 6(3):215-221.

Robbins, Bruce (ed) (1990) 'The Phantom Public Sphere', Special section of *Social Text* 25/26.

Rumsey, Alan (1990) 'Wording, Meaning and Linguistic Ideology', *American Anthropologist* 92(2):346-361.

Schieffelin, Bambi, Kathryn A. Woolard and Paul Kroskrity (eds) (1998) *Language Ideologies: Practice and theory*, New York: Oxford University Press.

Silverstein, Michael (2000) 'Whorfianism and the Linguistic Imagination of Nationality', in Paul Kroskrity (ed) *Regimes of Language: Ideologies, polities, and identities*, Santa Fe: School of American Research Press, 85-138.

Silverstein, Michael (1987) 'Monoglot "Standard" in America', *Working Paper Proceedings of Center for Psychosocial Studies*, 13, Chicago: Center for Transcultural Studies.

Taylor, Talbot (1990) 'Which is to be Master? Institutionalization of authority in the science of language', in J.E. Joseph and T.J. Taylor (eds) *Ideologies of Language*, New York: Routledge, 9-26.

Warner, Michael (1990) *Letters of the Republic*, Cambridge MA: Harvard University Press.

Woolard, Kathryn A. (1998) 'Introduction: language ideology as a field of inquiry', in Bambi Schieffelin, Kathryn Woolard and Paul Kroskrity (eds) *Language Ideologies: Practice and theory,* New York: Oxford University Press, 3-47.

Woolard, Kathryn A. and Bambi B. Schieffelin (1994) 'Language Ideology', *Annual Review of Anthropology* 23:55-82.

2. The Family Romance of Colonial Linguistics
Gender and Family in Nineteenth-Century Representations of African Languages[1]

JUDITH T. IRVINE

1. Introduction

My title comes from Lynn Hunt's (1992) book, *The Family Romance of the French Revolution*, a study of family and gender imagery in the discourse of Revolutionary politics. Hunt, in turn, takes the title from Freud, whose 1909 essay on 'family romances' describes the fantasies of neurotic children who create imaginary families more satisfying than their own.[2] But unlike Freud, Hunt is not directly concerned with the psychic dynamics of individuals. Instead, she explores the ways people collectively imagine the operation of power through their understanding of family relations (Hunt 1992:8). Ideas about family, she suggests, provide a pre-analytical model for understanding political experience – a model invested with emotional significance.

If ideas about family have a compelling imaginative force, its impact is not limited to 1789, or to political discourse in the narrow sense.[3] In this paper I consider family and gender discourse in a somewhat later time, a more distant political context, and a type of text that is less obviously about politics. The time is the nineteenth century, the context is the European colonial expansion into sub-Saharan Africa, and the texts are linguistic analyses. Ideologically based images of family relations pervade these texts, from descriptions of grammatical structure to discussions of language classification. And while these texts purport to be about languages,

[1] Research funding was provided through a Fellowship from the National Endowment for the Humanities. Thanks are also due to my fellow participants at the Center for Transcultural Studies' Working Group, and especially to Kathryn Woolard and Susan Gal for their comments on earlier versions.
[2] Freud's notion here is that the imaginary family is more emotionally satisfying, and more socially important, than the child's actual parents are. See Freud ([1909]1959), 'Family romances'.
[3] Hunt actually examines many kinds of texts, especially works of fiction, in addition to texts with explicitly political themes.

they also construct claims about those languages' speakers, their social and moral condition, and their place in a global community.

Family imagery as a way of understanding relationships among languages dates back before the nineteenth century, but the family idiom took on new significance and substance during that period, with the rise of comparative philology and rigorous methods for determining what we still call genealogical relationships among languages. Yet, comparative philology got its start and its rigor with analyses of Indo-European and Semitic languages. What of the languages of the colonized or soon-to-be-colonized peoples? How did the idea of 'family' apply to them? And how was it affected by the complex of ideas about race, sexuality, difference, and domination inherent in the construction of colonial power? Nineteenth-century studies of African languages not only employed family and gender imagery, but also gave special prominence to grammatical gender, as if this were the essence of language structure and the touchstone of language-family relationships. For many linguists of the time, how a language handled gender distinctions was the basis of its relationship to other languages, and (moreover) revealed its speakers' mentality and socio-political condition. Many linguists, too, appealed to (supposed) ethnographic facts about African family life to explain linguistic structures and relationships.

Among the authors who discussed African languages in this period (roughly, 1789-1914) there are groups whose views and political agendas sharply contrast. An early group, heirs to the French Revolution and the linguistic philosophy of the *Idéologues* Condillac and Destutt de Tracy, saw in African languages the proof of human equality and fraternity. Other scholars, later in the century, saw in African languages evidence of the importance of sexual and racial hierarchies. This was the view that predominated during the period of the 'scramble for Africa' and the establishment of European colonial empires.

2. The rise and fall of linguistic 'fraternity'

My first group of scholars shares the vocabulary and imagery of the 1789 Revolution. Instead of a king who embodied the state and was endowed with a father's authority over his subjects, Revolutionary political writers had emphasized the fraternal, thus equal, relations among citizens (rather than subjects). Fraternity was envisioned universally, as the appropriate relationship among men, whatever their nation or condition. (Among all these brothers not much was said about sisters, but never mind that for now.)

It was in these terms – of universal fraternity and the relations among citizens – that our first group of writers described exotic peoples and languages. We may start with Joseph-Marie Degérando, a charter member of the *Société des Observateurs de l'Homme* ('Society of Observers of Man'), founded in 1799 to promote anthropological study. Commissioned to draft recommendations on anthropological observation for a French expedition of round-the-world exploration, Degérando wrote a memoir outlining the principles and techniques of fieldwork, *The Observation of Savage Peoples*. Placing primary emphasis on the study of language, he remarked:

> It is a delusion to suppose that one can properly observe a people whom one cannot understand and with whom one cannot converse. The first means to the proper knowledge of the Savages, is to become after a fashion like one of them; and it is by learning their language that we shall become *their fellow citizens* (Degérando [1800]1969:70; my emphasis).

Describing such people as "our brothers" (ibid.:104), "former kinsmen separated by long exile from the rest of the common family" (ibid.:63), Degérando urged travellers setting out for distant shores, "You who, led by a generous devotion [...] will soon come near their lonely huts, go before them as the representatives of all humanity! Give them in that name the vow of brotherly alliance!" (ibid.:64). In contrast to Columbus, who "put in the New World only greedy conquerors" (ibid.:103), the French expedition was to inaugurate global community: "What more moving plan than that of re-establishing in such a way the august ties of universal society?" (ibid.:63).

The particular expedition to which Degérando's memoir was directed was not a great success, nor did the *Société des Observateurs de l'Homme* survive long. Still, its members and its recommendations remained influential. Among those fieldworkers who might be said to have applied Degérando's recommendations in Africa are two authors of works on languages of Senegal: Jean Dard and Jacques-François Roger. Both were French civil servants who spent several years in Senegal, learned Wolof, and published accounts of that language in the 1820s.[4] Both argued against

---

[4] These scholars were connected in more ways than just their shared intellectual orientation. Degérando was a member of the administrative council of the *Société pour l'instruction élémentaire*, sponsors of Dard's work in Senegal and of the publication of his Wolof Grammar. See Dard 1826:xxxi. Roger, a lawyer by training who ran an agricultural station in Senegal and then became governor of the

colour prejudice and saw their linguistic analyses as evidence of Africans' fundamental rationality, potential for civilization, and membership in a common human fraternity. As Dard wrote in the introduction to his Wolof grammar:

> Not wishing to found either a particular people or a sect closed within narrow boundaries, the divine legislator has reproduced in human nature that universal fraternity which results from the identity of its origin, its forms and its destination. [...] As for [the blacks'] sensitivity, their mutual affection, their intellectual capacity, their humanity, these are at least as great and as true as among whites; and whoever has lived as observer among the Africans can affirm that, if nature has put some difference among men in the colour of the skin, she has put none in the expression of those natural sentiments which she has placed in the heart of all beings belonging to the great family of humankind (Dard 1826:ii, vii).[5]

Roger, also arguing against colour prejudice, which he termed a "strange malady of the European spirit", a sort of "moral leprosy" (Roger 1828:193, 194), similarly found in the structure of the Wolof language evidence of "that common nature, that fraternity" of all humanity, which is endowed with the same intelligence, sensibility, and mental "organization" (Roger 1829:104-105).

Actually, in certain respects Roger finds the Wolof language more 'rational' than French. In particular, Wolof's lack of a grammatical gender system based on sex distinctions is, in his view, a definite advantage. Wolof is not prevented from expressing maleness and femaleness when the referents of nouns actually have these characteristics; it expresses sex differences lexically or periphrastically. So it avoids the arbitrariness and irrationality Roger finds in French, which makes all nouns masculine or feminine no matter what they refer to, "despite reason" (ibid.:30). Like earlier *Idéologues* such as Destutt de Tracy (1817:73, 170-171), Roger apparently thought languages would be better off without grammatical gender systems.

---

colony (1821-1826), came from the same region of France as Dard and had some of the same patrons in Paris. Roger's stay in Saint-Louis-du-Sénégal overlapped with Dard's for a time (1819-1820).

[5] My translation. For further discussion of Dard's work and his educational programme for indigenous literacy in African languages, see Irvine 1993. With African-language literacy, Dard argued, Africans "could in very little time take their place among the civilized nations" (Dard 1826:xi).

For these authors, then, the prevailing type of family imagery is that of the bond of brothers, a bond extending over the entire human species, Degérando's "universal society". The aim of linguistic research is to help bring Africans and other non-Europeans into a global public arena, where participation in discourse is accessible to all as fellow citizens, regardless of race, lineage, or gender (although, in contrast to the explicit discussion of race, social gender is seldom mentioned, perhaps because the image of fraternity implied a social circle inhabited only by men).[6] In language, grammatical gender systems – i.e., sex–gender systems, the only type these authors recognize – are consequently of little interest, if not deplorable. And the only family mentioned as relevant to language is the common, human family. Genealogical relationships among languages, such as would imply long-term historical separation and structural distinctiveness, are not the focus of attention.

It is unlikely that these scholars were simply ignorant of the rising schools of German and Danish philology that emphasized historical particulars and relationships. Rather, comparative philology did not appeal to them. And it was not yet clear whether its goals and methods could apply outside the Indo-European and Semitic families. Some of the most prominent philologists believed they could not. Friedrich Schlegel, for example, distinguished between 'organic' and 'inorganic' languages, a contrast he equated with inflecting and non-inflecting languages, thus between Indo-European and Semitic on the one hand, and the rest of the world's languages on the other. Only the organic languages had families (Schlegel [1808]1977:51-54).

For Schlegel the problem was that non-inflecting languages lacked the grammatical structures on which comparison could be based. So, for reasons partly methodological but partly deriving from the languages' essential nature, they could not be grouped genealogically. For other linguists the problem was the lack of written traditions that would fix a language's structures against uncontrolled variation and change. Descent, in such circumstances, was untraceable and virtually irrelevant. Even as late as 1866 Max Müller could write, "Genealogical classification [...] applies properly only to [...] languages in which grammatical growth has been arrested, through the influence of literary cultivation" (Müller 1866:174; see also 338-339).

---

[6] Many recent works have commented on the gendered construction of Revolutionary discourse and the difficulties this presented for female participation in a supposedly universalistic public sphere. See, for example, Landes 1988; Outram 1987; Fraser 1990.

Actually, Max Müller attributes the supposed lack of language families in Africa not only to the lack of written traditions but also to a supposed
lack of public meetings and, especially, lack of the kind of family life in
which children would be properly supervised by their parents. He quotes
the South African missionary Robert Moffatt's description of Kalahari
desert villagers:

> With the isolated villagers of the desert it is far otherwise; they have
> no such meetings; they are compelled to traverse the wilds, often to a
> great distance from their native village. On such occasions fathers
> and mothers, and all who can bear a burden, often set out for weeks at
> a time, and leave their children to the care of two or three infirm old
> people. The infant progeny, some of whom are beginning to lisp, while
> others can just master a whole sentence, and those still further ad-
> vanced, romping and playing together, the children of nature, through
> their livelong day, *become habituated to a language of their own.* [...]
> Thus, from this infant Babel, proceeds a dialect of a host of mongrel
> words and phrases, joined together without rule, and *in the course of
> one generation the entire character of the language is changed* (Müller
> 1866:64-65; original emphasis).

"Such is the life of language in a state of nature", concludes Müller.

In contrast, then, to the *Idéologues'* picture of human fraternity and
the universal society, a later generation of linguists revised the imagery of
family so as to exclude the possibility of African participation on an equal
plane. For some authors, such as Müller, Africans simply had no language
families as Europeans did, and perhaps not much in the way of domestic
units or public fora either. For other authors of the period, family imagery
did apply to Africans but with an emphasis on hierarchies of sex and age,
so that black Africans were described as if they were women or children
in relation to white European adult men.

This family-hierarchy imagery was perhaps most sweepingly applied
to Africans by the Saint-Simonian sociologist and linguist Gustave
d'Eichthal. Though claiming allegiance to the ideals of the 1789 Revolution (d'Eichthal and Urbain 1839:20), d'Eichthal argued that it was
unrealistic to discuss the human species in the abstract, as earlier scholars
had done, without full consideration of gender and generation:

> Every individual is *male* or *female*, and successively *son* and *father*
> [...] Thus [...] it was necessary to locate, in the development of the
> human species, not an *individual* life, but a *family* life; it was necessary

to say who, in this family, is the *male*, and who the *female*, who the *older generation*, and who the *newer generation* (d'Eichthal 1839:8; my translation; original emphasis).

In this "definitive constitution of the human family" – now cast in an explicitly gendered and developmental framework – the two races "form a *couple*, in which the white race represents the *male*, and the black race the *female*, and thus humanity reproduces the law of duality of the sexes which all organic beings obey" (ibid.:14-15).

Feminized imagery for black Africans and their languages persisted in European writing throughout the colonial period (and later too), as many recent works have noted. The same imagery appears in linguistic descriptions, as when (for example) Hausa is described as "impregnated with Semitism" (La Grasserie 1898:618). Though the idea that whole languages might be gendered and enter into sexual relations with one another was only a metaphor, some authors seem to have taken it quite seriously.[7] We shall see more of this metaphor later; for the moment, let us just note how altered is the imagined family of the 'family romance'. What was once envisioned as a band of brothers has become a reproductive couple, seen as a model for racial hierarchy.

3. Comparative philology: language families and racial hierarchy

Max Müller was one of the last scholars to exclude African languages from the arena of genealogical investigation. By the later decades of the nineteenth century, most linguists accepted that African languages could be grouped into families, and that the analytic methods of German comparative philology could be extended to them. By this time, enough African languages had been documented to make the possibility of systematically classifying them not utterly unrealistic. And as Darwinian ideas of evolution entered linguistics (see, e.g. Schleicher [1863]1869; Bleek 1869; Haeckel 1869), philological efforts could be linked with evolutionary hierarchies. The linguists of this period, then, took a global view of language classification, grouping African languages into families which, in turn, could be linked to a worldwide genealogy of humankind.

---

[7] Such views were consistent with the extreme organicism advocated by Schleicher ([1863]1869:20-21), for whom "languages are organisms of nature [...] subject to that series of phenomena which we embrace under the name of 'life'".

At this time a crucial question, paralleling the contemporaneous debate on the monogenesis or polygenesis of the human species – that is, whether the species had a single evolutionary origin or many – was whether the human acquisition of language came before or after racial differentiation. Some linguists, such as the Viennese scholar Friedrich Müller,[8] emphasized the priority of racial differentiation: only within a race could one speak of language families. Since races could (in his view, following Haeckel) be distinguished by hair form, Friedrich Müller's (1877-1888) four-volume survey of the world's language families is organized according to whether their speakers' hair is woolly, straight, curly, or tufted. Further racial distinctions apply within these groups, before language families – the narrowest level of a racially-defined classification – appear.

Friedrich Müller's classification, though widely cited, was vulnerable to criticism on its racial basis. As some of his contemporaries pointed out, hair form might not be the crucial marker of racial difference. Moreover, European history itself showed that language was not invariably linked with blood. Arguments such as these characterized another, competing line of Africanist linguistic scholarship, more sympathetic to the monogenesist position. These scholars recognized larger language-family groupings than Müller had, and they claimed to establish family groupings on the basis of linguistic facts alone. Although the groupings were still accorded a racial interpretation, supposedly this was only subsequent to the linguistic analysis. Among these linguists, three who produced general works on languages of the African continent were most important: Wilhelm Bleek, Richard Lepsius, and Carl Meinhof. The work of Meinhof in particular continued to be influential in African linguistics until after the Second World War.

The object of identifying language families, as Lepsius put it, was that:

> from the relations of separate languages, or groups of languages, to one another, we may discover the original and more or less intimate affinity of the nations themselves [...Thus] will the chaos of the nations in [Africa], Asia, America, and Polynesia, be gradually resolved into order, by the aid of linguistic science (Lepsius 1863:24).[9]

---

[8] The Viennese scholar Friedrich Müller is not to be confused with F. Max Müller, cited earlier. F. Max, though of German origin, spent most of his professional life at Oxford, and is the better remembered of the two today.

[9] In the full text of this passage, Lepsius discussed some specific aspects of the classification of African languages and nations before continuing, "in like manner will the chaos of the nations in Asia, [... etc.]".

To discover language-family relations, Bleek and Lepsius paid particular attention to noun morphology, comparing gender systems based on sex-distinction with systems of noun classification based on other principles, and with languages lacking noun classification systems altogether.[10] Africa has languages of all three types.[11] (See Appendix 1 for a typology, locating languages referred to by Bleek within larger groupings recognized today.)

Figure 1 shows Bleek's classification, with its identification of a "sexual stock" or "sex-denoting family" as against other language families.

For these nineteenth-century scholars, the essence of the language family, evidently, was how the language represented family in its grammatical structure. Lepsius claimed that the basis of noun classification lay in "the discrimination and separation of the sexes and their [...] moral ordering and opposition in marriage, whereupon the family is based" (Lepsius 1880:xxvi). Thus domestic family and language family depended on the same psychological principles, namely, those underlying a people's management of sexual relations. Bleek ([1867]1869:xvi) noted that languages that threw all humans into the same grammatical class (like the Bantu languages, with their 'person' class), and languages that showed no noun class distinctions at all, were associated on the social side with polygamy. Apparently, for Bleek and Lepsius, both Africans and their languages failed to identify the male–female monogamous couple as the proper basis of family life.[12]

Further consequences were to be found in religion and science. The speakers of languages lacking sex–gender systems and, instead, distinguishing a 'person' or 'human' class from non-human noun classes, were

---

[10] Bleek's 1851 dissertation seems to have been the first work to move beyond the Bantu languages in developing any systematic, large-scale genealogical classification of African languages on structural criteria, rather than regional criteria or wild etymologizing.

[11] The classifications proposed by Bleek and by Lepsius were sometimes genealogical, sometimes typological. Since their arguments for genealogical relationship depended above all on structural criteria, the difference between the two kinds of classification is not always obvious. Yet both authors recognized that genealogical classifications ultimately depend on establishing sound correspondences as well. Bleek, in particular, took some initial steps in this direction and towards reconstructing protolanguages (see Bleek 1862).

[12] See also La Grasserie (1904:227), who argued that the languages of uncivilized societies lack sex–gender systems "precisely because of that extreme easiness of sexual relations" among their speakers. Under conditions of promiscuity, the "sexualist idea" would be of relatively little power or interest.

Typological

1. Genderless languages

2. Prefix-pronominal
   languages

3. Suffix-pronominal
   languages

Genealogical

Bushman
languages

Lingua Mater   [other "archaic"
                       languages]

                       Great African
                       family

Bantu   Nilotic   West African
family   branch   branch

                                    Gor
                                    family:

         Masai,   Twi,   Fula,
         etc.   Bullom,   Wolof,
                    Temne,   Ga
                    etc.

"Sexual stock" (1851) /
"Sex-denoting family" (1871)

                Northern family

Hottentot   Indogermanic Semito-African   Coptic

                                    Galla,   Berber
                                    Hausa

                         Semitic

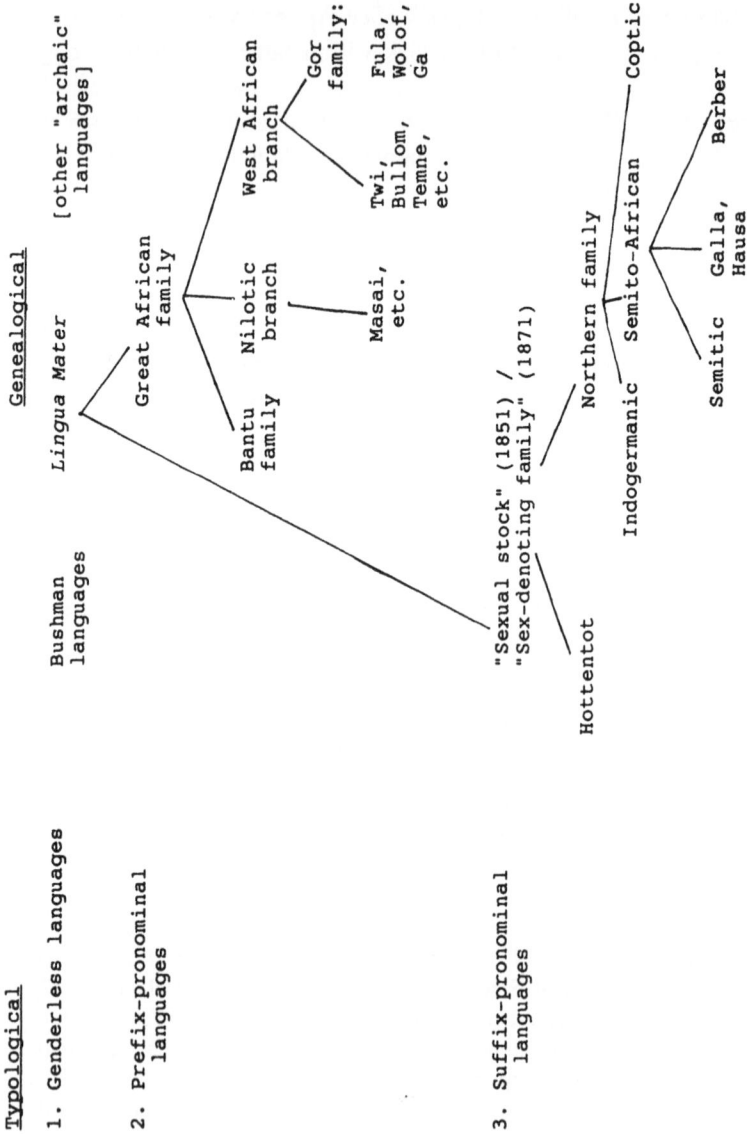

Figure 1: Bleek's (1871) classification

preoccupied with the hostility of the non-human environment, according to Lepsius (1880:xxii). For protection they looked to their deceased ancestors, whom they worshipped. Moreover, in a polygamous family, worship of the male ancestor merely extended the children's and grandchildren's customary attitude towards him beyond the grave, Bleek argued ([1867]1869:xvi). In contrast:

> [t]he nations speaking Sex-denoting languages are distinguished by a higher poetical conception, by which human agency is transferred to other beings, and even to inanimate things, in consequence of which their personification takes place, forming the origin of almost all mythological legends. This faculty is not developed in the Kafir [i.e. Bantu-speakers'] mind, because not suggested by the forms of their language (Bleek [1867]1869:ix-x).[13]

Other scholars extended this argument to economics and politics, especially after 1880 – also the period in which the European countries extended their political domination of the African continent. For some linguists, the basis of grammatical gender lay in distinctions of force and domination: masculine gender was associated with power, independence, and control; feminine gender with subordination, dependence, and passivity (see, e.g. Byrne 1892:9; La Grasserie 1898:613, 1904:241, and discussion in Royen 1929). Languages lacking sex–gender systems – such as most sub-Saharan African languages – revealed, to these scholars, a mentality not yet able to recognize social hierarchy or assert independence.

For Carl Meinhof, writing in 1915 (1915:146-148), sex–gender systems evolved from noun classification systems distinguishing humans from non-human referents. The change was due to the marriage practices of patriarchal warrior tribes, where the exchange of women for cattle resulted in transferring women from the 'person' class to a 'thing' class, the origin of the feminine gender. These warrior cattle-herders, speaking languages Meinhof classified as "Hamitic", were also (he supposed) the source of political hierarchy in Africa, through their putative conquest of darker-skinned peoples speaking "Sudanese" (or "Nigritic") languages.

Thus Meinhof interpreted African linguistic genealogies, as he constructed them, in terms of a construction of racial essences and racial history. Gender was not only a crucial aspect of grammatical structure

---

[13] Note that Bleek did not invent the notion that grammatical gender systems based on sex distinctions involved a superior and 'poetic' imagination. That idea goes back to Humboldt, Grimm, and Herder. See discussion in Royen (1929).

revealing these essences, but it also entered at the metaphorical level, contrasting 'feminine' Sudanese with 'masculine' Hamites. These metaphorically gendered languages might even mate and produce offspring. Meinhof described the Bantu language family, which has noun classes but not sex-based grammatical gender, as "a mixed language, such as I might say, [sprang] from a Hamitic father and a Nigritic mother" (Meinhof 1910-1911:164-165; see Figure 2 for Meinhof's classification scheme). Actually, Meinhof's text slides between suggesting metaphorical matings of languages and suggesting actual matings of their speakers, as giving rise to the mixed-language result.

The myth of the conquering Hamites proved an enduring representation of African history throughout the colonial period. Because Meinhof had earlier earned a considerable reputation for his painstaking work within Bantu linguistics, his 1912 book *Die Sprachen der Hamiten* lent to the Hamitic myth the weight of linguistic science. In that work, to which was appended an essay on Hamitic racial characteristics, he discussed at length the linguistic features that supposedly constituted the Hamitic language family. I say 'supposedly' constituted, and I call the Hamitic hypothesis a myth, not only because of its racial, political, and gender fantasies but also because the linguistic features detailed by Meinhof do not in fact support his "Hamitic" grouping at all. Although there were linguists who pointed out this difficulty (such as Edward Sapir, reviewing Meinhof's book in 1913), and many linguists who disagreed with the assignment of particular languages to the "Hamitic" group, the hypothesis did not really die until attacked by Greenberg in the 1950s – if even then. (See Appendix 2 for Greenberg's 1963 classification.)

4. Conclusion

We have seen that early colonial representations of African languages, and of Africans via linguistic evidence, were thoroughly entangled with ideologies of family relationships and of gender, racial, and political hierarchies. The tangle is particularly evident where genealogical classifications are concerned. There, Europeans came to represent Africans in terms especially of the management of sexual and family relations. And those linguists who openly disagreed with the views of Bleek or Meinhof, such as William Dwight Whitney (1873) and Edward Sapir (1913), were not primarily interested in African languages, and so provided no specific alternatives.

Of course I do not mean to suggest that historical relationships among languages should not be investigated, or that the idiom of 'family' and

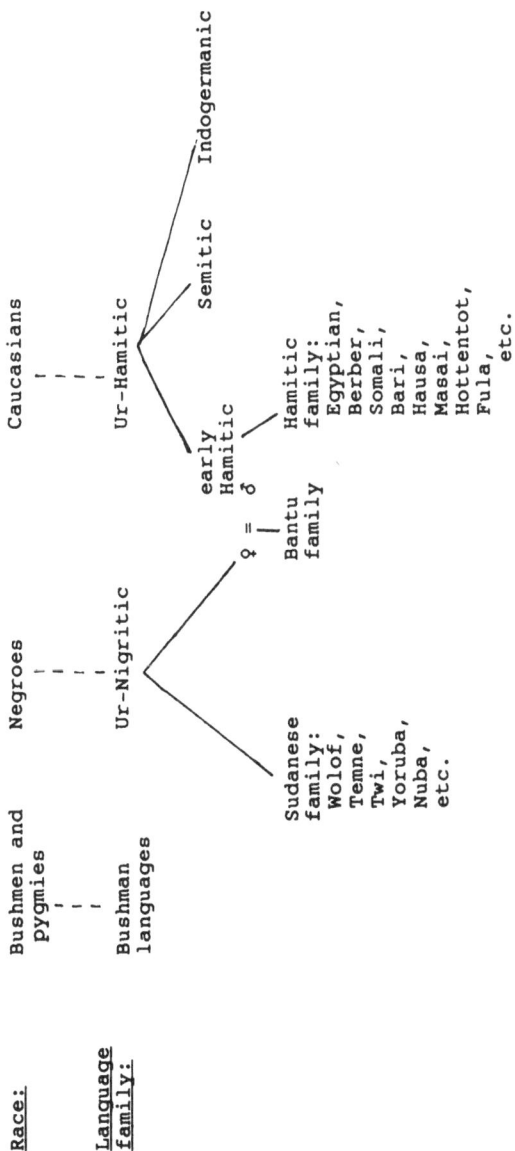

Figure 2: Meinhof's (1910-1911) classification

'descent' cannot be useful in linguistics. But, as Henry Hoenigswald (1990:122) has pointed out, it is not the only idiom one might have chosen. It is neither inevitable nor exactly suited to the case, although it was once thought to be so.[14] Instead, like any metaphor it carries baggage, extra implications about languages and about their speakers – such as whether those speakers share a common interest; whether they are co-participants in some global community; and whether their participation is (as some of the authors discussed here would have it) inevitably differentiated according to some hierarchical principle.

Such connotations may be particularly powerful if, as Hunt's book suggests, family relations are a model invested with special emotional significance. It is not just 'family' as the term might be defined analytically, but family romances – imaginative constructions based on ideologies of gender and politics – that have dominated the representation of linguistic relationships, and, thereby, the representation of discursive communities.

Appendix 1

Outline Typology of Noun Morphology in African Languages
Languages having grammatical gender systems involving sex distinctions:
    Indo-European languages
    Semitic languages (now recognized as a branch of Afro–Asiatic)
    Other Afro–Asiatic languages (e.g. Hausa, Somali, Galla, Berber)
    Some Nilo–Saharan languages (e.g. Maasai, Bari)
    Nama Khoi ('Hottentot')
Languages having noun classification systems based on other principles:
    Atlantic languages: Fula, Wolof, Temne, Bullom, etc.
    Voltaic languages
    Bantu languages and some other Benue–Congo languages
Languages having vestigial or no noun classification systems:
    Kwa languages (including Ga, Twi)
    Yoruba (usually no longer included in Kwa)

---

[14] See, for example, the following statement by E.A. Freeman (1877:723), concerning the languages of "the great Aryan family": "... we cannot avoid [...] the use of language which implies that the strictly family relation, the relation of community of blood, is at the root of the whole matter. We cannot help talking about the family and its branches, about parents, children, brothers, sisters, cousins. The nomenclature of natural kindred exactly fits the case; it fits it so exactly that no other nomenclature could enable us to set forth the case with any clearness".

Mande languages
Other Nilo–Saharan languages

Appendix 2

Greenberg's (1963) Classification of African Languages
(Some portions of this classification have been questioned and revised, but most of the well-accepted changes involve internal divisions and subgroupings of the four major language families. Languages referred to in this paper are given below.)

    I. Khoisan: includes Khoi ('Hottentot') languages and 'Bushman' languages. Some linguists now dispute the unity of this family.
    II. Nilo–Saharan: includes Maasai, Nuba languages, Bari, etc.
    III. Congo–Kordofanian: the main branch (Niger–Congo) includes:
        A. Atlantic: includes Fula, Wolof, Temne, Bullom, etc.
        B. Mande
        C. Voltaic
        D. Kwa: includes Twi, Ga, etc., and Yoruba (later excluded)
        E. Benue–Congo: includes Bantu languages
        F. Adamawa–Eastern
    IV. Afro–Asiatic
        A. Semitic
        B. Egyptian
        C. Berber
        D. Cushitic: includes Somali, Galla, etc.
        E. Chadic: includes Hausa

References

Bleek, Wilhelm (1871) 'The Concord, the Origin of Pronouns, and the Formation of Classes or Genders of Nouns', *Journal of the Anthropological Institute* Vol. I, Appendix VIII/8: Proceedings of the Ethnological Society, lxiv-lxxxix.

------ (1869) *A Comparative Grammar of South African Languages*, Vol. II/2: *The Concord*, London: Trübner.

------ ([1867]1869) *On the Origin of Language*, ed. E. Haeckel; trans. Thomas Davidson. New York: L.W. Schmidt. (First published 1867 as *Über den Ursprung der Sprache*.)

------ (1862) *A Comparative Grammar of South African Languages*, Vol. I/1: *Phonology*, London: Trübner.

------ (1855) 'On the Languages of Western and Southern Africa', *Transactions of the Philological Society* for 1855, 40-50.

------ (1851) *De nominum generibus: Linguarum africae australis, copticae, semiticarum aliarumque sexualium*, Bonn: Karl George.

Byrne, James (1892) *General Principles of the Structure of Language*, 2nd ed. London: Kegan Paul, Trench, Trübner.

Dard, Jean (1826) *Grammaire wolofe*, Paris: Imprimerie royale.

Degérando, Joseph-Marie ([1800]1969) *The Observation of Savage Peoples*, trans. F.C.T. Moore. Berkeley and Los Angeles: University of California Press. (First published 1800 as *Considérations sur les méthodes à suivre dans l'observation des peuples sauvages*.)

Destutt de Tracy, Antoine-Louis-Claude (1817) *Elémens d'idéologie*, Vol. II/2: *Grammaire*, 2nd ed. Paris: Courcier.

Eichthal, Gustave d' and Ismail Urbain (1839) *Lettres sur la race noire et la race blanche*, Paris: Paulin.

Fraser, Nancy (1990) 'Rethinking the Public Sphere: A contribution to the critique of actually existing democracy', *Social Text* 2:56-80.

Freeman, Edward Augustus (1877) 'Race and Language', *Contemporary Review* 29:711-741.

Freud, Sigmund ([1909]1959) 'Family Romances', *The Standard Edition of the Complete Psychological Works of Sigmund Freud*, trans. James Strachey. London: Hogarth. Vol II/2:238-239.

Greenberg, Joseph (1963) 'The Languages of Africa', *International Journal of American Linguistics* 29(1):Part II.

Haeckel, Ernst (1869) 'Editor's Preface', in W. Bleek *A Comparative Grammar of South African Languages*, London: Trübner:iii-viii.

Hoenigswald, Henry (1990) 'Descent, Perfection and the Comparative Method since Leibniz', in T. de Mauro and L. Formigari (eds) *Leibniz, Humboldt, and the Origins of Comparativism*, Amsterdam: Benjamins,119-132.

Hunt, Lynn (1992) *The Family Romance of the French Revolution*, Berkeley & Los Angeles: University of California Press.

Irvine, Judith T. (1993) 'Mastering African Languages: The politics of linguistics in nineteenth-century Senegal', in Dan Segal and Richard Handler (eds) *Nations, Colonies and Metropoles*, *Social Analysis* No. 33:27-46.

La Grasserie, Raoul de (1904) 'De l'expression de l'idée de sexualité dans le langage', *Revue philosophique de la France et de l'étranger* 58:225-46.

------ (1898) 'La catégorie psychologique de la classification révélée par le langage', *Revue philosophique de la France et de l'étranger* 45:594-624.

Landes, Joan (1988) *Women and the Public Sphere in the Age of the French Revolution*, Ithaca: Cornell University Press.

Lepsius, Carl Richard (1863) *Standard Alphabet for Reducing Unwritten Languages and Foreign Graphic Systems to a Uniform Orthography in European Letters*, 2nd ed. London: Williams & Norgate; Berlin: W. Hertz.

------ (1880) *Nubische Grammatik mit einer Einleitung über die Völker und Sprachen Afrika's*, Berlin: W. Hertz.

Meinhof, Carl (1915) *An Introduction to the Study of African Languages*, trans. Alice Werner. London: J. M. Dent.

Meinhof, Carl (1912) *Die Sprachen der Hamiten*, Hamburg: Friederichsen.

------ (1910-1911) 'Sudansprachen und Hamitensprachen', *Zeitschrift für Kolonialsprachen* 1:161-166.

Müller, Friedrich (1877-1888) *Grundriss der Sprachwissenschaft*, Vienna: Alfred Hölder.

Müller, F. Max (1866) *Lectures on the Science of Language Delivered at the Royal Institution of Great Britain in April, May and June 1866*, 2nd ed. rev. New York: Scribner.

Outram, Dorinda (1987) 'Le langage mâle de la vertu: Women and the discourse of the French Revolution', in Peter Burke and Roy Porter (eds) *The Social History of Language*, Cambridge: Cambridge University Press, 120-135.

Roger, Jacques-François (1829) *Recherches philosophiques sur la langue ouolofe, suivies d'un vocabulaire abrégé français-ouolof*, Paris: Dondey-Dupré.

------ (1828) *Fables sénégalaises, recueillies de l'ouolof, et mises en vers français*, Paris: Nepveu.

Royen, Gerlach (1929) *Die nominalen Klassifikations-Systeme in den Sprachen der Erde*, Vienna: Anthropos.

Sapir, Edward (1913) 'Review of Carl Meinhof, "Die Sprachen der Hamiten", *Current Anthropological Literature* 2:21-27.

Schlegel, Friedrich ([1808]1977) *Über die Sprache und die Weisheit der Indier*, ed. S. Timpanaro. Amsterdam: Benjamins.

Schleicher, August ([1863]1869) *Darwinism Tested by the Science of Language*, trans. Alexander Bikkers. London: John Camden Hotten. (First published 1863 as *Die Darwinsche Theorie und die Sprachwissenschaft*.)

Whitney, William Dwight (1873) 'Dr. Bleek and the Simious Theory of Language', *Oriental and Linguistic Studies*, New York: Scribner, Armstrong & Co., 292-297.

3. Linguistic Theories and National Images in Nineteenth-Century Hungary[1]

SUSAN GAL

1. Introduction

Johann Gottfried Herder published the following comment in his 1791 work *Ideen zur Philosophie der Geschichte der Menschheit*:

> as for the Hungarians or Magyars, squeezed between Slavs, Germans, Vlachs and other peoples, they are now the smallest part of their country's population and in centuries to come even their language will probably be lost.[2]

The remark forms a single subordinate clause in a four-volume work; Herder had little more to say about Hungarians. Yet in Hungary Herder is popularly recognized not so much for the philological and philosophical contributions that make him renowned in the west, but rather for this prophecy of language loss. Throughout the nineteenth century, Hungarian writers repeatedly argued with the prophecy, trying to vitiate it through linguistic and educational reform. Its influence on Hungarian thinking about language continued into the twentieth century. In 1979 a book entitled *Herder arnyékában* ('In Herder's shadow') appeared in a popular paperback series and warned yet again of the dangers of language death.

The difference in magnitude between Herder's brief, offhand remark and the extended, complex Hungarian response accurately reflects the power disparity between regions and between scholarly traditions. So does the fact that the influence of western scholars on eastern European thinkers has been studied more thoroughly than eastern views about the west. Like writers on colonial discourse who have shifted attention away from the European centre, I propose to reverse the usual perspective, viewing German and English thinkers on language from a distinctly peripheral –

---

[1] Many thanks to Kit Woolard for her stimulating questions, and to Bill Hanks for his comments at the AAA symposium.
[2] My translation from Pukánszky (1921), who cites this passage and carefully describes the few paragraphs Herder devoted to the Hungarian language and people, tracing the reception and influence of this part of Herder's work on Hungarian scholarship and literary life in the nineteenth century.

that is Hungarian – point of view. Accordingly, I focus not on the familiar orientalist project of the metropole building its vision of itself by constructing a devalued, homogeneous and changeless 'other', but rather on what some of the changing and diverse objects of western European scrutiny did with these ideas.

The analogy with colonial discourse is not entirely farfetched. Much of eastern Europe can be considered among western Europe's first dependencies, territories that were increasingly harnessed to provide agricultural products, lucrative investment opportunities and labour for the Prussian state and the Habsburg Empire. As was the case in many overseas colonies, elites of eastern Europe were in constant contact with German, French, and English scholarship during the eighteenth and nineteenth centuries; indeed, Hungarian, Romanian, and Slavic elites helped create many of the reigning ideas about 'east' and 'west.' Sometimes they did this in an effort to form their own 'eastern' or 'Asian' identities in opposition to 'Europe.' At other times they argued for their own 'Europeanness' and thus for political and military support from western powers for various internal projects, or to guard their frontiers against invaders from further east. This dichotomous discourse about 'Europe/ Asia' or 'east/west' has worked for centuries as an elaborate fractal distinction, a linguistic shifter of identity (Gal 1991). Ideas about languages and about linguistic difference played a central role in shaping and justifying the moral and aesthetic qualities that were attributed to 'east' and 'west' by scholarly as well as popular audiences (Gal and Irvine 1995; Irvine and Gal 2000).

To explore the logic, social context, and effects of such ideas about language, I focus on two well-known linguistic debates that preoccupied literate Hungarians between 1870 and 1890. The first took up the origins and genetic relationships of the Hungarian language. The second concerned the ways in which the language should be modernized, expanded and reformed to meet the needs of an increasingly urban and capitalist society. The two debates, while contemporaneous and equally discussed in Hungarian historiography, are rarely treated together. Yet the participants wrote for the same few journals and were involved in close collegial, familial, or mentoring relationships. Those best known for their contribution in one discussion occasionally also commented on the other.[3] I suggest

---

[3] For biographical information as well as evidence on friendship links between the linguists of the period, see Pinter (1934), who provides much more straightforward information, especially on religious and ethnic background, than works produced during the state-socialist period.

that the links between the two debates become clear if we view them not only as advancing scholarly arguments about specific linguistic problems but, in addition, as engaging alternate images of nationhood and of 'national publics'. In justifying their views and rendering them compelling, linguists made claims to various forms of authority, especially that of natural science. Hence the debates were also part of the social process that established linguistic expertise as disinterested, scientific knowledge which could be relied upon to provide the ostensibly neutral, factual basis for defining social and political units.

Both debates drew on ideas about the nature of language and its relation to social life that were developed earlier in German, French, and English writings. By reworking these ideas and inscribing them in everyday practices, Hungarian linguists and writers were changing the structure of the Hungarian language, along with its popular image. In this process, they created *external* boundaries defining the place of 'Hungarian' *vis-à-vis* the rest of the world. They also formed *internal* boundaries defining the social groups that would become the taken-for-granted 'public' or 'people' who spoke Hungarian in what came to be seen as the best way. The question of internal boundaries was particularly salient for the Kingdom of Hungary in the late nineteenth century because it was a linguistically heterogeneous polity with large populations that spoke German, Slavic, Romanian, and Greek, among other languages. Its unifying ideology, shared in earlier eras by the populations speaking these diverse languages, was loyalty to the Crown of St Stephen. But this form of political unity was being actively challenged during the nineteenth century by nationalisms imagined in ethnolinguistic terms. Accordingly, the Hungarian state encouraged 'magyarization' and some segments of the urban population responded with alacrity. Both kinds of boundaries were thus matters of interest not only to linguists and politicians; they were vital as well to publishers, literati, journalists, government administrators and to the socially mobile urban populations for whom such 'language experts' created new identities through new forms of mass media and education.

In analyzing these nineteenth-century arguments, I draw on the concept of 'public' understood as an ideological construct that is dependent on technologies such as print, which highlight the potential of language for recontextualization and thus emphasize and exploit the inevitable gap between speakers and their utterances. A public in this view is not an empirically countable audience, nor even a notion of readership understood on analogy with face-to-face interaction. Rather, it is a logic for the legitimation of political power that gets its authority from supposedly including 'everyone'. This notion of a public has been identified in a number of forms in studies of post-absolutist Europe and North America. Building on Habermas' early work on European publics, Warner (1990) argues that the legitimacy of eighteenth-century American republicanism was based on the idea of disinterested individuals who, because the anonymity of print allowed them to be no-one-in-particular, could claim to represent the 'people'. Anderson's ([1983]1991) notion of an 'imagined community' plays on this same conception of a non-face-to-face social group identified through simultaneous reading as everyone-because-no-one-in-particular. The related idea of the *Volk* as defined by their oral traditions has the same logic: collections of tales whose individual authors were deliberately effaced thereby forming the authentic, anonymous rural voice that is 'everyone' because no one. In nineteenth-century Hungary, arguments about the national language worked in just this way to create the image of a political unit defined and legitimated through a standard language supposedly linked to no particular group. Linguists argued that correct speech need not be modelled on a social class or stratum, that it could be derived from the language's inherent laws. These laws, in turn, would be discovered through the disinterested expertise of linguistic science.

2. External boundaries

By the middle of the nineteenth century, the earlier influence of Herder in Hungary was outstripped by the ideas of the Victorian scholar, Max Müller. Müller's *Lectures on the science of language*, delivered to the Royal Society in the 1860s, argued for the view that linguistics is a natural science, and languages are organisms of the natural world. In Lecture Eight he proposed a hierarchy of language types – isolating, agglutinating, inflecting – linked to cultures of increasing complexity. The simplest of the types was the category of isolating languages, in which grammatical relations were not signalled by suffixation at all but by the ordering of elements. In agglutinating languages, by contrast, suffixes were added but without altering the roots. The languages of this group, exemplified by what Müller called the 'Turanian' language family of Central Asia, were spoken by nomadic hordes whose forms of life made them unsuited to state-making. The third and highest evolutionary category included the Semitic and Aryan languages which were characterized by inflection, so that the root was systematically changed by affixation to signal grammatical relations. In Müller's scheme these were the languages of high civilizations.

Müller's lectures were reviewed in Hungary soon after their publication and, unusually for contemporary linguistic works, were translated into Hungarian by the 1870s. This interest was not entirely scientific, but owing in part to political considerations. Müller had far-flung political contacts and significant international influence as a philosopher, linguist, and orientalist with a professorship at Oxford. In 1874 he was President of the Orientalist Congress; his researches on eastern languages were sometimes undertaken at the behest of the British government, and often funded by the East India Company. Though of German origin, he wrote in English and was regularly translated into several other European languages. Most importantly, he had discussed Magyar directly, placing it among the Turanian family of languages, whose speakers were categorized as unfit for state-making. Such news came at a bad time for Hungarian elites, who were just embarking on yet another effort at political independence, trying to undo the effects of their defeat in the 1848 revolution against Habsburg rule.

In addition, Müller's work arrived in the midst of a long-standing debate among Hungarian nobility and literati about the origins of their language and its linguistic relations. The idea of genetic relationship was well established in theory, but methods for determining it were far from fixed at this time. On the issue of Hungarian provenance one could find apparently contradictory opinions even within the work of a single author. The view that Hungarian was related to Hebrew or Sumerian was sustained alongside other theories: that it was related to Persian, Chinese, Hun, or Tatar, or without any relatives at all, and older than Sanskrit and Hebrew (Láncz 1987:93-4). The relationship with Finnish and Estonian that later became (and remains) the accepted orthodoxy had also been written about for centuries, inside as well as outside Hungary. However, in contrast to the other hypotheses which had ardent supporters, this view was not widely embraced. On the contrary, despite increasing information from scientific expeditions to the Scandinavian countries, inner Asia, and northern Siberia, all pointing to the existence of a Finno–Ugric language group in which Hungarian could be considered part of the Ugric branch, disputes about this matter continued well into the twentieth century and received not only scholarly but also much popular attention. At the end of the nineteenth century, the question occupied the picture magazines as well as the political and cultural weeklies of Budapest.

By the 1880s, the arguments were sharper and the possibilities had narrowed: champions of the Finno–Ugric relation faced off against those arguing for a link to Turkish. There was linguistic evidence for both positions. Much depended on how one defined genetic relationship, and well-trained linguists could be found on both sides. Nevertheless, subsequent accounts of this debate, dubbed the 'Ugric–Turkish War', have cast the Finno–Ugric camp as the exponents of truth and scholarly progress, matched against obfuscating myth-makers. It would be more accurate, however, to read this as a later construction, a history written by the institutional victors (Békés 1991). The Finno–Ugric side regularly appealed to the authority of scientific expertise by arguing about methodological issues: the proper application of the comparative method, the importance of eliminating loan words before making judgements about genetic relation, the centrality of affixation and regular sound change (Pusztay 1977). They accused their opponents of amateurism and romanticism. The other side defended its view with alternate sources of evidence, painstakingly documenting the indisputable and widespread presence of Turkic lexical elements in Hungarian vocabulary.

But for the general reading public in the cities, the linguistic details mattered much less. Taking advantage of economic niches created by turn-of-the-century capitalist expansion, these urban migrants were forming new middle strata. Encouraged by government policies as well as their own mobility, they were looking for ways to be Magyar, as they abandoned their multilingual pasts. What proved to be crucial for them were the very different images of the 'Magyar' offered by these contrasting linguistic histories. Both histories acknowledged the 'Asian' as opposed to 'European' provenance of Hungarian. Both relied on the metaphor of 'family' and 'relatedness', but had contrasting political implications. One set of linguists, in the name of science and thus a higher Europeanness, accepted the politically less attractive family relation with the simplest of North-Central Asian societies. They wrote about the Hungarian kinship with Voguls, Samoyeds, and Ostyaks, small fishing communities of the upper Volga, living in 'primitive' conditions in the wilds of Siberia. The supporters of the Turkish connection, in contrast, fed the popular appetite for Turkic imperial exoticism. They relied on a widespread sympathy for the empire of the Ottoman Turks that supported Hungary against Pan-Slavism, and that had given refuge to Lajos Kossuth (leader of the 1848 revolution) when he was fleeing from Habsburg persecution.

Those linguists and literary men who rejected the Finno–Ugric hypothesis later summarized their view in the contemptuous motto *halszagú atyafiság*, 'a kinship connection that smells of fish'. For instance, the linguist Gábor Szarvas, in remembering his early years as a provincial gymnasium teacher, tells how he had refused to read the journal that published evidence of the Finno–Ugric connection on the grounds that: "We don't need a science that smells of fish" (Szarvas 1893:441). He had preferred to see the Magyars as descended from the conquering hordes of the Asian steppe. This more heroic view was well represented in a popular handbook of Hungarian literature that saw six printings and was long used in schools. Opening with a chapter entitled "From the banks of the Volga: A few ancient characteristics of the Magyar soul", it pictures a single "eagle-eyed horseman" in "leopard-skin with Persian sword" calmly scanning the horizon, awaiting his enemy. "If only a few of them come, he will fight them alone; if they come in a horde he will call the others" (Beöthy 1896:15-16). This fitted well with national ideals and self-conceptions of proud, calm, mysterious horsemen, born warriors and leaders.

The most prolific writer embracing the image of Turkish kinship was Ármin Vámbéry, a Turkologist, eccentric journalist and political correspondent who in his travels in Asia had managed to gain notoriety by penetrating several sacred Islamic sites in disguise. He frequently reported to the British press on conditions in Turkey and the Caucasus. On several lecture tours to England in the course of the 1870s and 1880s, his eyewitness accounts of military activity in the Balkans were especially welcomed. His books on the east, including a history of the Hungarians, appeared in popular editions in English as well as German and Hungarian (e.g. Vámbéry 1895). Among those on the Finno–Ugric side were József Budenz, Finno–Ugrist and general linguist, and the eminent polymath Pál Hunfalvy, who was founder of Hungary's first technical linguistics journal and first president of the Hungarian Ethnographic Society. While opposing Vámbéry bitterly at home, Hunfalvy was no less attuned than he to foreign audiences and to a larger international context that could potentially influence Hungary's political claims and alliances.

In 1874 Hunfalvy attended the Second Orientalist Congress held in London and delivered a scathing attack on the theories of Max Müller. Hunfalvy questioned Müller's 'Turanian' rubric; he tore to shreds the categories of isolating, agglutinating and inflecting languages by demonstrating that agglutination and inflection were not mutually exclusive processes, and could occur together in a single language. Most radically, Hunfalvy asserted that one cannot logically and scientifically infer, from a categorization of languages, any hierarchical ordering of associated cultures or levels of political development. The implication was that the scientifically established link between Hungarian and the languages of simpler, stateless societies should have no necessary political entailments. When reporting on the Congress to his own colleagues, Hunfalvy noted with some irritation that Müller seemed unaffected by these arguments, apparently having political commitments to his own position. Yet Hunfalvy gained visibility for himself and his science at home by writing about his dispute with Müller, (see Hunfalvy 1875, 1876; Zsigmond 1977).

For all concerned, the debate involved representations projected not only to domestic audiences that were looking for ways to signal their upward mobility, but also to western metropolitan elites. These images were part of the means by which Hungarians tried to build international alliances for their political project of the moment which, as I have noted, centred on establishing a semi-independent state within the Habsburg sphere. Qualities of calm yet powerful leadership were important in claiming the moral right to rule over an ethnically diverse and increasingly restive population.

The two opposed positions in the Ugric–Turkish War were not without their further ironies. The expeditions to Russia, Siberia, and Mongolia that ultimately provided the evidence to clinch the Finno–Ugric case also created the opportunity for Turkic exoticism. Such expeditions were dished up in lurid detail by the popular weekly magazines for the delectation of the urban audiences that were intensely interested in their own relation to a romantic orient. The press offered detailed travelogues but 'begged to differ' from the scholarly conclusions drawn on the basis of the newly gathered evidence. Nor did the defenders of the Finno–Ugric connection necessarily believe that the linguistic relationship they so strongly supported carried implications for their practical relations with these 'cousins'. When József Budenz, in the 1880s, was writing his ground-breaking works on the grammar of the Samoyed language, he was able to consult some native speakers of that language who had been brought to Budapest. A newspaper report of the period remarks, in passing, that the Samoyed couple were forced to reside in the Budapest zoo.

3. Internal boundaries

Hunfalvy and Budenz both suffered attacks in the press and in literary circles for their supposedly unpatriotic opinions on the origins of the Hungarian language. Such charges of disloyalty were especially outrageous in the case of Hunfalvy who had been jailed by the Habsburg police for his pro-independence activities in the 1848 revolution. Both men claimed loyalty to Hungary, but both were vulnerable to charges of disloyalty because neither was ethnically Hungarian. Nor were many of the major figures on the opposite side. Vámbéry was the son of poor Jewish tradesmen in northwestern Hungary; Hunfalvy was from a Saxon German family in what is now Slovakia; Budenz was born in German Fulda and only came to Budapest as an adult to teach in a German-speaking Lutheran gymnasium. None was a native speaker of Hungarian (Pinter 1934).

These men can therefore serve here as emblems of the major social processes – capitalist development, ethnolinguistic diversity, urban class formation – that, as I have already suggested, were transforming Hungary in the second half of the nineteenth century. As a relatively undeveloped region within the Habsburg Empire, Hungary attracted western investment especially after the Compromise with Austria that created the Dual Monarchy in 1867. What followed was a great movement of people to cities, especially Budapest, and a consolidation of socially and culturally diverse elements into a class-stratified urban centre. The Hungarian-speaking gentry and Hungarian-identified ruling aristocracy were only a small part of this urban population which came to include as well Hungarian-speaking peasants migrating from the countryside and from smaller cities, along with migrants who were speakers of Romanian, Ukrainian, and German. Important too were the existing urbanites: German-speaking craftspeople, and German-speaking Jews engaged in small industry and commerce. These groups were now joined by a new Jewish migration from Moravia in the west and from Poland, Russia, and Ukraine in the east. In addition, the administrative and clerical workers of the Dual Monarchy were German-speaking Austrians, and they made up a sizable part of Budapest's population. Until the last three decades of the century, Budapest was largely German-speaking; large segments of government administration, scholarly life, and commerce were conducted in German.[4]

Within this social and linguistic mix, it was the Hungarian-speaking gentry and the aristocracy that traditionally constituted the artistically and politically active segments of the population. They produced the literary men and politicians who initiated the reform of the Hungarian language at the end of the eighteenth century. One impetus for this first linguistic reform was the 'enlightened' Language Decree of 1784, in which the Habsburg court, aiming for bureaucratic efficiency, attempted to make German the official administrative language of the Hungarian as well as German parts of the Empire. The Hungarian nobility's resistance to this decree was intense, and took the form of ever stronger initiatives to defend and develop national consciousness through the use of the Hungarian language. Works from that period attest to the nobility's frustration as they attempted to translate western literatures into Hungarian. The effort convinced many that Hungarian was an inadequate language and persuaded

---

[4] The classic account of the social processes in late nineteenth-century Hungary that are very briefly sketched here remains Hanák (1975); for economic history covered in detail, see Berend and Ránki (1974).

them of the necessity to develop it if Hungary was to participate in European artistic movements, science, nation-craft, and especially the advances of capitalist industry and technology. By the first decades of the nineteenth century, thousands of new words had been coined, roots were 'discovered', and word-formation devices invented, along with stylistic and genre experiments in poetry, prose, and drama.[5]

However, the anticipated technical and commercial changes did not materialize until some eighty years after the first language reforms, and the social strata most immediately involved were not the Hungarian-speaking gentry and nobility that had led the earlier movement to 'renew' the language. Much more active in Hungarian economic life, state administration and scholarly life at the end of the nineteenth century were the migrant populations and their children. Many were learning Hungarian, and the coining of Hungarian words continued throughout the nineteenth century. But those who created the scientific and economic vocabularies for Hungarian in this later period were usually not themselves native speakers of Hungarian (Fábián 1984:42-50).

With respect to language and linguistic practices, there was a significant gulf between literary life, which was largely Hungarian, and the newspapers, technical publications, and commercial press which had for centuries been written mostly in German. When Hungarian-language newspapers started to appear in increasing numbers in the 1860s, they were often no more than Hungarian versions or bilingual versions of German papers. Articles were translated directly, and German stylistic models were freely adopted. Indeed, the Hungarian papers were written by the same journalists as the German ones, or by others who were similarly newcomers to Hungarian: the children of German, Slovak, Jewish, or Romanian migrants. The readership itself was largely bilingual. Thus the debates about correct Hungarian usage I describe below, and which preoccupied the popular magazines and newspapers, are parallel to the travelogues and Turkic exoticism published by these same papers. Both are best seen as the means by which these upwardly mobile migrants tried to imagine themselves and finally actually to make themselves Hungarian. For, although the literary heirs of the Hungarian gentry who had controlled the eighteenth-century language reform retained enormous

---

[5] This important episode has a voluminous literature. Among the better known works: Szegedy-Maszák (1988) gives a useful outline of Hungarian romanticism and its linguistic component; Fábián's (1984) work is a complete history of the language reform movement in Hungary. Fábri (1987) provides a detailed view of the literary salons of the early nineteenth century and their linguistic ideologies.

prestige in the eyes of the new middle classes, they were no longer the undisputed leaders of cultural and linguistic change.

One response of Hungarian literary men and aristocrats to this challenge to their cultural authority at the end of the nineteenth century was to complain about the 'ruination', 'deterioration', and 'corruption' of the Hungarian language, its increasing 'unhungarianness'. To address these problems they mobilized the Academy of Sciences to establish a journal called *Nyelvőr* ('Language Guardian'), with the express aim of once again saving the language from destruction, this time not by expanding it and inventing new forms but rather by 'cleaning' it of foreign elements. This initiated the second wave of reform, a purist movement whose descendants, still fighting 'in Herder's shadow' to save the language, remained active in the cultural life of Hungary throughout the twentieth century.[6]

This second linguistic debate, occurring simultaneously with the arguments about the origins of Hungarian, centred around the activities of the *Nyelvőr*, the conceptions of its editors about proper Hungarian, the notions about language in general that determined the journal's policies, and its recommendations for reform. The scholars embroiled in the Ugric–Turkish debate contributed to the *Nyelvőr* as well, but were less active in its editorial policy. Like Hunfalvy, Budenz, and Vámbéry, the editors and other contributors of the *Nyelvőr* were mostly the sons of newly mobile and newly Hungarian-speaking families. For instance, Gábor Szarvas, who was the first editor – and whose views on 'fishy kinship' I have already noted – migrated to Budapest from a Hungarian town in what is now Slovakia; his close assistant György Volf was from a German-speaking family from the outskirts of the city; Zsigmond Simonyi, who later replaced Szarvas as editor, was from a German-speaking Jewish family and had started as a teacher in a Budapest rabbinical academy.

Again, like their contemporaries in the Turkish debate, Szarvas and his allies drew on the theoretical proposals of writers like Max Müller, August Schleicher, and other German and English linguists, changing these ideas while deploying them for new purposes in Budapest's cultural scene. Central for Szarvas, as for many others, was the view that language is an

---

[6] For this description of the late nineteenth-century culture wars, and the language ideologies espoused by the various contesting parties, I have relied primarily on Németh's (1970) astute analysis, on Láncz's (1987) detailed account of the philosophical assumptions and scholarly issues of the second language reform, and a selective reading of the contemporary popular and scholarly press. Also useful is the encyclopaedic history of the Hungarian press of the period (Kosáry and Németh 1985).

organism with laws of growth and change independent of its users.[7] He added, however, that these laws could best be ascertained by linguists studying older varieties and forms used in the countryside. Rural dialects and the stylistic devices of the rural gentry were considered to be less susceptible to language-external damage. But even these rural speakers were sometimes led astray, argued Szarvas, away from the immanent laws by which their language develops. The linguists of the *Nyelvőr* considered themselves the guardians of these laws, using the entire apparatus of European linguistics as their authorization (Láncz 1987:55-63).

In effect, they attempted to create what they called a *népnyelv* ('language of the people') that would belong equally to everyone because its rules would be outside social life, emanating directly from the language itself. Under the stewardship of the linguists, this would be an anonymous yet all-inclusive national language. The linguists claimed no direct power to define linguistic correctness, but saw themselves as the experts who had the knowledge to decode the laws of nature. Thus they could argue that the language would not be linked to any particular class or group; no region or stratum would have priority. Indeed, the common or even elegant usage of their educated contemporaries was irrelevant to them. The printed forms appearing in the *Nyelvőr* were meant to be models of usage and to constitute, in themselves, the standard of correctness.

Although brought into being by the Hungarian-speaking literary establishment in the Academy of Sciences, the *Nyelvőr* was soon at odds with it. The literati were appalled that the *Nyelvőr* refused to consider matters of beauty in language, and that it refused to acknowledge the ability and discernment of talented native speakers. The literary men, drawing on a competing tradition of European linguistic theorizing, insisted on the primacy of poets in inventing new linguistic forms and judging acceptability. The *Nyelvőr*, in contrast, denied the importance of what the literary men called their *nyelvérzék* ('feeling for the language'). The linguists at the *Nyelvőr* even rejected the efforts of the earlier generation of writers to expand and reform the language. They attempted to outlaw many of the neologisms invented in the late eighteenth century that had in fact become common in everyday usage. Instead, Szarvas and his colleagues insisted

---

[7] As in the wider European discussions, however, this was hardly the only position. There were Hungarian linguists (e.g. Sándor Imre) who differed profoundly from Szarvas, and viewed language as a historical and social phenomenon that depended in part on the will of its speakers. On Imre's views, see Láncz (1991); for a discussion of the larger issue, Taylor (1990), and in a different vein Olender (1992).

that only by following the scientifically discoverable paradigms of the language could 'correct' new forms be made. Convention, aesthetics, and current usage were devalued. 'Nothing can be beautiful that is not correct' was one of their mottos.

Much of the popular press also disagreed with the *Nyelvőr*, while being equally obsessed with linguistic correctness. The Hungarian-language newspapers and magazines frequently printed articles on language, often with long lists of 'incorrect usage', 'faulty translations from German', and recommended neologisms. Their general ability to be arbiters of taste and style for the new middle classes was accepted in areas of consumption, family form, entertainment, and moral uplift. Only in the central sphere of language was their authority attacked, as the *Nyelvőr* attempted to keep usage under strong surveillance by printing and ridiculing supposedly mistaken forms found in other journals and magazines. Questions of translation, 'foreignness', and style were problems faced constantly by journalists and their readership who were forced to negotiate daily between two or more languages. The linguists of the *Nyelvőr* could perhaps have helped the journalists with such issues, or recommended alternative solutions. Ironically, however, such problems of language contact and everyday bilingual practice were never explicitly addressed by the *Nyelvőr*, which was focused on linguistic issues understood to be internal to Hungarian.

The linguists of the *Nyelvőr* opposed their language-from-nowhere to both the linguistic resources of the Hungarian-speaking literati and to the opinions of the popular press that shaped and reflected the concerns of the multilingual middle classes. While critics insisted that the *Nyelvőr*'s judgements often represented the forms typical of Hungarian rural life, especially the speech of the conservative rural gentry, the linguists steadfastly claimed to be doing no more than protecting the inherent laws of the language itself. In the midst of this controversy, unequivocal support for the *Nyelvőr* came only from the publications and policies of the national government, which was pleased to be associated with a scientific standard – also billed as a 'language of the people' – that could claim to be authentically Hungarian, yet supposedly favoured no particular social group.

4. Conclusion

I have shown the way in which elements of metropolitan linguistic theories were implicated in the making of Hungarian self-imaginings in the periphery of Europe at the end of the nineteenth century. Science, professionalism, and political authority were intertwined. Metropolitan linguistic theories were part of an orientalist discourse that Hungarian linguists rejected. But such theories, along with the linguistic evidence itself, also provided them with the materials for arguing about a national self, built on metaphors of 'family' and linguistic 'kinship'. Thus, images of Hungarians were created in part by arguments about the kinds of people to whom Hungarians were historically and linguistically related. These images were important first for external audiences who heard at least two versions of the Hungarian self – Turkic and Ugric – both denying, in different ways, the evolutionary category into which some western linguistic theories had thrust the Hungarians. They were important as well for internal audiences, who were socially and culturally heterogeneous, but who were often seduced by the popular press, literary handbooks, and school texts to imagine themselves as Magyars of a particular kind: sober, conquering Asian heroes.

As metropolitan linguistic theories were inserted into the Hungarian cultural scene they were transformed by various groups of Hungarian linguists. In their new guises, these theories produced another kind of domestic effect. Linguistically heterogeneous Hungary was faced with the question of what kind of language its assimilating populations would speak. With new classes forming and vying with older social strata for political as well as cultural authority, who would be the arbiters of linguistic correctness, and thereby – in part – of upward mobility? The theories of Müller and Schleicher, among others, enabled one group of linguists to challenge both the Hungarian-speaking literati and the popular press, and to construct their own professional authority through an alliance with European science. They made the argument for a national standard that only they could reveal. This would be a code supposedly based on the inherent, objective, linguistic characteristics of the Hungarian language; a language that they claimed would be 'everyone's', because it purported to be 'no one's-in-particular'.

References

Anderson, Benèdict ([1983]1991) *Imagined Communities: Reflections on the origin and spread of nationalism*, London: Verso.

Békés, Vera (1991) '"Nekünk nem kell a halzsiros atyafiság" – Egy tudomány történeti mitosz nyomában', in J. Kiss and L. Száts (eds) *Tanulmányok a magyar nyelvtudomány történetének témaköréből*, Budapest: Akadémiai Kiadó, 89-95.

Beöthy, Zsolt (1896) *A magyar irodalom kis-tükre*, Budapest: Franklin Társulat.

Berend, I. and Gy. Ránki (1974) *Economic Development in East-Central*

Europe in the Nineteenth and Twentieth Centuries, New York: Columbia University Press.

Fábián, Pál (1984) *Nyelvmüvelésünk évszázadai*, Budapest: Gondolat.

Fábri, Anna (1987) *Az irodalom magánélete*, Budapest: Magvető.

Gal, Susan (1991) 'Bartók's Funeral: Representations of Europe in Hungarian political rhetoric', *American Ethnologist* 18(3):440-458.

Gal, Susan and Judith T. Irvine (1995) 'The Boundaries of Languages and Disciplines: How ideologies construct difference', *Social Research* 62(4):967-1002.

Hanák, Peter (1975) *Magyarország a Monarchiában*, Budapest: Gondolat.

Hunfalvy, Pál (1875) 'Jelentések az orientalisták Londonban 1874-ben tartott nemzetközi gyűléséről', *Értekezések a nyelv és szép tudományok küréből*, Vol.VI/6. Magyar: Tudományos Akadémia.

Irvine, Judith T. and Susan Gal (2000) 'Linguistic Ideology and Language Differentiation', in Paul Kroskrity (ed) *Regimes of Language: Ideologies, polities, and identities*, Santa Fe: School of American Research Press, 35-84.

Kosáry, D. and G.B. Németh (eds) (1985) *A magyar sajtó története: 1867-1892*, Vol. II/2. Budapest: Akadémiai Kiadó.

Láncz, Irén (1991) 'Imre Sándornak a nyelvről valott nézetei', in J. Kiss and L. Száts (eds) *Tanulmányok a magyar nyelvtudomány történetének témaköréből*, Budapest: Akadémiai Kiadó, 435-440.

------ (1987) *Az új ortológia korának általános nyelvészeti nézetei*, Újvidék: Hungarológiai Intézet.

Németh, Béla G. (1970) 'A századvégi Nyelvőr vita', in *Mű és személyiség*, Budapest: Gondolat, 465-520.

Olender, Maurice (1992) *The Languages of Paradise: Race, religion and philology in the nineteenth century*, Cambridge MA: Harvard University Press.

Pinter, Jenő (1934) *A magyar irodalom története: A magyar irodalom a XIX század utolsó harmadában*, Vol. VII/7. Magyar: Tudományos Akadémia.

Pukánszky, Béla (1921) 'Herder intelme a magyarsághoz', *Egyetemes Philológiai Közlöny*, 35-39.

Pusztay, János (1977) *Az 'ugor-török háború' után*, Budapest: Magvető.

Szarvas, Gábor (1893) 'Keressétek az igazságot', *Nyelvőr* 22:441-449.

Szegedy-Maszák, Mihály (1988) 'Romanticism in Hungary', in R. Porter and M. Teich (eds) *Romanticism in national context*, New York: Cambridge University Press, 217-239.

Taylor, Talbot (1990) 'Which is to be Master? Institutionalization of authority in the science of language', in J.E. Joseph and T.J. Taylor (eds) *Ideologies of Language*, New York: Routledge, 9-26.

Vámbéry, Ármin (1895) *A magyarság keletkezése és gyarapodása*, Budapest: Franklin.

Warner, Michael (1990) *The Letters of the Republic*, New York: Cambridge
    University Press.
Zsigmond, Gábor (1977) 'Hunfalvy Pál útja az embertudománytól az etno-
    gráfiáig', in Gy. Ortutay (ed) *Népi kultúra – népi társadalom,* Budapest:
    Akadémiai Kiadó, 20-251.

4. Representing Native American Oral Narrative
The Textual Practices of Henry Rowe Schoolcraft[1]

RICHARD BAUMAN

1. Introduction

The burgeoning philological researches of the nineteenth century established the foundations not only for the scholarly production of languages,
but also for the production of a significant class of texts, specifically, texts
gathered from oral tradition under the aegis of the developing field of
folklore. In Europe, the twin linguistic and folkloristic labours of the Brothers Grimm exerted a formative influence on conceptions of both language
and folktales, but while the revolutionary significance of Jakob Grimm's
Deutsche Grammatik is well known to linguists, the Grimms' textual practices figure not at all in standard histories of linguistics. Nevertheless, the
increasing centrality of narrative textuality to a number of contemporary
lines of linguistic enquiry, including discourse analysis, conversational
analysis, pragmatics, ethnopoetics, and performance-centred study of
verbal art, suggests that conceptions of narrative textuality and the
metadiscursive practices that have been employed in identifying, recording, extracting, and interpreting oral narrative texts are worthy of linguists'
attention as well. Charles Briggs (1993) has offered an illuminating analysis
of the Grimms' textual practices and the rhetorics they employed in support of those practices. Briggs' investigation is part of a joint project in
which he and I are engaged, centring on poetics and performance in linguistics, linguistic anthropology, folklore, and adjacent disciplines (see
Bauman and Briggs 1990, 2000; Briggs and Bauman 1992, 1999; Briggs

[1] An initial draft of this essay was written during my tenure as a Fellow of the
Center for Advanced Study in the Behavioral Sciences, Stanford, California, with
the support of funds from the Andrew W. Mellon Foundation. I am deeply grateful to the Center and the Foundation for this support. Thanks also to Don Brenneis,
Charles Briggs, Susan Gal, Bill Hanks, Michael Silverstein, and Kit Woolard for
their helpful comments on an earlier version of the paper, delivered at the 1993
Annual Meeting of the American Anthropological Association; I have benefited
greatly from their help.

1993). The present paper is intended as a complement to Briggs' investigation of the Brothers Grimm, examining a similarly formative moment in the Americanist tradition, namely, the work of Henry Rowe Schoolcraft (1793-1864), whose career was roughly contemporaneous with that of the Grimms.[2]

2. Schoolcraft's discovery of Native American narrative

Schoolcraft is accorded by intellectual historians a status similar to that of the Grimms as founding ancestor of folklore and anthropology. A.I. Hallowell has observed that, "historically viewed, Schoolcraft was a pioneer in the collection of the folklore of any non-literate people anywhere in the world" (1946:137); Rosemary Zumwalt has called him "the first scholar of American Indian culture to collect and analyze a large body of Indian folklore" (1978:44); and W.K. McNeil credits him with being "the man generally recognized as the father of American folklore and anthropology" (1992:1). As with the Grimms, critics are divided or ambivalent concerning the scholarly validity of Schoolcraft's work. Some, like Stith Thompson, are strongly negative: "Ultimately, the scientific value of his work is marred by the manner in which he reshaped the stories to suit his own literary taste. Several of his tales, indeed, are distorted almost beyond recognition" (1929:xv). The vocabulary and rhetoric here are strikingly similar to some of the assessments of the Grimms cited in Briggs' (1993) article. Others, like Zumwalt and William Clements, credit many of Schoolcraft's pronounced methodological principles, but fault him for his lack of adherence to those principles in practice (Zumwalt 1978:49; Clements 1990:181). Finally, like the Grimms, Schoolcraft's statements concerning textual practice are framed centrally in terms of a rhetoric of authenticity and the problematics of intertextual relations.

Schoolcraft's first encounter with Ojibwe oral narrative occurred within weeks of his arrival at Sault of St. Marie in early July of 1822 as newly appointed Indian agent for the Michigan Territory.[3] Eager from the beginning to learn about his charges, he was initially frustrated by having to rely on traders and interpreters who were disappointingly ignorant

---

[2] Concerning Schoolcraft's life and career, see Bieder (1986); Bremer (1987); Freeman (1959); Marsden (1976).

[3] Ojibwa, Ojibwe, Odjibwa, and Chippewa are all alternate spellings for the same group; Ojibwe is the currently preferred form.

concerning the finer points of the native languages and incapable of man-
aging his more subtle inquiries into the "secret beliefs and superstitions"
of the Indians (Schoolcraft 1851a:106). When he moved into the home of
John Johnston and his family, however, a week and a half after arriving at
his post, a new world was opened to him. Johnston was a highly successful and respected Indian trader, Irish-born but of long experience on the
frontier, and married to an Ojibwe woman of high status and political
influence. Their children, bridging both cultures, were accomplished
individuals, one of whom became Schoolcraft's wife. I will deal with
the Johnston family further below, but suffice it to say here that they
provided a privileged vantage point for Schoolcraft on Ojibwe language
and culture.

Two weeks after entering the Johnston household, Schoolcraft recorded
his exciting and energizing discovery of the existence of oral narratives
among the Indians, revealed to him by his hosts:

> Nothing has surprised me more in the conversations which I have had
> with persons acquainted with the Indian customs and character, than
> to find that the Chippewas amuse themselves with oral tales of a mytho-
> logical or allegorical character.[...]The fact, indeed, of such a fund of
> fictitious legendary matter is quite a discovery, and speaks more for
> the intellect of the race than any trait I have heard. Who would have
> imagined that these wandering foresters should have possessed such
> a resource? (Schoolcraft 1851a:109)

The sense of importance surrounding this discovery never left Schoolcraft;
he saw it as being at the same time the basis of a major contribution to
knowledge that would enhance his scholarly reputation, a matter of interest to his patron, Governor Cass, who encouraged his further enquiries as
a basis for the formulation of a national Indian policy, and a point of entry
into Ojibwe culture more broadly (Schoolcraft 1839:17). Especially significantly, the existence of oral storytelling among the Indians was for
Schoolcraft the key to their essential humanity; it transformed his vision
of who they were:

> That the Indians should possess this mental trait of indulging in lodge
> stories, impressed me as a novel characteristic, which nothing I had
> ever heard of the race had prepared me for. I had always heard the
> Indian spoken of as a revengeful, bloodthirsty man, who was steeled
> to endurance and delighted in deeds of cruelty. To find him a man
> capable of feelings and affections, with a heart open to the wants, and

responsive to the ties of social life, was amazing. But the surprise reached its acme, when I found him whiling away a part of the tedium of his long winter evenings in relating tales and legends for the lodge circle. (Schoolcraft 1851a:196)

One of the significant implications of this sense of discovery was that Schoolcraft felt a lack of models and precedents to guide his collection, understanding, and rendering of these materials for dissemination to a wider audience. He was eager to get the word out concerning his discovery, but how? What were these tales? What was their significance? Who would be interested? In effect, Schoolcraft felt that he had to start from scratch in gathering the narratives, understanding their nature, meaning, and significance, identifying and engaging a public, and making his discovery available and comprehensible to this audience. All of these factors had a formative effect on his textual practices.

As regards Schoolcraft's understanding of the nature of Indian narratives, he conceived of them simultaneously and in varying degrees and combinations as literary forms and ethnological data. Schoolcraft himself employed the term 'literary' repeatedly in his writings in referring to his narrative materials (e.g. 1839:iii; 1851a:254, 631), but it is necessary in developing this point to specify what 'literary' implied for Schoolcraft and his readers.[4] First of all, 'literary' meant, in its most general sense, 'to be read'. Insofar as literacy and access to books were tied to particular social strata, serving as a touchstone of bourgeois attainment, 'literary' also carried a dimension of moral meaning, as implying *polite* learning, marked by standards of taste, decorum, and refinement that needed to be cultivated in the process of literary production. This element will figure significantly at a later point in my consideration of Schoolcraft's textual practices. At the same time, in the period comprehended by Schoolcraft's career, 'literary' was connected as well with a heightening awareness of authorship, of literary works as intellectual property, commodities oriented to a growing bookselling market. This too will receive further attention later in the paper.

Finally, during the first half of the nineteenth century, the term 'literary' came increasingly to designate creative, imaginative, aesthetically shaped works, and this sense of the term also marks Schoolcraft's usage. For example, he remarks on the "poetic" quality of the Indian narratives

---

[4] I am grateful to Michael Silverstein for pointing out to me the need to elucidate the meanings that 'literary' carried in Schoolcraft's writings. My discussion draws centrally from Williams (1983:183-188).

(e.g. 1825:409; 1839:iii), not a matter of verse, but of aesthetic properties, as the narratives are rendered as prose and distinguished from "measured songs or poetry" (1825:427). That he conceived of them more particularly as *narrative* literature is amply attested by his pervasive – if loose – employment of such generic labels as 'tale', 'legend', and 'story', and his references to "narration" (1839:17), "narrators" (1839:17; 1851a:216), and "narrated" (1848:130) in describing their provenance. In addition to their poetic qualities, a further dimension of Schoolcraft's conception of the Indian narratives as literature in this more marked sense of the term is revealed by his repeated reference to their "imaginative" and "fanciful" qualities (1825:403, 409; 1839:15, 17; 1848:68; 1851a:109, 678; 1853:314), which is to say that they were, for the most part, "fictitious" (1839:iii; 1851a:109, 196; 1851b:216; 1853:313). It is this last cluster of meanings that warrants Schoolcraft's use of the compound term, "oral literature": an early entry in his journal, dated 27 September 1822, bears the heading "Oral Literature of the Indians" (1851a:120). Whether this heading appeared in the original journal or was added for publication in 1851 we cannot know, but the term is also employed in his 1848 volume, *The Indian in his Wigwam, or Characteristics of the Red Race of America.* It is worth remarking that from the vantage point of the first sense of 'literary' offered above, that is, 'to be read', 'oral literature' is an oxymoron; it becomes intelligible to the extent that 'literary' designates primarily poetic, imaginative, creative works. Indeed, the tension encapsulated in the term 'oral literature' highlights some of the most salient problems Schoolcraft had to confront in formulating and implementing his textual practices.

At the same time that Schoolcraft conceived of the Indian tales as literature, he recognized them from the beginning of his enquiries as privileged sources of insight into the Indians' culture. In his first publication of Indian narratives, the subject matter of the final chapter of his *Travels in the Central Portions of the Mississippi Valley* (1825, hereafter *Travels*), Schoolcraft prefaces a narrative entitled "The Funeral Fire" with a statement that makes clear the close interrelationship between narrative and custom (or tradition):

> For several nights after the interment of a person, a fire is placed upon the grave. [...] The following tale is related as showing the origin of this custom. It will at once be perceived that their traditions and fictions are intimately blended. It would be impossible to decide whether the custom existed prior to the tale, or the tale has been invented to suit the custom. We may suppose that their customs and imaginative tales have alternately acted as cause and effect. (Schoolcraft 1825:404)

The realization that Indian belief and custom were accessible through their narratives was for Schoolcraft an exciting and significant breakthrough.[5] His early attempts to obtain such ethnological information by more direct enquiry were notably unsuccessful, a problem he attributed variously to misapprehension, evasion, and "restlessness, suspicion, and mistrust of motive" on the part of the Indians and the inadequacies of his early interpreters (1851a:106; 1856:xv). But when he turned his attention to the narratives, the veil of secrecy was lifted. Indeed, this rhetoric of revelation, of bringing secrets to light, pervades Schoolcraft's framing of his Indian tales throughout his career. "Hitherto", he writes, "Indian opinion, on abstract subjects, has been a sealed book" (1856:xv). In the tales, however, "the Indian mind unbends itself and reveals some of its less obvious traits" (1851b:216). The narratives:

> furnish illustrations of Indian character and opinion on subjects which the ever-cautious and suspicious minds of the people have, heretofore, concealed. They reflect him as he is. The show us what he believes, hopes, fears, wishes, expects, worships, lives for, dies for. They are always true to the Indian manners and customs, opinions and theories. They never rise above them; they never sink below them. [...] Other sources of information depict his exterior habits and outer garb and deportment; but in these legends and myths, we perceive the interior man, and are made cognizant of the secret workings of his mind, and heart, and soul. (Schoolcraft 1856:vii; see also 1848:68, 1851a:196)

Ultimately, Schoolcraft believed that the "chief value" of the tales lies in "the insight they give into the dark cave of the Indian mind – its beliefs, dogmas, and opinions – its secret modes of turning over thought – its real philosophy", and he considered that his revelation of these aspects of Indian life constituted the basis for the lasting importance of his work (1851a:655; see also 1851a:585).

---

[5] It is worth noting here the correspondence between Schoolcraft's discovery and the Herderian programme, rooted in mid-seventeenth-century classical and biblical philology, of looking to folklore forms as sources of insight into culture. The centrality of this strategy to Americanist anthropology in the tradition established by Powell and Boas underscores the importance of Schoolcraft as intellectual precursor.

3. Schoolcraft's textual practices

Schoolcraft's dual conception of Ojibwe narratives as simultaneously
literary forms and ethnological data ramifies throughout his statements
concerning his textual practices. The first of these is a revealing footnote
from Schoolcraft's first major publication of Indian narratives, in the con-
cluding chapter of *Travels*:

> These tales have been taken from the oral relation of the Chippewas,
> at the Sault of St. Mary, the ancient seat of that nation. Written down
> at the moment, and consequently in haste, no opportunity for literary
> refinement was presented; and after the lapse of some time, we have
> not judged it expedient to make any material alterations in the lan-
> guage adopted, while our impressions were fresh. A literal adherence
> to the sense of the original, to the simplicity of the narration, and, in
> many instances, to the peculiar mode of expression of the Indians, is
> thus preserved, while the order of the incidents is throughout strictly
> the same. Our collections on this subject are extensive. We do not feel
> assured that the selections here given present a just specimen of their
> merits – particularly in relation to the poetical machinery or invention
> of the Indians (Schoolcraft 1825:409).

In this passage, we may observe clearly the play of meanings that shaped
Schoolcraft's understanding of the Indian tales as literary. Note, for example, the coupling of 'literary' with 'refinement', suggesting that taking
down the tales in writing was not sufficient to render them fully literary,
for which further refining work was necessary. Writing the tales down
makes them available for reading, but literary refinement distances them
from their original oral qualities of expression. Even unrefined, however,
they remain literary insofar as they are the products of "the poetical machinery" and "invention" of the Indians. The passage testifies to the
difficulty Schoolcraft experienced in reconciling these various dimensions of the tales' literariness. We are immediately struck in this passage
by Schoolcraft's effort to minimize the intertextual gap between the texts
he has presented and "the oral relation of the Chippewas". What is emphasized here is freshness, immediacy, directness, preservation, adherence
to an original, while the potential distancing effect of textual "alterations"
is explicitly disclaimed.

   Now, while it is clear that Schoolcraft had ample opportunity to experience storytelling directly, it is equally clear that his narrative materials
did not come to him in as unmediated a fashion as this passage might

suggest. Certainly, Schoolcraft's own observations of Indian storytelling constitute one of the chief bases for the rhetoric of revelation and authenticity that marks his presentation of the Indian tales. For example, in contrasting the public and formal demeanour of Indians "before a mixed assemblage of white men" with their more relaxed manner in their own villages, "away from all public gaze", Schoolcraft writes, "Let us follow the man to this retreat, and see what are his domestic manners, habits, and opinions". He continues, "I have myself visited an Indian camp, in the far-off area of the NORTHWEST, in the dead of winter, under circumstances suited to allay his suspicions", and then goes on to describe a sociable occasion of storytelling (1851b:184; see also 1851a:109). It is such direct experiences that allow Schoolcraft to discover and reveal the secrets of Indian life, including the grand discovery of their storytelling. "It requires observation on real life", he insists, "to be able to set a true estimate on things" (1851a:138), an early appeal to the authority of fieldwork, with all its rigors and remoteness and claims to privileged access to the 'real stuff'. And, of course, the magnification of his own role in gathering these significant materials was quite consistent with his lifelong concern for his scholarly reputation (see, e.g. 1851a:639, 655, 672, 703).

While we do not have direct information concerning the circumstances under which three of the four tales presented in *Travels* were collected, we do know the source of one of the narratives, "Gitshee Gauzinee" (1825:410-412). This tale, recounting a dream-vision of an Ojibwe chief relating to burial practices, was part of the repertoire of John Johnston, Schoolcraft's father-in-law, to whom it was earlier told by Gitshee Gauzinee himself (McKenney 1827:370; for a fuller discussion, see Bauman 1993). While Johnston was fluent in Ojibwe, he would undoubtedly have recounted the narrative to Schoolcraft in English. Nevertheless, the mediation of the story through Johnston to Schoolcraft is elided in Schoolcraft's methodological statement, which implies that he himself recorded the tale directly from "the oral relation of the Chippewas". I shall have more to say about dimensions of mediation in Schoolcraft's textual practices below.

To be sure, Schoolcraft does suggest the intertextual gaps that are opened by the twin processes of intersemiotic and interlingual translation, that is, the taking down of the oral narratives in writing and their translation from Ojibwe into English, in his references to the haste with which the texts were recorded and to his lack of assurance that they adequately represent "the poetical machinery or invention of the Indians". These problems are minimized, however, by the claim that "a literal adherence to the sense of the original, to the simplicity of the narration, and, in many

instances, to the peculiar mode of expression of the Indians, is [...] preserved, while the order of the incidents is throughout strictly the same".
There is an implication here, as well, of a form–content differentiation,
insofar as Schoolcraft's statement suggests that "poetical machinery" fares
less well in the translation process than "the sense of the original" and
"the order of the incidents", that is, the meaning and the plot. This distinction assumed a still greater place in Schoolcraft's subsequent discussions
of his textual practices, correlated with the dual nature of the narrative
materials as literature and ethnological data.

The issues of intersemiotic and interlingual translation figure in a somewhat more problematic way in Schoolcraft's next major collection of Indian
narratives, *Algic Researches* (1839), the work on which his reputation as
a student of folklore principally rests and for which he is best known
beyond folklore and anthropology because of its role as the central source
of Indian lore for Henry Wadsworth Longfellow in his composition of
The Song of Hiawatha (1855). In an introductory section entitled "Preliminary Observations on the Tales", the reader encounters Schoolcraft's
claim that his investigations of Ojibwe culture led him to the discovery
"that they possessed a story-telling faculty, and I wrote down from their
narration a number of these fictitious tales" (1839:17-18). As with the
statement in *Travels*, this assertion suggests a lack of mediation, a directness of recording, that is belied by the historical record, for we know that
Schoolcraft's Johnston kinsfolk, including prominently his wife Jane as
well as his sister-in-law Charlotte and his brothers-in-law George and
William, collected a significant number of the narratives included in
Schoolcraft's collection and conveyed them to him already in writing
and in English.

Later in the volume, in a note immediately preceding the texts themselves, Schoolcraft acknowledges these and other individuals for their
assistance as interpreters and translators of the narratives, though not for
the actual recording of the tales. The terms of the acknowledgement are
significant:

> These persons are well versed in the respective tongues from which
> they have given translations; and being residents of the places indi-
> cated, a reference to them for the authenticity of the materials is thus
> brought within the means of all who desire it. (Schoolcraft 1839:26)

Here, then, for the first time, is an explicit indication of mediation in the
text-making process, but the recognition of the intertextual gap opened by
the need for translation of the tales into English is framed in terms

designed to minimize its distancing effects. The linguistic competence of
the translators and their residence in Indian country is a warrant both for
the accuracy of their translations and for the authenticity of the materials,
a claim akin to the fieldworker's appeal to the authority of direct contact
with the source.

The matter is rendered more complex, however, by a pair of entries in
Schoolcraft's journal (published in 1851) concerning his textual practices
in the preparation of *Algic Researches* for publication. These entries are
worthy of quotation at length. The first is dated 26 January 1838:

> Completed the revision of a body of Indian oral legends, collected
> during many years with labour. These oral tales show up the Indian in
> a new light. Their chief value consists in their exhibition of aboriginal
> opinions. But, if published, incredulity will start up critics to call their
> authenticity in question. [...] If there be any literary labour which has
> cost me more than usual pains, it is this. I have weeded out many
> vulgarisms. I have endeavoured to restore the simplicity of the origi-
> nal style. In this I have not always fully succeeded, and it has been
> sometimes found necessary, to avoid incongruity, to break a legend in
> two, or cut it short off. (Schoolcraft 1851a:585)

The second entry dates from 21 June 1839, after the publication of *Algic
Researches*:

> [I]t is difficult for an editor to judge, from the mere face of the vol-
> umes, what an amount of auxiliary labour it has required to collect
> these legends from the Indian wigwams. They had to be gleaned and
> translated from time to time. [...] They required pruning and dressing,
> like wild vines in a garden. But they are, exclusively[...]wild vines,
> and not pumpings up of my own fancy. The attempts to lop off excres-
> cences are not, perhaps, always happy. There might, perhaps, have
> been a fuller adherence to the original language and expressions; but
> if so, what a world of verbiage must have been retained. The Indians
> are prolix, and attach value to many minutiae in the relation which not
> only does not help forward the denouement, but is tedious and witless
> to the last degree. The gems of the legends – the essential points – the
> invention and thought-work are all preserved. Their chief value I have
> ever thought to consist in the insight they give into the dark cave of
> the Indian mind – its beliefs, dogmas, and opinions – its secret modes
> of turning over thought – its real philosophy; and it is for this trait that
> I believe posterity will sustain the book. (ibid.:655)

Both of these entries, especially the first, reveal clearly the depth of Schoolcraft's concern that his narratives be recognized as authentic, that they not be taken as "pumpings up of my own fancy." Tellingly, however, his anxiety on the matter is acknowledged as the principal motivation for the intensity of the editorial labours he has invested in the revision of the texts. These labours are enumerated in some detail: the weeding out of vulgarisms, the restoration of the simplicity of the style, the breaking of compound tales into two, the abbreviation of texts, the lopping off of excrescences.

These operations open ever more widely the gap between form and content. While literary refinement remains a salient concern, Schoolcraft clearly and explicitly assigns primary importance to the cultural content of the tales as he views them, the "beliefs, dogmas, and opinions" which are given expression in the narratives – these are what must be preserved. By the standards of Schoolcraft's literary aesthetic, the tales are flawed, and any effort to achieve "a fuller adherence to the original language and expressions" or to other formal features of native expression would only detract from their literary appeal for his readers. Their chief flaw, in Schoolcraft's view, lay in verbal excess – prolixity, excessive verbiage, proliferation of minutiae, excrescences – that renders them "tedious and witless to the last degree" and offers nothing to the realization of the essential plot, the denouement.

To a degree, Schoolcraft saw the stylistic deficiencies of the Indian narratives as inherent in their language itself. He noted his apprehension, for example, "that the language generally has a strong tendency to repetition and redundancy of forms, and to clutter up, as it were, general ideas with particular meanings" (1851a.:141). In a further indictment of Ojibwe morphology, he observed that "the Indian certainly has a very pompous way of expressing a common thought. He sets about it with an array of prefix and suffix, and polysyllabic strength, as if he were about to crush a cob-house with a crowbar" (ibid.:151). (This is certainly in striking contrast to Sapir's aesthetically appreciative suggestion that "single Algonkin words are like tiny imagist poems" (1921:228).) And again, in a sweeping dismissal of the communicative capacities of Indian languages, "one of the principal objections to be urged against the Indian languages, considered as media of communication, is their cumbrousness. There is certainly a great deal of verbiage and tautology about them" (Schoolcraft 1851a:171). Small wonder, then, that he considered the style of the narratives to be in need of repair by the standards of polite literary taste.

In the light of these considerations, Schoolcraft's statement that he has "endeavored to restore the simplicity of the original style" might appear contradictory. It is not entirely clear what he means by the notion of "original style", but the sentence that follows, about breaking a legend in two or cutting it off, would suggest that Schoolcraft had in mind a conception of tales as properly consisting of unitary plots which were compromised by storytellers' occasional tendency in certain contexts to chain or blend multiple narratives into a single extended narration. This too had to be adjusted for an 'original' quality to be restored.

Ultimately, while there is some sense of loss attendant upon the stylistic repairs he has carried out, an admission that they "are not, perhaps, always happy", literary taste requires such intervention, and the repairs do not detract from the preservation of "the essential points". Indeed, they enhance their accessibility and appeal to his readers.

Finally, in 1856, Schoolcraft published a collection of tales, derived largely from *Algic Researches*, but entitled *The Myth of Hiawatha*, in the hope of capitalizing on the popularity of Longfellow's *The Song of Hiawatha*, published in the preceding year and inspired in significant part by Schoolcraft's publications of Indian lore. In the Preface to *The Myth of Hiawatha*, Schoolcraft offered the following:

> There is but one consideration of much moment necessary to be premised respecting these legends and myths. It is this: They are versions of oral relations from the lips of the Indians, and are transcripts of the thought and invention of the aboriginal mind. [...] To make these collections, of which the portions now submitted are but a part, the leisure hours of many seasons, passed in an official capacity in the solitude of the wilderness far away from society, have been employed, with the study of the languages, and with the very best interpreters. They have been carefully translated, written, and rewritten, to obtain their true spirit and meaning, expunging passages, where it was necessary to avoid tediousness of narration, triviality of circumstances, tautologies, gross incongruities, and vulgarities; but adding no incident and drawing no conclusion, which the verbal narration did not imperatively require or sanction. (Schoolcraft 1856:vii-viii)

In this final statement of textual practice, the intertextual gaps I have noted in earlier passages are widened still further. Here, for example, the texts are claimed as "versions of oral relations from the lips of the Indians," the term 'version' conveying a lack of full identity with an original. Likewise, this passage acknowledges a still greater degree of editorial intervention, in the writing and *re*-writing of the texts and in the addition of incidents and conclusions, albeit ones that are required or sanctioned by the verbal narration. Significantly, the "true spirit and meaning" of the tales, "the thought and invention of the aboriginal mind", are not "preserved", as before, but *obtained*, brought out and in part created by Schoolcraft's own editorial work in repairing the literary deficiencies of "tediousness of narration, triviality of circumstances, tautologies, gross incongruities, and vulgarities". Accuracy and clarity of content must be won back from literarily flawed narration.

My emphasis thus far on Schoolcraft's negative assessment of Indian tales as literature and his judgement that their chief value lay in their content as a key to the native mind must not be taken to imply that he considered the beliefs, values, opinions, or "thought-work" that he was at such pains to preserve to be of positive worth, for such was decidedly not the case. Indeed, his assessment of native thought was fully as negative, notwithstanding occasional sympathetic gestures toward the Indian as a feeling human being. His common evaluation of both style and thought are clear in the following passage from *Algic Researches*:

> The style of narration, the cast of invention, and the theory of thinking, are imminently peculiar to a people who wander about in woods and plains, who encounter wild beasts, believe in demons, and are subject to the vicissitudes of the seasons. The tales refer themselves to a people who are polytheists; not believers in one God or Great spirit, but of thousands of spirits; a people who live in fear, who wander in want, and who die in misery. The machinery of spirits and necromancy, one of the most ancient and prevalent errors of the human race, supplies the framework of these fictitious creations. Language to carry out the conceptions might seem to be wanting, but here the narrator finds a ready resource in the use of metaphor, the doctrine of metamorphosis, and the personification of inanimate objects; for the latter of which, the grammar of the language has a peculiar adaptation. Deficiencies of the vocabulary are thus supplied, life and action are imparted to the whole material creation, and every purpose of description is answered. The belief of the narrators and listeners in every wild and improbable thing told, helps wonderfully, in the original, in joining the sequence of parts together. (Schoolcraft 1839:18-19; see also 1851a:196; 1856:xix-xx)

Style, plot, and error are all of a piece. There is an important point to be made here concerning the interrelationship between form and content. This passage makes clear that Schoolcraft did in fact perceive certain dimensions of connection between the two, especially in regard to the relation between personification, agency, and the grammatical marking of animacy. In Lisa Valentine's description of Ojibwe gender:

> The two genders are animate and inanimate, classifications that are roughly logical, i.e., people, animals, and many plants are catego- rized as animate, whereas things such as moccasins, blankets, and sticks are considered inanimate. There are many systematic excep- tions to this generalization, e.g., heavenly bodies (sun, moon, stars), traditional religious articles (tobacco, pipes, drums, etc.), close per- sonal possessions (mitts, spoons, snowshoes, etc.) and an odd assortment of unrelated items including among many others certain berries, stones, and tires. (Valentine 1995:219)

Animate, personified stars or berries would have struck Schoolcraft as "wild" and "improbable," signs of "error". From Schoolcraft's vantage point, then, grammatical form, narrative function, and cultural meaning are mutually implicated, at least to this extent.

Schoolcraft's negative judgement of Indian thought did not extend to a belief in innate mental inferiority (1848:67). Rather, he held that "it was not want of mental capacity, so much as the non-existence of moral power, and of the doctrines of truth and virtue, that kept them back" (ibid.:68). For "moral power" and "the doctrines of truth and virtue" here, read "Chris- tian moral power" and "the Christian doctrines of truth and virtue", for Schoolcraft was a devout Christian, an energetic champion of missionary efforts, and a strong believer in the need for the Indians to accept Christi- anity in order to secure their future in this world and save their souls in the next. Here, then, is the key to Schoolcraft's preoccupation with offering texts that foreground cultural content at the expense, if necessary, of fi- delity to native style. Opening up "the dark cave of the Indian mind" is a critical prerequisite to bringing the Indian to the light of Christian belief, an essential basis for the formulation of a national policy toward these inevitable losers in "the contest for supremacy" on the North American continent. The relationship between tales and policy is explicit: "by obtaining – what these legends give – a sight of the inner man, we are better able to set a just estimate on his character, and to tell what means of treatment are best suited for his reclamation" (1856:xxii). The treatment must be humane, for the narratives establish the Indians' essential human- ity, but it must be a policy of reclamation nevertheless. The crucial point for my argument is the mutual consistency in Schoolcraft of textual prac- tices and political ideology. The intertextual gaps between the oral form of native storytelling and Schoolcraft's published texts are intended to serve the minimization of intertextual gaps in content, all in the greater service of cultural and political dominance.

But of course, Schoolcraft had other agendas and motivations beyond political ideology and policy. He was profoundly concerned with the commercial viability and success of his published work, and indeed, he made his living by writing after his dismissal from his government position in 1841. If he was to reach an audience – which is to say, a market – with his work, he needed to shape his writings to appeal to publishers, booksellers, and readers. Still further, Schoolcraft was motivated by a life-long desire to build a scientific reputation, which demanded a proper display of scholarly knowledge and rigor in his writings as well. We must recall, in this connection, that the second quarter of the nineteenth century in America was a period in which the professionalization of scholarship was in its most nascent stages, especially in regard to philology and ethnology, and if we recall as well the novelty of Schoolcraft's findings concerning American Indian oral narrative, we can recognize the scope of his task in devising a mode of presentation for his Indian tales. To a considerable degree, he was compelled to exploration and experimentation in his textual practice. The concern to unveil the secrets of the Indian mind was paramount, but the practical considerations of commercial viability and scholarly respectability weighed strongly as well, and the achievement of a proper balance among these forces required real effort.[6]

The practical effects of this dilemma may be perceived in Schoolcraft's actual textual practices as revealed by an examination of his texts (see the Appendix to this paper for two contrasting renderings of the 'same' tale), and here, once again, we turn to Schoolcraft's dual conception of Indian narratives as literature and ethnological data. Notwithstanding School-craft's conviction that the native tales were literarily flawed, they remained a species of literature with a potential appeal to a literary audience. More-over, they had a dual potential of their own in this regard, standing as

---

[6] In the light of the dual focus of the papers in this collection on languages and publics, it may be appropriate to say a word concerning Schoolcraft's orientation to a public, as well as to an audience and a market, though this is not a central concern of my paper. I take a public to be an audience (in the general sense of receivers and consumers of communicative forms) that is held to share some commonality of attitude and interest and that may be mobilized to collective social action (cf. Crow 1985). In this sense, then, insofar as Schoolcraft intended his publication of Indian tales to influence people's attitudes towards Indians in support of particular national Indian policies, he was attempting to shape a public as well as an audience and a market.

literature in their own right while also representing a resource for the development of a distinctively American national literature.[7]

As I have established, Schoolcraft considered that to render the tales acceptable in a literary garb required editorial intervention and repair. Schoolcraft employed a number of means and devices to enhance the literary quality of his tales, some of which are suggested by his statements concerning textual practice. For example, polite literary taste required the weeding out of vulgarisms, and sexual and scatological references in the tales. Likewise, the felt need to avoid tedious prolixity and repetition manifested itself in the abridgement or elimination of form–content parallelism in the sequencing of narrative episodes. A further means of enhancing literary appeal was the adoption of a flowery and elevated register, full of high emotion, sentimental observations of nature, archaic pronominal usage ('thou', 'thee', 'ye'), and heavily sentimental rhymed poetry to index the inclusion of songs in native narrative performance. A still further device was the advancement of the narrative by means of direct discourse. All of these marked the texts as literature in regard to standards of polite taste, and were available to enhance their appeal to a literary audience.

On the other hand, Schoolcraft had a corresponding set of textual means for highlighting the ethnological 'authenticity' and scholarly validity of his texts. Some of these involved the manipulation of the same sets of elements that could be utilized to foreground literary refinement, tempering, reducing, or eliminating them to foreground ethnological content and expository clarity. Thus, Schoolcraft might employ a less ornate, more expository register, reduce direct discourse, or eliminate the poems from the texts. At the extreme, this would yield a brief, informationally focused précis of what might elsewhere be a more extended 'literary' narrative. Also related to the language of the texts, one device favoured by Schoolcraft to enhance ethnological verisimilitude was the employment of native-language words, idioms, or phrases, frequently with an

---

[7] Schoolcraft emphasizes this potential in his dedication of *Algic Researches* to Lt. Col. Henry Whiting:
  SIR
  The position taken by you in favour of the literary susceptibilities of the Indian character, and your tasteful and meritorious attempts in imbodying their manners and customs, in the shape of poetic fiction, has directed my thoughts to you in submitting my collection of their oral fictions to the press. (Schoolcraft 1839:v)Likewise, the dedication of *The Myth of Hiawatha* to Henry Wadsworth Longfellow lauds Longfellow's work as demonstrating "that the theme of the native lore reveals one of the true sources of our literary independence" (1856:v). See also Dippie (1982:16-17).

accompanying English gloss in the text or a footnote. For still more scholarly effect, these Ojibwe forms might be further accompanied by linguistic commentary explicating their morphology or etymology. To cite one further device in the service of rendering cultural content accessible, Schoolcraft resorted frequently to metanarrational commentary, noting a particular action, behaviour, or other feature as customary, or explaining its function. Some such comments might be interpolated into the texts or presented as framing matter before or after a given narrative for all audiences, but for a more scholarly tone, they might be rendered as expository footnotes. Being especially concerned with moral issues, Schoolcraft used a special set of metanarrational devices to key a moral interpretation, including genre designations in subtitles, such as 'allegory' or 'fable', and explicit moral exegeses appended to the text.

Schoolcraft employed all of these devices in varying degrees, combinations, and mixtures to calibrate the framing of particular texts and collections as relatively more literary or ethnological, popular, or scholarly. Thus a given tale might be rendered in a more literary guise for publication in a literary magazine but in a more expository register for inclusion in *Algic Researches*. For its part, *Algic Researches* is marked by a proliferation of ethnological and linguistic metacommentary; *The Myth of Hiawatha* draws some of these more scholarly 'ethnological' texts from *Algic Researches*, but includes also an admixture of more 'literary' texts previously published in other venues. One would not want to say that Schoolcraft was fully and rigorously systematic in his calibration of textual practice, for there is a certain *ad hoc* quality about some of his compilations, but the general patterns and tendencies can be adduced from an examination of the published texts. Nor, ultimately, were Schoolcraft's efforts fully successful, at least in his own estimation, for he repeatedly expressed his dissatisfaction with the degree of recognition and commercial success he achieved – or, by his lights, failed to achieve (see, e.g. 1851a:585, 631, 634, 655, 672, 697, 703).

4. Conclusion

Successful or not, however, Schoolcraft's career-long struggle to devise a viable set of methods for the representation of Indian narratives and a productive rhetoric for the effective framing of those methods for his readers (and for himself) illuminates a formative moment in the history of textual representation, of significance to the subsequent development of linguistic anthropology, folklore, and adjacent disciplines. I have attempted to elucidate in this brief examination of Schoolcraft's metadiscursive practices a range of factors that defined the field of tensions that shaped his efforts. One set of relevant factors had to do with personal, biographical circumstances, such as his position as Indian agent, his relationship with the Johnston family, and his personal ambition. A second set related to broader historical factors: the lack of precedents for the representation of oral narratives in print, the related need to identify – even to create – an audience and a market for his work, the desire to influence national Indian policy. I have given most prominence to the tension between Schoolcraft's dual conception of the Indian tales as literary forms and ethnological data, with special attention to contemporary conceptions of literariness. To be sure, all of us who are engaged in the study of oral discourse are susceptible to just the same sorts of tensions in our work, though we may differ in the degrees to which we are able and willing to acknowledge them openly and confront them directly in our own practices. Unlike Schoolcraft, however, we do not lack for precedents – again, whether we acknowledge them or not – among which are the pioneering and vexed efforts of Schoolcraft himself.

References

Bauman, Richard (1993) 'The Nationalization and Internationalization of Folklore: The case of Schoolcraft's "Gitshee Gauzinee"', *Western Folklore* 52:247-259.

Bauman, Richard and Charles L. Briggs (2000) 'Language Philosophy as Language Ideology: John Locke and Johann Gottfried Herder', in Paul Kroskrity (ed) *Regimes of Language: Ideologies, polities, and identities*, Santa Fe: School of American Research Press, 139-204.

------ (1990) 'Poetics and Performance as Critical Perspectives on Language and Social Life', *Annual Review of Anthropology* 19:59-88.

Bieder, Robert E. (1986) *Science Encounters the American Indian, 1820-1880*, Norman: University of Oklahoma Press.

Bremer, Richard G. (1987) *Indian Agent and Wilderness Scholar: The life of Henry Rowe Schoolcraft*, Mt. Pleasant: Clark Historical Library, Central Michigan University.

Briggs, Charles L. (1993) 'Metadiscursive Practices and Scholarly Authority in Folkloristics', *Journal of American Folklore* 106:387-434.

Briggs, Charles L. and Richard Bauman (1999) '"The Foundation of all Future Researches": Franz Boas, George Hunt, Native American texts, and the construction of modernity', *American Quarterly* 51(3):479-528.

------ (1992) 'Genre, Intertextuality, and Social Power', *Journal of Linguistic Anthropology* 2:131-172.

Clements, William M. (1990) 'Schoolcraft as Textmaker', *Journal of American Folklore* 103:177-192.

Crow, Thomas (1985) *Painters and Public Life in Eighteenth-century Paris*, New Haven: Yale University Press.

Dippie, Brian W. (1982) *The Vanishing American*, Lawrence: University of Kansas Press.

Freeman, John F. (1959) *Henry Rowe Schoolcraft*, Ph.D. dissertation, History of American Civilization, Harvard University.

Hallowell, A. Irving (1946) 'Concordance of Ojibwa Narratives in the Published Works of Henry R. Schoolcraft', *Journal of American Folklore* 59:136-153.

Marsden, Michael T. (1976) 'Henry Rowe Schoolcraft: A reappraisal', *The Old Northwest* 2:153-182.

McKenney, Thomas L. (1827) *Sketches of a Tour to the Lakes*, Baltimore: Fielding Lucas. Repr. ed. Minneapolis: Ross & Haines, 1959.

McNeil, W.K. (1992) 'New Introduction', in Henry Rowe Schoolcraft (1839), *Algic Researches, First Series: Indian tales and legends*. Repr. ed., Baltimore: Clearfield Co., 1-18.

Rhodes, Richard A. (1985) *Eastern Ojibwa–Chippewa–Ottowa Dictionary*, Berlin: Mouton.

Sapir, Edward (1921) *Language*, New York: Harcourt, Brace & World.

Schoolcraft, Henry Rowe (1962) *The Literary Voyager or Muzzeniegun*, ed. Philip P. Mason. East Lansing: Michigan State University Press.

------ (1856) *The Myth of Hiawatha and Other Oral Legends, Mythologic and Allegoric, of the North American Indians*, Philadelphia: J.B. Lippincott & Co.

------ (1853) *Information Respecting the History, Condition and Prospects of the Indian Tribes of the United States, Part I*, Philadelphia: Lippincott, Grambo & Co.

------ (1851a) *Personal Memoirs of a Residence of Thirty Years with the Indian Tribes on the American Frontiers*, Philadelphia: Lippincott, Grambo & Co.

------ (1851b) *The American Indians, their History, Condition and Prospects*, Rochester: Wanzer, Foot & Co.

------ (1848) *The Indian in his Wigwam, or Characteristics of the Red Race of America*, New York: W.H. Graham.

------ (1839) *Algic Researches, First Series: Indian tales and legends*, 2 vols. New York: Harper & Bros. Repr. ed. in one vol. Baltimore: Clearfield Co., 1992.

------ (1825) *Travels in the Central Portions of the Mississippi Valley*, New York: Collins and Hannay. Repr. ed. Millwood: Kraus Reprint Co. 1975.

Thompson, Stith (1929) *Tales of the North American Indians*, Cambridge, MA: Harvard University Press.

Valentine, Lisa (1995) *Making it their Own: Severn Ojibwe communicative practices*, Toronto: University of Toronto Press.

Williams, Raymond (1983) *Keywords*. Rev. ed. New York: Oxford University Press.

Zumwalt, Rosemary (1978) 'Henry Rowe Schoolcraft, 1793-1864', *The Kroeber Anthropological Society Papers* 53/54 (Spring/Fall 1976):44-57.

Appendix

Text 1: From Schoolcraft ([1826]1962:7-8)

Trance

Suspended respiration, or apparent death, is not common among the Chippewa Indians. Some cases have however happened.

Wauwaunishkum or Gitshee Gausinee of Montreal river, after being sick a short time, died, or it turned out, fell into a trance. He was a good hunter, & among other things left a gun. His widow still flattered herself he was not dead, & thought by feeling his head she felt some signs of life. After four days had elapsed he came to life, & lived many years afterwards – He related the following story to his companions – That after his death he traveled on towards the pleasant country, which is the Indian heaven, but having no gun could get nothing to eat, & he at last determined to go back for his gun – On his way back, he met many Indians, men & women, who were heavy laden with skins & meat, one of these men gave him a gun, a squaw gave him a small kettle, still he kept on, determined to go back for his own gun which had not been buried with him. When he came to the place, where he had died he could see nothing but a great fire, which spread in every direction. He knew not what to do, but at last determined to jump through it, thinking big forests were on the other side. And in this effort he awoke, & found himself alive. – Formerly it had been customary to bury many articles with the dead including all his effects, clothing etc & even presents of food etc from friends wishing them well. After this the practice was discontinued.

Text 2: From Schoolcraft (1839:180)

Git-Chee-Gau-Zinee or the Trance

(The following story is related by the Odjibwas, as semi-traditionary. Without attaching importance to it, in that light, it may be regarded as indicating Indian opinion on the temporary suspension of nervous action in trance, and on the (to them) great unknown void of a future state. The individual, whose name it bears, is vouched to have been an actual personage living on the shores of Lake Superior, where he exercised the authority of a village chief.

In former times, it is averred, the Chippewas followed the custom of interring many articles with the dead, including, if the deceased was a male, his gun, trap, pipe, kettle, war club, clothes, wampum, ornaments, and even a portion of food. This practice has been gradually falling into disuse until at present, it is rare to see the Indians deposit any articles of value with adults. What effect tales like the following may have had, in bringing this ancient pagan custom into discredit, we will not undertake to decide. Much of the change of opinion which has supervened, within the last century, may be fairly attributable to the intercourse of the Indians with white men, and in some situations, to the gradual and almost imperceptible influence of Christianity on their external manners and customs. Still, more is probably due to the keen observation of a people, who have very little property, and may naturally be judged to have ascertained the folly of burying any valuable portion of it with the dead.

Git-Chee-Gau-Zinee, after a few days' illness, suddenly expired in the presence of his friends, by whom he was beloved and lamented. He had been an expert hunter, and left, among other things, a fine gun, which he had requested might be buried with his body. There were some who thought his death a suspension and not an extinction of the animal functions, and that he would again be restored. His widow was among the number, and she carefully watched the body for the space of four days. She thought that by laying her hand upon his breast she could discover remaining indications of vitality. Twenty-four hours had elapsed, and nearly every vestige of hope had departed, when the man came to life. He gave the following narration to his friends:

"After my death, my Jeebi* traveled in the broad road of the dead toward the happy land, which is the Indian paradise. I passed on many days without meeting with anything of an extraordinary nature. Plains of large extent, and luxuriant herbage, began to pass before my eyes. I saw many beautiful groves, and heard the songs of innumerable birds. At length I began to suffer for the want of food. I reached the summit of an elevation. My eyes caught the glimpse of the city of the dead. But it appeared to be distant, and the intervening space, partly veiled in silvery mists, was spangled with glittering lakes and streams. At this spot I came in sight of numerous herds of stately deer, moose, and other animals, which walked near my path, and appeared to have lost their natural timidity. But having no gun I was unable to kill them. I thought of the request I had made to my friends, to put my gun in my grave, and resolved to go back and seek for it.

"I found I had the free use of my limbs and faculties, and I had no sooner made this resolution, than I turned back. But I now beheld an immense number of men, women, and children, traveling toward the city of the dead, every one of whom I had to face in going back. I saw, in this throng, persons of every age, from the little infant – the sweet and lovely *Penaisee*,** to the feeble gray-headed man, stooping with the weight of years. All whom I met, however, were heavily laden with implements, guns, pipes, kettles, meats, and other articles. One man stopped me and complained of the great burdens he had to carry. He offered me his gun, which I however refused, having made up my mind to procure my own. Another offered me a kettle. I saw women who were carrying their basket work and painted paddles, and little boys, with their ornamented war clubs and bows and arrows – the presents of their friends.

"After encountering this throng for two days and nights, I came to the place where I had died. But I could see nothing but a great fire, the flames of which rose up before me, and spread around me. Whichever way I turned to avoid them, the flames still barred my advance. I was in the utmost perplexity, and knew not what to do. At length I determined to make a desperate leap, thinking my friends were on the other side, and in this effort, I awoke from my trance." Here the chief paused, and after a few moments concluded his story with the following admonitory remarks:

"My chiefs and friends," said he, "I will tell you of one practice, in which our forefathers have been wrong. They have been accustomed to deposit too many things with the dead. These implements are burthensome to them. It requires a longer time for them to reach the peace of repose, and almost every one I have conversed with, complained bitterly to me of the evil. It would be wiser to put such things only, in the grave, as the deceased was particularly attached to, or made a formal request to have deposited with him. If he has been successful in the chase, and has abundance of things in his lodge, it would be better that they should remain for his family, or for division among his friends and relatives."

Advice which comes in this pleasing form of story and allegory, can give offense to no one. And it is probably the mode which the northern Indians have employed, from the earliest times, to rebuke faults and instill instruction. The old men, upon whom the duty of giving advice uniformly falls, may have found this the most efficacious means of molding opinion and forming character.

---

*[*jiibay* 'spirit' (Rhodes 1985:580) – R.B.].
**The term of endearment for a young son. [H.R.S.]. [Probably *bneshiinh* 'bird' (Rhodes 1985:425) – R.B.].

5. From the Meaning of Meaning to the Empires of the Mind
Ogden's Orthological English[1]

MICHAEL SILVERSTEIN

1. Introduction: creating a register

As part of a project I have been engaged in on 'Modern Prophets of Language,'[2] I have been investigating the creation of so-called Basic English, the word *BASIC* being an acronym for *B*ritish – *A*merican –*S*cientific – *I*nternational – *C*ommercial, and the various realms or spheres in which it is to be useful at least as an auxiliary language, if not a first language. Of course, for British, American, and even Australian, New Zealander, etc. speakers of English as their primary language, this takes the form of a specific *lexical register* that contains, other than numerals and such, 850 permissible or included lexical primes. For others, as for example the immigrants who were taught it in Massachusetts during the 1940s, it became the primary exposure to at least a form of usable English, one that functionally instantiates something of what we now recognize as a *pidginized variety* of English.

It would be of some interest in its own right to examine Basic English from these points of view. One might try to see whether or not, for example, a non-English-speaking learner could go on and build on the pidginized variety so as to convert it into a functional lexical register of more fully developed English competence. And one might try to see what paradigms

---

[1] I thank Michael Locher for his help as my research assistant during the initial period of bibliographic search and gathering of materials on Ogden and Richards, tasks he carried out with distinction.
[2] A manuscript of this title was produced as a preliminary report for a lecture to the Institute for the Humanities and the Department of Anthropology at the University of Michigan on 23 October 1992. I thank these institutions and their then respective heads, Professors James Winn and Richard Ford, as well as Professor Bruce Mannheim, for the arrangements and support that facilitated that project and presentation. For this project, in addition to the compilation of an archive of newspaper, magazine, and journal articles, and the reading of the works of the authors themselves, a number of other sources have been especially useful for basic biographical information; for Ogden, see Florence and Anderson (eds) 1977, and for Richards, see Russo 1989.

of lexical conjugates[3] are associated with the lexical register of Basic English in such a person's competence, and how various indexical values emerge in the use of such conjugate sets. But that is not my purpose here.

Nor, moreover, is it my purpose merely to practise what I have come to call 'smirk anthropology', here in particular 'smirk linguistic anthropology': I do not wish merely to hold up the specimen of my own culture to the necessarily ironic – and frequently ridiculing or dismissive – postmodern gaze, the ostensive display being actually all there is of argument in such a rhetorical move, which indexes a recognition that it would be drowned out by knowing laughter. To be sure, there is something of crackpot science here in C. K. Ogden and I. A. Richards, respectively the impresario and the ringmaster of this transcontinental circus. But Ogden and Richards' real problem in this respect was not that they were wrong, even ludicrously wrong, for we are all 'wrong' in the technical sense if we are scientists. The example they present to us here lies in showing (1) the particular location – institutional, ideological, and processual – of 'language' as a phenomenon (and phenomenon of contemplation) in the Anglo–American sociocultural universe, and particularly (2) the location of social rights that render authoritative or legitimate certain people's construals of language, with all their profound practical consequences.

2. Only a science of mind-in/and-society need apply

This I take to be the central importance of the particular example, the wild, attention-grabbing success of the Basic English movement for nearly twenty years, from about 1930, when Ogden's scheme was becoming widely known, to 1950, when he closed his Orthological Institute in London. For in the Anglo–American sociocultural universe, language is something situated in what one would indeed call the 'public sphere'. And in this particular moment of high intellectual modernism and heightened inter-war despair of the well-intentioned liberal left, it was the mobilization in the public sphere of the paraphernalia of applied science, even such insurgent science as Ogden professed in 'orthology', the intersection of psychology, philosophy, and linguistics,[4] that was the basis for

---

[3] The term comes from Geertz's ([1960]1968:287) usage "sets of linked conjugates" for the paradigms of lexicalized register-alternants in Javanese honorification. For a more adequate analysis, see Silverstein 1979:216-27; Errington 1985 and 1988.

[4] Observe that this intersection developed as an 'insurgency' within the American academy in two forms in recent decades, first as 'cognitive studies' at, for

the authority with which Ogden and Richards eventually reached their wartime success in the governmental realms of both the United States and Britain (gaining the attention and approval of both FDR and Churchill). Literate, literary man of science and practical, scientifically inclined man of letters, Ogden and Richards united the imaginative duality at the cultural boundary where language as a phenomenon is in fact theorized by the institutional structures of the educated elite.

And, of course, in the cultural ideology of this elite, language is the indicator of thought. So in this respect in particular, Ogden and Richards elaborate on the dualistic folk-view of language-form-as-accidence and conceptual-thought-as-essence in our non-technical cultural view of the matter. At this boundary of literate art and mental science, Ogden's orthology, like Korzybski's 'general semantics', wishes to apply a therapy of reworking language-form to cure the disease of conceptual thought. A talking cure, as it were, where, in contrast to psychoanalysis, the control over the mode of talk that the lexical enregisterment of Basic English demands of its users will lead them into denotational utopia, marked by clear, unambiguous, and easily communicated thoughts.

Note how consonant are these aspects of the Basic English movement with intellectual trends in Europe and the US during this period, all being expressed in the emergence of a suspiciousness of ordinary phenomenal language-as-discourse (not to be countered until the heyday of J. L. Austin et al. and the last years of Wittgenstein, at Ox- and -bridge, respectively). As a social phenomenon that for them constituted the *pars pro tota* of all human symbolic behaviour, language-as-discourse came to view for intellectuals and professionals in the public sphere as something to be given a critical, theoretically based interrogation or 'reading' on behalf of the culture-hero, the individual human psyche, who could, in a sense, be victimized – the term is decidedly of our own political era, note – by being led astray by its own talk.

---

example, Harvard-MIT and then more broadly as 'cognitive science' in a number of these and other institutions, incorporating the computer as both vehicle and metaphor for the object of study-and-simulation, mind. In a sense, Ogden was far in advance of his contemporaries in theorizing the existence of interesting work at this triple intersection, in the Mertonian sense of the historical sociology of scientific knowledge. Note, however, that both Ogden's orthology and later cognitive science are firmly rooted in the tradition of conceptualizing an autonomous, individual mind as the locus of knowledge, action, etc., rather than recognizing an order of social (or sociocultural) factuality that is predicable only of groups of people to the extent one can recognize organization of the groupness and of individuals' membership-orientation to that groupness.

Imagine with what great force this was driven home to Ogden and Richards on Armistice Day – the original one – in 1918, as they watched Ogden's bookstore in Cambridge being thoroughly trashed by an angry mob led by medical students. Ogden had been publishing pacifist-leaning and mildly German-tolerant material in the war years; this was his punishment by the crowd of semiotic victims who were, our theorists concluded, reacting more to the 'emotive' than to the 'symbolic' and 'referential' meanings in the verbal and other signs that were the tools of publishing (as of other intellective endeavour). Thus, they report, was *The Meaning of Meaning* (Ogden and Richards 1923) born as a project and thesis.

3. Orthology as the curing talk for 'madness'

Through this connection, one can perhaps appreciate how vividly the 'madness' of the war was presented to the Cambridge–Bloomsburyite network (the Woolfs, the Bells, Bertrand Russell, Keynes, the Stracheys, etc.), and how such an incident of the public suppression and destruction of the artefacts of thought was construable as essentially thoughtless. That is, it could be seen as a result – like the war itself – of the way that language in a pathological form mediates social (i.e., aggregate and communicable) pathologies of thought that lead inevitably to war, destruction, and social pathology. (Note then that the individual's inherent, logical reasonableness is masked by pathologies of language and thus leads, under the communicative reconstruction of a sociality-of-monads, to what appears to be a social-level pathology.)

And even the intellectuals and professionals concerned with language elsewhere than Bloomsbury – even those in German-speaking Europe, indeed! – were formulating parallel kinds of theories that were at once clarifying the nature of mathematico-logical thought, holding 'natural' languages up to this clarificational model by seeing them through it, and at the same time finding 'natural' languages deficient with respect to it by conceptual undercoding or semiotic superplenitude.[5] There is thus the potential for a kind of *ex cathedra* priestly access to the refined or purified

---

[5] One has in mind here the development of formal mathematical logic (in which Russell was a major early player) and the use of it to clarify the nature of scientific empiricism in the philosophy of science, under conceptions of operationalism, physicalism, logical constructivism, and so forth, one such trend culminating, for example, in Vienna Circle doctrines and perspectives that proved to be so influential for more than a generation in such fields as psychology and linguistics, especially in the US.

version of language-used-for-pure-symbolic-and-creative-thought, an enregisterment of an almost diglossic situation for those who have mastered the discursive style of scientific-expository register.

Now Ogden, to be sure, was not recommending that everyone learn how to perform the kinds of operations on everyday English to render it orthologically purified, even as Basic. But he was taking the stance of the socially aware and concerned scientist – just as, inversely, Richards was always encouraging the masses (of Harvard students, at any rate) to be each and every one of 'em his own practical critic. And as concerned scientist, Ogden was formulating and launching a tool toward the end of clarified and rationalized 'pure' denotation, free of messily-encoded emotion and calibrated to 'reality'.

And with such a metric, developed out of Jeremy Bentham's theory of '(linguistic) fictions', which Ogden edited and published with an extensive commentary, the natural English language is found wanting: too luxuriously hypertrophied in lexicon, with many words and lexicalized expressions that seem to be used to denote 'the same thing'; with, indeed, many words that seem to be used to refer to what Bentham and Ogden and their like consider nothing at all. Like Bentham, Ogden had no use for verbs, in fact precious little use for predication at all as a functional concept. One can see that he might well have been happy as one of Jonathan Swift's Sages of Lagado, who dispensed altogether with words in favour of the 'real' things of verbal referring, which they merely exhibited (*demonstratio ostentiva*). For 'real' things, successfully and correctly referable to by means of 'literal' lexical simplexes[6] independent of other, contextual encumberments, was what Ogden was after. By eliminating synonyms and other elements of lexical-conjugate sets that are 'emotively' based, by invoking phrasal and compositional paraphrasis whenever possible (e.g. *tears = eye-water*), Ogden and his devoted assistants, principally Miss L.W. Lockhart, managed, by spring 1928, to achieve a pruning or slash-and-burn clearing through the *OED* and yielded 850 such lexical primes or word units as the elements of Basic·English.

What is of interest is *not* the obviously 'positioned' nature of the resulting list.[7] To be sure, the fierce socio-historical locatability of the items

[6] Note that, in phrasal-head position, with their minimal obligatory inflections, if any, such lexical simplexes occur as word forms, sometimes identical with the citation forms of metalinguistic operations by native speakers.

[7] In symposium presentation, this was reproduced and distributed from the chart in Leonard Bloomfield's presentation copy of Ogden's *Psyche Miniature* series essay, *Debabelization* (London: Kegan, Paul, Trench, Trubner and Co. 1931),

(e.g., *ink, porter*) is almost too sad for us to contemplate retrospectively, given the pretensions of the list to *universality* in the mode of John Wilkins and other seventeenth-century Puritan scientists. And also quite apparent is the expected semiotic myopia of the native speakers Ogden and Co. such that the whole grammar of English disappeared from view in their creation, except for the morphological paradigm of 'plural' –s and a few other such things. The real grammar, organizing the grammatical catego-ries of Saussurean sense for us linguists in highly intricate and complex patterns of arrangement, appears here as merely commonsense modes whereby, for the native speaker, lexical units are combined in 'natural' phraseology. After all, shouldn't the grammar of transitive *take* as quasi-causative to intransitive *go* be, well, obvious? Tell that to a contemporary like Sapir, Bloomfield, or Whorf![8]

---

now in the library of The University of Chicago. The inscription, dated February 1934, 'To Professor Bloomfield from the Author' sends Bloomfield to pp. 155 ff., where he could have read:

> It will thus be seen that Basic English fulfils in a high degree all the conditions laid down by professors Sapir, Bloomfield, Boas, Gerig, and Krapp as requisite for the success of an International Auxiliary Language.

We can understand, perhaps, why Bloomfield quietly passed the volume on to the library, saving the institution having to pay for it.

[8] Whorf addresses Basic English directly in a passage of his ca. 1936 manuscript, posthumously published (Carroll (ed.) 1956:65-86) called 'A linguistic consid-eration of thinking in primitive communities'. Noting (ibid.:82-83) that such "social prophets" as H.G. Wells had been promoting "Ogden's ingenious artificial lan-guage called Basic English", Whorf goes on to observe that:

> Basic English appeals to people because it seems simple. But those to whom it seems simple either know or think they know English – there's the rub! Every language of course seems simple to its own speakers be-cause they are unconscious of structure. But English is anything but simple – it is a bafflingly complex organization, abounding in covert classes, cryptotypes, taxemes of selection, taxemes of order, signifi-cant stress patterns and intonation patterns of considerable intricacy. English is indeed almost in a class by itself as regards prosodic com-plexity, being one of the most complex languages on earth in this respect; on the whole, it is as complicated as most polysynthetic lan-guages of America, which fact most of us are blissfully unaware of. The complex structure of English is largely covert, which makes it all the harder to analyze. Foreigners learning English have to absorb it unconsciously – a process requiring years – by dint of constant expo-sure to bombardment by spoken English in large chunks; there exists at this time no grammar that can teach it. As with Basic English, so with

4. Achieving institutional warrant and biographi cal *gravitas*

It is of particular interest that Ogden, who even as a Cambridge under-graduate carried organizations and publications on his back and shoulders as their chief or only responsible party, operated outside academia *per se*, having no regular Cambridge or London appointment in a recognizable field. But ever the intellectual entrepreneur, Ogden promoted the adoption of Basic English through the institutions of applied science in the public sphere that he himself created and staffed. By 1931, Ogden and Richards were situated transatlantically, Ogden in Cambridge and London, Richards on an extended visit in Cambridge, MA. where he was to

---

other artificial languages – underlying structures and categories of a few culturally predominant European tongues are taken for granted; their complex web of presuppositions is made the basis of a false simplicity. We say 'a large black and white hunting dog' and assume that in Basic English one will do the same. [...] The English adjectives belong to cryptotypes having definite position assignments, and their formula is a definite and complex one, but lo, the poor Indian organizes his thinking quite differently. The person who would use Basic English must first know or learn the immensely intricate covert structure of actual 'English as she is spoke.'

We see here the error made by most people who attempt to deal with such social questions of language – they naively suppose that speech is nothing but a piling up of LEXATIONS, and that this is all one needs in order to do any and every kind of rational thinking; the far more important thought materials provided by structure and configurative rapport are beyond their horizons. It may turn out that the simpler a language becomes overtly, the more it becomes dependent upon cryptotypes and other covert formations, the more it conceals unconscious presuppositions, and the more its lexations become variable and indefinable. Wouldn't this be a pretty kettle of fish for the would-be advocates of a 'simple' international tongue to have had a hand in stewing up! For sound thinking in such fields we greatly need a competent world survey of languages.

Observe the echoes here both of Bloomfield's innovative 1933 terminology 'eme'-icizing grammar in terms of minimal units of formal grammatical arrangement, called *taxemes*, that are completely autonomous of the facts of surface segmentability or *lexical* form, and, in its moralistic punch-line, of Sapir's earlier discussions of international auxiliary language, to be based on universal grammar of grammatical processes and grammatical concepts, and illustrated in the monographs "Totality," "Grading," and "The expression of ending-point relations...," and other work stimulated by Sapir's encounter with Alice Vanderbilt Morris of the International Auxiliary Language Association.

remain after 1939. In the early 1920s, Ogden had created *Psyche*, an organ of his Orthological Institute and of the humanist sensibility of the movement he hoped to foster in educated highbrow circles. He founded, edited, and vigorously contributed to, Kegan, Paul's *International Library of Philosophy and Science* (of which some 110 volumes were ultimately to be published), his reprint-packaged *Psyche Miniature* series (many extracted from Ogden's own prose in the magazine), and others as well. He founded – and, it might be said, essentially constituted – the Orthological Institute, first in Cambridge, then in Bloomsbury. He wrote voluminously for the middle-to-highbrow press – even in America, *Saturday Review*, *Harper's*, etc.

Richards, too, was, from his nominal Harvard appointment as lecturer in the English composition and rhetoric programme at its School of Education (he was only much later to become the prestigious university professor he was in later years), somewhat more of a public intellectual, vigorously publishing accessible material on bringing science – especially orthological science (though he did not, in this cis-Atlantic context, faithfully adhere to the term) – to criticism and thereby, through reading and writing, to thought.

So note the foundation laid among the educated reading public, and the semblance of authority these writers were building up for themselves and their programmatic extensions-of-self. We can trace the index of the increase in their emergence to public view in the magazine accounts of their work on Basic English and related matters. Over the course of time, from 1923, when *The Meaning of Meaning* was published, Ogden and Richards appear as authors in book reviews of their textual productions, to be sure. But increasingly in the press, there are what we can term *personalia* articles, focused on the personages themselves as well as on their specific texts.

5. Through the war with Basic's imperial politics

By the time of the second world war, the work promoting Basic through teaching texts and a vast panoply of media innovations becomes a recurrent feature that combines the personalia aspect of the work with the contribution of this metonymic British–American transatlantic cooperation to win the war and get on with the reconstruction of the world order. This movement in exposure is not, of course, an accident. As early as an editorial on 'The future of English' published by Ogden in the January 1928 edition of *Psyche* (Vol. 8, No. 3), he trumpets the importance of the orthological approach to this question:

> Philologists will surely be the last to discover the bearing of modern
> psychology on their devoted labours, the last to appreciate the uses of
> the gramophone in linguistic technique, and the last to realize that on
> the application of their labours and that technique the future of Em-
> pires may now depend. [...] The future of Africa lies with those who
> can master African languages, and still more with those who can de-
> vise a more practical medium of communication, in commerce and
> in racial interchange, for our black brethren. That medium is likely to
> be some form of American, but there is no reason why it should not
> be English. The future, in fact, will be with the language which can
> simplify itself most rapidly, and the simplification of English is one
> of the most important branches of Orthology. [...] [W]ith a command
> of 1000 easily memorized names of common objects, situations, and
> occurrences, and some 500 linguistic devices for operating and con-
> necting them, a foreigner could make himself more fluent and
> intelligible after a three months course in English than most Scotchmen
> and any bucolic after fifty years. Chaucer's English, Milton's English,
> or Oxford English, would then take their place with Latin, Welsh, or
> Chemical formulae as accomplishments for antiquarian, literary, local,
> scientific, or polite society, and the business of international commu-
> nication might leap forward a thousand years. (Ogden 1928:1-8)

So the dream of winning, as it were, the World War of words, and of
making English – particularly British-based English – already has its roots
in how Ogden links simplification of vocabulary, *"names"*, note, "of common objects, situations, and occurrences", to "the business of international
communication" and thence to "the future of Africa" and "the future of
Empires" more generally.

In the domain of the public sphere that articulates the social utility of
scientific knowledge, orthologists, like others, were offering a way of
making language into a well-honed instrument of essentially Bauhaus
design, form following function just so as to allow us, Humpty-Dumpty-
like, to be masters of the words rather than vice versa. Everyone on the
political left or right seemed to recognize the essentially political nature
of Basic English. In writing of 'The meaning of C. K. Ogden' for the *New
Republic* in 1934, the late Kenneth Burke draws out the urgency left-
inclined intellectuals gave to the task:

> If language is the fundamental instrument of human cooperation, and
> if there is an 'organic flaw' in the nature of language, we may well
> expect to find this organic flaw revealing itself throughout the texture
> of society. If the 'nature of our thinking is determined by the nature of

our productive forces,'[9] it becomes vitally necessary to consider what
part the genius of man's key productive force, language, has played in
determining the nature of his thinking, his notions as to what 'real
issues' are, and thence his ways of dealing with them. [...] For such
reasons, a thoroughly documented technique of linguistic scepticism
might be considered as essential to human welfare as any single line
inquiry. [...] We have reached a point in culture where our speech,
which evolved out of use, must be made still more useful – otherwise
it will continue to serve best the needs of salesmanship, political land-
slides, wars and Hitlerite 'sanitation.' (Burke 1934:328-331)

One can only be impressed by the prescience of Burke (was he writing
tongue-in-cheek?) in invoking the Benthamite orthological project as a
machine-shop for instruments to counter Nazism. For this is what ultimately prevailed, in the end.

   Indeed, Franklin D Roosevelt and Winston Churchill eventually came
around, mid-war, to endorse and even embrace Basic English as a kind of
Pax Anglophonica for the post-Axis world. Churchill, in his address at
Harvard (then Richards' university) on 6 September 1943, declared that
"[T]he empires of the future are the empires of the mind", and he sought
such empires by "spread[ing] our common language even more widely
throughout the globe and, without seeking selfish advantage over any,
possessing ourselves of this invaluable amenity and birthright" (cited in
Time 22.82 [20 September 1943]).[10] By this time, Richards had long since

---

[9] Note here the superstructure/(infra)structure relationship characteristic of
Marx-influenced formulations, which would be both said and (of necessity) un-
said for the savvy readership of the *New Republic*. I have found no evidence of
this particular Marxist turn-of-phrase in Ogden – quite the contrary – but Burke's
political affiliations and positions were, of course, and are well-known. Note
further down in the quotation the nicely Vygotsky- or Bakhtin-like functionalism
of 'our speech [=language]', which evolved out of use, again echoing the prac-
tice-before-thought/structure orientation here.

[10] Albert Guérard wrote in answer to this Churchillian and, as he discovered,
orthologist's attitude in the 20 September 1943 issue of the *New Republic*
(109:400), in his review of 'Basic English and its uses by I.A. Richards', then
recently published. Entitled 'Linguistic imperialism', Guérard's piece finds that
"Mr. Richards betrays, or rather displays, the magnificent insularity which is the
pride of the Anglo-Saxon mind" – with a wonderful pun on *insularity* – and
invites Richards to show that he is not "a chauvinist in 'orthological' clothing" by
agreeing that "[a]ll dreams of 'imperialism' should be exorcized, including linguistic imperialism, which sums up all the rest".

been collaborating with Walt Disney Studios to produce animated teaching cartoons to take Basic to such places as China, one of the sites of imperial struggle yet to be resolved. And Ogden had begun negotiations, eventually ill-fated, to have His Majesty's government take over the work of the Orthological Institute in this practical realm of Basic.

So the curious oppositional irony existed, as Churchill was accepting his honorary Harvard degree that September, of having the American professional linguistic establishment mobilized at 165 Broadway in New York City to crank out the Army Language courses in a variety of intensities so as to make contact across languages and cultures feasible, while on the West Coast, Walt Disney and Richards had been preparing for linguistic homogenization through the instrumentality of Basic. That ultimately things changed in the demobilization, the Army Language Program becoming the famous or infamous 'oral-aural' or 'direct' or (barbarous) 'linguistic' method teaching programme in departments of language and literature across America, the Basic programme for places like China falling with Chiang Kai-Shek's government to be replaced by Mao's applied linguistics, is merely a historical eventuality of a continuous cultural era.

6. Elite liberalism and applying 'science' in its public sphere

In retrospect, we can, I think, see the particular coming together of orders of ideological licensing of the Ogdenian project, and the very emblematic embodiment of that project in the Ogden–Richards dyad and its particular institutional location. At its heyday emblematizing an Anglo–American partnership between Britain (and Cambridge) and the United States (and Cambridge, Mass.), between a main Orthological Institute and its branch office at the particularly anglophile oldest private university (historically connected to the other Cambridge), Ogden and Richards were distinctively public figures in the circles in which, in those years, 'educated public opinion' translated into important decision-making. In the United States, certainly, support by the Rockefeller Foundation for a Harvard project constituted an important imprimatur of legitimacy and authority, for example. Such a project would, perhaps, more easily enter the consciousness of an FDR (Harvard class of 1904), surrounded as he was by people such as Stuart Chase and others of his 'Brain Trust'. (Harvard and the Rockefeller Foundation were 'private' institutions, to be sure, but still perhaps a mere quarter-step away from governmental power at this time.)

Of course in Depression-era and wartime US and Britain, the ideological project focused on saving the polity from fascisms, communisms, etc. on right and left, while ameliorating the lot of truly suffering populations within the orbit of liberal political institutions, based on individual rights – grounded in absolutes beyond those institutions, recall, in political theory – and the rational participation of individuals. It is in such a context that the specific dualisms and dichotomies of the Ogden–Richards project – like Korzybski's project of 'general semantics' that flourished coevally – have such an appeal: the amelioration and spreading of rationality as a thera-peutic antidote to these political threats, which are constituted as the antithesis of individual, freely exercised rationality. Basic English is the instrumental route into rational English (that most rational of languages!), a route that is quick, efficient, and achievable in the pressed circumstances of a world needing a quick fix before it spins out of control. So as *The Meaning of Meaning* articulated the distinction between referential (read: Rational) and emotive (read: Irrational) functions of words, Basic was presented and promoted as the quick way into the strictly referential con-tent of English, the strict adherence to which, it can be seen, constituted a longed-for condition beyond the malaise located in this very dualism of the human psyche.[11] Ogden and Richards' position, grounded in philo-sophical analysis and the paraphernalia of academic, even scientific, research, is licensed as embodying the disinterested position of rational-ity as much as it theorizes that very positioning and a route to it for everyone-and-anyone who will learn Basic. It is, in short, 'science' ap-plied, i.e., applied science, with therefore the confidence that this licensed authority brings.

   The question now is, to what extent we ourselves as students of lan-guage in our society still live in this location in the public sphere. We might note that the very concept of a 'public sphere' might be analyzed as really constituted out of a projection of certain necessary conditions for rational discourse to be broadcast from anywhere-and-hence-everywhere-yet-nowhere – such as Wilkins and Bentham and Ogden have been after – on to a structure of supposedly inhabitable role-relations abstractable from everything else sociocultural, especially positioned interests differentially valorized. But here is, perhaps, where our own expository expertise about language actually makes its authoritativeness indexically – even

---

[11] As noted by Russo in his comprehensive biography of Richards, this dichotomy of 'rationality' vs. 'affect' underpins all of Richards' literary criticism, which, like the Basic English project, flowed out of the orthological analysis of sign phenomena and mind in the Edwardian Cambridge milieu of humanism. See esp. Russo 1989:35-385.

emblematically – manifest. There are, to be sure, theories around in our professional academic field – think of Anna Wierzbicka or of George Lakoff – which duplicate in large part one or another of the presumptions of the Ogdenian mission, with at least as much evangelical fervour. And there are 'applied linguistics' projects galore under such a departmental rubric, from saving to reforming to suppressing languages and varieties, each making its authoritative appeal to governments which, as the old saying implies, create 'languages' out of 'dialects' by calling in the army and/or navy on their behalf. But as anthropologists we must examine the very culturally and historically specific class- and sector-bound modernism of this cluster of institutionalized activities. So doing constitutes a probing of the possibly essential, or inherently presupposing, relationship between the very concept of a 'public sphere' and its 'public' on the one hand, and, on the other, the location in some embodiable scientific authority of the mystical power to create or project 'language' from text (entextualizations) in the applied science mode. These authoritative scientific statements have the dangerous effect of seeming abductively to turn otherwise leaden surface tokens of ideologically democratic rationality into underlying golden semiotic types. And we must beware of the tendencies to alchemy in each of us that may seem to come with the professional–intellectual licence.

References

Burke, Kenneth (1934) 'The Meaning of C.K. Ogden', *New Republic* 7:328-31.
Carroll, J.B. (ed) (1956) *Language, Thought and Reality: Selected writings of Benjamin Lee Whorf*, Cambridge, MA: MIT Press.
Errington, J. Joseph (1988) *Structure and Style in Javanese: A semiotic view of linguistic etiquette*, Philadelphia: University of Pennsylvania Press.
------ (1985) 'On the Nature of the Sociolinguistic Sign: Describing the Javanese speech levels', in E. Mertz and R.J. Parmentier (eds) *Semiotic Mediation*, Orlando, FL: Academic Press, 287-310.
Florence, P. Sargant and J.R. Anderson (eds) (1977) *C.K. Ogden: A collective memoir*, London: Elek Pemberton.
Geertz, Clifford ([1960]1968) 'Linguistic Etiquette', in J.A. Fishman (ed) *Readings in the Sociology of Language*, The Hague: Mouton.
Guérard, Albert (1943) 'Linguistic Imperialism: Review of Basic English and its uses by I.A. Richards', *New Republic* 10:400.
Ogden, C.K. (1928) 'The Future of English', *Psyche* 8(3):1-8.
Ogden, C.K. and I.A. Richards (1923) *The Meaning of Meaning: A study of the influence of language upon thought and of the science of symbolism*, London: Kegan Paul, Trench, Trubner.

Russo, John Paul (1989) *I.A. Richards: His life and work*, Baltimore: Johns
    Hopkins University Press.
Silverstein, Michael (1979) 'Language Structure and Linguistic Ideology', in
    P. Clyne, W.F. Hanks and C.F. Hofbauer (eds) *The Elements*, Chicago:
    Chicago Linguistic Society, 193-247.

6. Mock Spanish, Covert Racism, and the (Leaky) Boundary between Public and Private Spheres

JANE H. HILL

1. Introduction

To attend to 'constructing languages' and 'constructing publics' implicates two directions of thought. A constructionist perspective problematizes and de-naturalizes the idea of 'language', and suggests how the fragile textuality of our talk is the result as much of ideological processes as of neurobiological constraints. To consider the construction of 'publics' draws linguistic anthropology in new directions. While the idea that the arenas in which opinions are formed and decisions are made are the products of social work is not new (cf. Myers and Brenneis 1984), 'publics' suggests a particular kind of arena, Habermas' ([1962]1991) "public sphere, [...] a category of bourgeois society". The concept of 'public sphere' exposes a new arena for our attention, distinct from the interactional field of the market or the kin group, where people who live in states speak 'as citizens', with reference to public affairs, yet not as agents of the state. Habermas of course argued that the bourgeois public sphere flourished only ephemerally before it was captured by the culture industry with its capacity to manufacture inauthentic 'public opinion'. Habermas has been much criticized for his nostalgic commitment to the freedom and rationality of the bourgeois public sphere, as well as his neglect of the way in which it functioned as much to exclude as to include (see Calhoun 1992; Robbins 1993). The concept of 'public' is, however, productive precisely because it sketches in the broad outlines of an important arena for the reproduction of exclusions in contemporary societies.

I do not use the term 'public' here, however, as a category of sociohistorical theory in the way that Habermas attempts. Instead, I take 'public' and 'private' to designate 'folk categories', or, perhaps better, 'ideologies', for certain speakers of American English. (These ideological complexes are obviously closely related to the theoretical ones proposed by Habermas, and, as he points out, exhibit historical continuities going back at least to Roman times.) The English words are polysemous, referring to contexts ('publicity', 'public figure', 'in public', 'go public'), and to social entities (broad ones, as in 'public opinion' or more narrowly defined groups, such as 'the public' of an actor or singer). This paper aims to suggest that what is most important about the public-private distinction in the United States today is not the zones of life clearly included within each category, but the play of meaning along the ambiguous boundary between them, especially between kinds of talk defined as 'public' and those defined as 'private'. The sense of boundary between these spheres involves several dimensions: of the social spaces where talk occurs, of the topics and themes which it engages, of speakers, of styles, and genres. All of these are sites for contestation about how talk may 'count' and how speakers may be held responsible for it.[1] I will be concerned here with how a particular ideology about appropriate styles for 'public' talk facilitates the persistence in this sphere of "elite racist discourse" (van Dijk 1993), and thereby constructs the publics for such discourse as 'white', excluding people of colour as audiences and participants. I discuss the case of what I call 'Mock Spanish', a way that Anglos in the United States can use light talk and joking to reproduce the subordinate identity of Mexican–Americans. Mock Spanish, and elite racist discourse in general, seems to oscillate along the boundary between 'public' and 'private' talk, making the public reproduction of racism possible even where racist discourse is supposedly excluded from public discussion. Mock Spanish is, of course, only one of a whole complex of discourses that have been recognized as covertly 'coded' as racist (for instance, talk by white politicians about 'teenage welfare mothers' or 'gangbangers' does not conjure up an image of misbehaving white children, in spite of the fact that whites constitute a high percentage of such groups). Mock Spanish is, however, relatively easy to identify and 'decode', facilitating our exploration of the leaky boundary between racist joking construed as 'private' and 'serious public discussion'.

Two dimensions of language ideology facilitate this persistence of a racist discourse in public talk. The first is a set of tensions about interest, between a 'presumption of innocence' for public discourse – that talk offered up as serious public discussion will be presumed to be addressed to the general good in an unbiased way – and a 'presumption of interest' – that such talk will be biased and interested in favour of speakers or those they represent. The second is a set of tensions about style that dates back to the earliest period of the American republic. Cmiel (1990) has traced the history in the United States of what he calls the "middling style": the

---

[1] Nancy Fraser (1990) identified this boundary as a particularly interesting phenomenon.

idea that a speaker in a democracy will eschew the high language of gentility appropriate to monarchies and strike a more popular tone that admits the possibility of plain speaking including slang and colloquialisms. The preference for the middling style blurs the boundary between serious public discussion and light private talk, such that elements of the latter, in this case Mock Spanish slang, may leak into public usage. Once such slang is used 'in public' it gains access to the contest over innocence and interest, and can make claims to the former quality. At the same time, this light talk is protected by conventions of privacy, especially those of solidarity among interlocutors and the idea that private talk should not be taken too seriously. These two ideological complexes protect racist (and sexist) discourse, and make possible its continued reproduction, even where convention proscribes it. By examining the ways in which the racist register of Mock Spanish can leak across the public-private boundary, we may perhaps make progress in understanding how this reproduction occurs, and thereby develop strategies for intervention.

2. Racist discourse in the public sphere

Michael Warner (1990) pointed out that conventions of 'public' speech that formed at the time of the foundation of the American republic required that those engaging in it should not be, "byass'd by any private or partial View, prejudicial to your Country's Service" (Warner 1990:41).[2] It is this convention that precipitates the contest between innocence and interest. Those making public representations make a claim of innocence, the absence of bias; those opposing them make a claim that the representation is interested. However, ideas about what sort of talk, and what sort of speaker, is likely to be 'interested' are themselves contestable. It is very easy to attack as 'interested' a pronouncement on economic policy by the head of an investment bank, or a defence of Social Security by the president of the American Association of Retired Persons. But in the case of racist discourse the contest is heavily weighted, at least for white speakers, in the direction of a presumption of innocence. One of the most important reasons for this is that the fact that 'whites' are a 'race' is simply invisible to most members of this group, who take themselves to have

---

[2] Yet as Warner pointed out, these "unbiased" speakers could not be imagined as other than white male property owners. By this means, the point of view of this group was made universal, unmarked, its bias invisible. Thus the cultural construction of the public sphere in the United States functioned from its beginning as a powerful device for masking and mystifying racism and sexism.

no 'race' and take their own positions to be universal (cf. Morrison 1992).[3] Thus, attacks on the speech of African–American or Latino leaders as racially 'interested' are a common feature of public discourse in the United States, but the idea that Felix Rohatyn or Ellen Goodman might be speaking for the interests of 'whiteness' is considered by most people to be a very strange notion indeed (one that could be advanced only out of a 'racial' bias by a person of colour). Not only is 'whiteness' universalized and invisible, the persistence of racism as an ideology is denied. Most white people believe that 'racists' are found only among marginalized white supremacist groups who are behind the times, inadequately educated and socialized. Thus to accuse a speaker of racism is a deep insult that evokes a whole range of highly undesirable qualities.

Van Dijk (1993) takes the denial of racism to be a key component of racist discourse, one that protects the positive self-image of the racist and in turn the positive image of whites more generally, and second, permits racist discourse and its negative and exclusionary functioning to proceed. I believe, however, that van Dijk's account is not complete in that it misses the fundamental fact that denials of racism become relevant only within the terms of the contest over innocence and interest. This explains an important element of racist rhetoric that van Dijk himself has identified: that people making racist representations in public often claim that they are being 'fair'. The idea of 'fairness' acquires coherence only within a context in which a claim of lack of bias is relevant. For instance, consider the rhetoric in defense of California's Proposition 187 and similar legislation proposed elsewhere.[4] The *Los Angeles Times* (19 November 1994,

---

[3] Lest there be any confusion here, my position is that "race" is not a biological category, but is a category available for the purposes of social exclusion that is essentially empty, available to be filled with whatever semiotic elements are most appropriate to a particular epoch (Goldberg 1993).

[4] I am indebted here to the work of Rogelio García (1994). Proposition 187, which passed overwhelmingly in the November 1994 election in California, denies access to public education to illegal immigrants and to their children (even where these children are US citizens), and also denies them access to many other social benefits that are normally universally available, including non-emergency medical care. Most analysts of the rhetoric in support of the proposition find that it is clearly racist, including nearly all the well-known tropes of elite racist discourse directed at a vision of an 'illegal immigrant' who is a person of colour, Asian or Latin American. Furthermore, a good deal of the money backing 187 and similar legislation proposed in other states comes from organizations with well-known racist agendas. García presents in evidence the following telling quote, elicited by *USA Today* from Don Barrington, a Tucson retiree who led the charge for

cited in García 1994:13) quotes a woman who supports the proposition, who says, "I work full time for benefits for my family, and I don't feel it is fair for illegals to be coming in and getting health care free". The *Arizona Daily Star* has received a number of letters from legal immigrants (from Canada and Western Europe) who argue that 'fairness' requires that benefits be available only to those who follow the demanding road of legal immigration. Precisely the same rhetoric is used by opponents of such legislation: in a letter to the *Arizona Daily Star* (26 December 1994), Xavier Enriquez says, "opponents of Proposition 187 do not desire anything to be 'free,' but rather fair": previous generations of immigrants contributed to the US economy and benefited from public education, and this should not now be denied to a new generation of hard-working immigrants. In addition to the 'fairness' argument, contributors to the debate invoke market 'rationality', which makes a strong claim of disinterestedness. For instance, the *Los Angeles Times* (15 November 1994, quoted in García 1994:12) quotes a supporter of 187 who says, "We're exporting jobs and importing poverty. And unless something is done, this state has nothing to face but fiscal havoc". *USA Today* (8 November 1994, quoted in García 1994:14) cites a "financial counselor" who says, "Everyone would like to provide all services to all people, but we just can't afford it". Again, opponents of the proposition also use market arguments, trying to quantify the contribution of illegal immigrants in the form of taxes paid, jobs created, and prices of the products of their cheap labour kept low for consumers.

3. Dimensions of the public–private boundary

For many Americans, the contest about innocence and interest is relevant only when talk is 'public': when a person speaks 'in public' (as in a letter to the editor or in a public meeting), or when a person speaks as a 'citizen' about topics held to be appropriate to 'public opinion', even if the talk is conducted within the domestic or intimate sphere. For instance, a speaker telling a racist joke at a family gathering might be judged by her relatives to have poor judgement, or bad character, but she would not be thought of as 'advancing an interest', of saying something that might 'count' in the formation of opinion.[5] Here, however, we enter the slippery realm of the

---

187-style legislation in Arizona. Barrington says, "And it's not a racial issue. My friends have never heard a racist word out of me. I just don't like wetbacks' (*USA Today*, 18 November 1994, cited in García 1994:11).
[5] Scholars, of course, recognize such 'private' talk as a very important site for the reproduction of racism.

boundary between spheres, where the social spaces in which speech occurs, topics and themes for discussion, kinds of persons who are speaking,
and styles and genres interact in complex ways.

3.1 Space

Consider an interesting case of the ambiguity of a social space, the classroom. On the one hand, it is argued that students and their teachers must
be free to voice frank opinions, in the interests of seeking the truth. While
many teachers try to move students toward a preference for 'objective'
grounds for opinions (thereby inculcating the conventions of 'public
speech'), personal experience is also admitted (as part of a general
privileging of individuality that is beyond the scope of the present discussion), thereby eroding the proscription against private bias. This suggests
that classroom discussion is not precisely 'public'. On the other hand, it is
argued (probably out of exactly the same ideology that privileges personal experience), that students as individuals have the right to be protected
against epithets that may threaten their pride and identity. This drive towards protection against the damage of conflict suggests that the classroom
is somehow 'public', that what is said there 'counts' in a way that a slur
shouted across a street would not.[6] Some sites are less seriously contested.
Especially in the worlds of business and commerce, there are occasions
defined as 'off the record' or 'backstage' when sexist and racist talk are
actually highly conventionalized. Thus a business leader or politician may
be known to possess a large repertoire of grossly racist and sexist jokes,
deployed when socializing among cronies in the appropriate interstices of
business discussion, yet be celebrated for progressive views on diversity
advanced in talk framed as 'public'. These backstage zones are increasingly entering the contested boundary realm, as the courts carve out the
rights of employees to an environment that is not threatening or demeaning on grounds of race or gender, but there is, of course, a substantial
backlash against this enlargement of what is 'public'.[7] Many people

---

[6] On at least one occasion, a slur shouted out of a window was counted as 'public'
and accountable, because the window was in a dormitory at the University of
Pennsylvania. There is a famous case from 1992, in which a student shouted
"Shut up, you water buffalos" at a group of African-American women whom he
judged to be making too much noise late at night. The student, brought before a
disciplinary panel for making a racist slur, claimed that he had learned the 'water
buffalo' insult in Israel and did not believe that it had any racist content.

[7] A case in point occurred as I was preparing the revision of this paper. A staff
member from the Affirmative Action Office of the University of Arizona came to

continue to recognize a backstage, an uncontested private zone. When interlocutors are speaking within this zone, it is not considered appropriate to censure their talk, even when it is possible to construe it as racist and sexist, even as grossly so. To censure breaks a contract of intimacy and solidarity, and exposes the censurer as in turn censurable, as a pettifogging killjoy.[8]

3.2 Topic

Topic and theme also influence judgements as to whether speech is somehow aimed at the formation of opinion. For instance, Nancy Fraser (1990) pointed out an interesting case of a more-or-less successful struggle to move a topic into the public sphere. Feminist discourse extracted what is now called 'domestic' violence from the realms of non-momentous gossip and boasting into a zone of 'serious public discussion'. This required considerable work in assimilating the question of 'beating your wife', a matter that might reflect on judgement or character, to the terms of talk about 'public issues'. It required the creation of a public that accepted that a woman at the domestic site was not just Joe's long-suffering wife, but a 'citizen' whose treatment could be considered within the zone of legal 'rights'. It required the widespread recognition that interactions within the family were not always and everywhere 'personal', but could constitute a site where larger political structures, specifically those of a gender hierarchy that compromised an ideal of individual rights, were produced and reproduced. However, domestic violence remains ambiguous; neighbours who would not hesitate to call the police if they saw a stranger breaking into Joe's house may still feel that they are 'poking their noses into other people's business' if they make a call when they overhear

---

brief members of my department on sexual harassment policy. She pointed out that it was university policy that sexually offensive material could not be exhibited on university property. This prohibition was issued when a visitor complained to the president of the university about a 'Sexual Harassment Consent Form' poster that was taped to a filing cabinet in the Department of Physics, in an area that would probably have been conventionally defined as 'backstage'. The presentation of this university policy was met with outrage from several members of the faculty, who realized that it applied to what they had hitherto considered to be their own 'backstage', the 'personal and private' dimension, of their offices and labs, containing material such as nude postcards taped to their whiteboards or pornographic coffee cups half-hidden in their desk clutter.

[8] Hence, the classic light bulb joke:
> Q: "How many feminists does it take to screw in a light bulb?"
> A: "That's not funny."

the sounds of Joe smacking his wife around, and in many communities police are still reluctant to make arrests in such cases.

3.3 Speaker

Persona or reputation of the speaker is an important factor along the public–private boundary.[9] Certain persons are defined as 'public figures' (a formal category in libel law); the term 'role model' is also gaining currency, implying that certain people are influential and accountable simply by virtue of reputation. Talk by such a personage may become the object of censure as an accountable 'public' utterance even if it is uttered backstage. Exemplary are the recent cases of backstage remarks involving Marge Schott, owner of the Cincinnati Reds baseball team, and Jesse Jackson, a prominent African–American politician.[10] In contrast, there exist other kinds of persons who are judged as absolutely without influence, who can utter racist statements without censure in a context that is unambiguously 'public'. For example, in a feature on *Sixty Minutes* during the 1992 presidential campaign, Mike Wallace interviewed an elderly, obviously working-class, white man in a bar, asking him his opinion on what the most important issues were facing the country. The man, obviously conscious of constraints on public discourse, said something like, "Well, I probably shouldn't say what I really think". Wallace reassured him that his opinions were valuable. The old man then said, "Well, I think the biggest problem is that the coloured people are just trying to get too much". Wallace's facial expression made it clear (at least to some viewers) that he was not pleased with this remark, but he thanked the man politely for participating. The interview was aired nationally with absolutely no public reaction. The notion that a person who is an obvious nonentity should

---

[9] Warner (1990:38) notes that in the eighteenth century, public discourse was taken to be "impersonal by definition"; public discourse was impersonal "both as a trait of its medium and as a norm for its subjects" (ibid.). Yet this 'impersonality' apparently can become a property of 'persons'. Fraser (1990) suggests that public spheres do not in fact exhibit pure impersonal rationality, in spite of this 'bourgeois' conception; instead, they are very importantly "arenas for the formation and enactment of social identities [...] construct[ed] and express[ed] [...] through idiom and style" (Fraser 1990:68).

[10] Schott apparently used rough racist language such as 'nigger' with great frequency. Jackson's problems involved his reference to New York City as 'Hymietown'. In these cases, the colourful and slangy language was of course provocative, but as the following example shows, the 'public' nature of these persons was probably the main reason the language was censurable.

hold such views, even in his role as a citizen asked for his opinion on national television, was unsurprising and undiscussed. This case is disturbing not only because there was no challenge to this obvious racism, but precisely because the old man was not 'taken seriously'. The incident makes clear the difficulty of making any vernacular opinion into 'public' opinion.

3.4 Style

A fourth very important zone of ambivalence at the boundary between 'public' and 'private' talk involves style. The contest over innocence and interest in the public zone requires that stylistic choices here index rationality over emotional commitment, the latter being taken as intrinsically more 'interested' (Kochman 1984). Cmiel (1990) has traced major changes in the relationship between public talk and stylistic choice:

> Neoclassical notions of discourse assumed that the *homo rhetor* was a gentleman, that his ethos, or character, would guide his every act and word. His refined taste, his avoidance of vulgar speech, was essentially tied to his sense of self, that *humanitas* presumed to commit him to the public good. (Cmiel 1990:14)

Several trends worked during the nineteenth century to undermine this association. First, technical and professional languages achieved equal footing with the refined literary language of gentility. Second, within the democracy, basic skills of 'civil speech' spread widely, and ideas of 'refinement' and 'vulgarity' came to refer to styles, and not to social groups. Finally, the democratic masses supplanted the small 'rational elite' as the most important audience for public discourse, requiring the incorporation of popular styles of discourse. The resulting triumph of what Cmiel calls the "middling style", defined by informality (including regional and colloquial language and slang), calculated bluntness (including both 'plain speaking' and deliberate insult), and inflated speech (including bombast, jargon, and euphemism) is obvious in American public speech today. Among the dominant classes of American English speakers, it is appropriate to inject a light note even into the most serious expression of public opinion. Jokes are a highly institutionalized component of public speaking, and even written opinion, as by newspaper columnists, may be punctuated by light elements including slang, with only a few expressions still widely considered off-limits in the mass media. Some political columnists, like Mike Royko and Molly Ivins, have built a reputation for their command of a light style, and the slang and regionalisms that punctuate their writing construct their opinions as especially honest and authentic. Public figures thought to be of patrician origin are especially constrained to salt their discourse with vernacular jests; George Bush's efforts to achieve a rhetorical 'common touch' during his years as vice president and president became something of a national joke.[11] Yet style presents ambiguities similar to those posed by the classification of social spaces, topics, and persons; style and sphere are intricately related. Some forms of vernacular expression are proscribed in 'serious public discussion' (the worst racist and sexist epithets fall into that category).[12] Other forms, however, are acceptable, and again, there is a contested zone, rendered especially complex by the efforts of stigmatized groups to reclaim pejorative labels (such as 'black' and, more recently, 'Mexican').

To the degree that a particular stretch of talk is keyed as 'light', I believe that it may be relatively resistant to proscription. This resistance derives from cultural models that associate style, person, and space in simplistic default configurations. Light talk and joking are prototypically private, associated with the spaces of intimacy, and they are prototypically vernacular, associated with persons of a type whose talk would be unlikely to have public significance. Thus their use 'in public' constitutes a sort of metaphorical code-switch, permitting 'privacy' to be evoked within a larger public context. In private spheres, the contest of innocence and interest is not in play, or at least it is less likely to be in play than in the public sphere. Indeed, the assumption of a key of lightness constructs a context of intimacy, and to reject the content of such talk is thereby to reject the intimacy itself. Censurers of offensive talk in the prototypical light style/private space/intimate relationship context must attack not interest, but character or judgement, a much 'heavier' threat to the face of the speaker. They run the risk of being accused of violating the contracts of intimacy that hold 'in private', of being overly precious and correct, of

---

[11] Cramer (1991) suggests that the presentation of a public front with no trace of snobbery was a special obsession of Bush's parents, who tried to distinguish themselves from what they considered to be the untoward aristocratic pretensions of some members of their social universe. Thus Bush's preppy light style was not a mask assumed only when he tried to get into Texas politics, but dated back to his earliest upbringing.

[12] Apparently, conventions against gross racist and sexist talk are being eroded on so-called 'talk radio', where members of the public phone in to express their opinions. While there seems to be a general agreement in the mainstream press that talk radio is an increasingly important forum for public opinion (national leaders, including candidates for the presidency, have appeared on these shows), I don't listen to it and have nothing to say about it here. Obviously linguistic anthropologists should be attending to it.

'not having a sense of humour'. A censurer will be accused of 'political correctness', a position that is held to deprive speakers of their legitimate right to use light talk and humour. When light talk appears as a code-switch 'in public', this complex of rights seems to come with it. Those who censure the content of public light talk, who accuse it of unfair 'interest', as in accusations of racism and sexism, are vulnerable not only to the above accusations, but to additional ones: they may be accused of elitism, of undemocratically rejecting plain everyday language and, in turn, the 'common sense' that has been held to reside in it since the days of Thomas Paine.

4. Mock Spanish on the blurred boundary

I devote the remainder of this paper to the use within the public sphere of a light register of American English that I have called Mock Spanish. I show that Mock Spanish is regulated through a powerfully racist semiotic. Spanish loan elements in this register are consistently pejorated and pejorating, which can be shown to derive, by metonym, from a racist view of Spanish speakers (and to continually reproduce that opinion). There are two lines of evidence for racism in Mock Spanish. One is that in order to 'get the joke' of Mock Spanish expressions, one must have access to negative stereotypes of 'Mexicans'. The second is the fact that Mock Spanish is often accompanied by racist visual imagery of stereotypical 'Mexicans' (Hill 1993a, 1993b). For instance, a farewell card with the caption '*Adios*' may be accompanied by a picture of a 'Mexican' asleep under an enormous sombrero (the equivalent, in the representation of Mexican-Americans, of a picture of a black man with an ear-to-ear grin, rolling eyes, and a huge slice of watermelon). I have collected many greetings cards and other paraphernalia with this sort of imagery, which would invite lawsuits if it were to appear on, say, a corporate logo or in a political cartoon in a newspaper.[13] The position that I am trying to develop here

---

[13] An anthropology graduate student at the University of Arizona (whose name won't be used here so she won't lose her job) recently found a particularly egregious case of the use of the image of a 'Mexican' asleep under his sombrero while leaning against a cactus, on the Christmas giftwrap of a local chain of kitchenware shops, Table Talk. The image was part of a 'Southwest collage' that included the 'sleeping Mexican' image, a howling coyote wearing a bandana, and a striped snake wearing a cowboy hat. A Mexican-American student complained to the manager of a branch of the chain in a major Tucson shopping mall and was told the paper would be withdrawn, but when I checked back at this branch just

suggests that images of this type on greetings cards, for instance, are acceptable because they are 'private', a matter between intimates. Yet the language of Mock Spanish, separated from these kinds of racist images, is permissible and even welcome in public discourse, and in fact is used by people who are universally credited with 'progressive' opinions on racism and sexism.

I will briefly summarize what Mock Spanish is (and what it is not).[14] Mock Spanish is a set of strategies for incorporating Spanish loan words into English in order to produce a jocular or pejorative key. Three major strategies govern this borrowing. The first is the semantic pejoration of Spanish expressions, by which they are stripped of elevated, serious, or even neutral meanings in the source language, retaining only the 'lower' end of their range of connotations (and perhaps even adding new lowering). For instance, the polite and neutral Spanish farewell, *Adiós*, has meanings in Mock Spanish ranging from a marking of laidback, easygoing, South-western warmth to the strong suggestion that the target is being insulted, 'kissed off'. An excellent example of the latter (which also exemplifies Chicano awareness of these usages) is a cartoon in the series *La Cucaracha* by Lalo Alcarez, published in the *Tucson Comic News* (December 1994; cited in García 1994), shortly after the passage of Proposition 187. The cartoon shows an Anglo man holding a 187 flag and calling, "Hooray, we saved our state". Next to him is an Anglo woman jumping up and down in hysterical post-election exuberance, shouting "*Adios*, Pedro!" (The joke is that the supposedly solid ground on which the two are standing turns out to be a mighty fist labelled "Latino Activism".) The second strategy involves the recruitment of Spanish morphological material in order to make English words humorous or pejorating. For instance, in a Joe Bob Briggs movie review (Briggs 1987), we find the expression "mistake-o numero uno". The third strategy produces ludicrous

---

before Christmas 1994, not only was this giftwrap still available, but large pre-wrapped packages using it were stacked in the aisles of the store.

[14] What it is *not* is 'Spanglish' or 'Caló', or 'Border Spanish'. I take 'Spanglish' to be a practice where the target language is Spanish, but a Spanish that is wide open to English loans, often treated in a jocular way. However, from what I know about 'Spanglish', it is a much richer and more open set of practices than Mock Spanish, which is, when all is said and done, a narrow, constipated little register of insults that doesn't really offer much potential for play or originality. This is in sharp contrast to the extravagant anglicisms of Cholos, or the rich play with the two languages found in Chicano authors or performers such as Guillermo Gómez Peña.

and exaggerated mispronunciations of Spanish loan material. For instance, a greetings card shows the rear ends of a row of undulating Hawaiian dancers dressed in grass skirts. Opened, the card reads, "Grassy-ass".[15] All of these strategies directly index that the utterance in which they are found should be taken to be humorous, and that the person who produced them has that valued quality, 'a sense of humour'.[16] However, in order to achieve their humorous effect, it is clear that a second, indirect indexicality is required, which reproduces an image of Spanish, and, in turn, of its speakers, as objects of derision.[17] Most Spanish speakers with whom I have discussed these issues concur, and in fact report that they are acutely aware of Mock Spanish and find it irritating and offensive.

Mock Spanish is very widely used in public (on television programmes, in films, and in magazines and newspapers). Because of the ambiguities of social space discussed above, I give here only examples of the use of Mock Spanish in what is, very explicitly, public discussion: the realm of political talk intended to help form public opinion. One notable history involves the use of the phrase *'Hasta la vista*, baby'. This tag exemplifies the strategy of pejoration. In Spanish, *Hasta la vista* is a rather formal mode of leave-taking, that expresses a sincere hope to meet again. The pejorated line, taken from Mock Spanish by an alert team of screenwriters, was placed on the lips of Arnold Schwarzenegger in his role as the Terminator in the film *Terminator II: Judgement Day*.[18] It was then exported into public political talk by Schwarzenegger in another role, as a Republican celebrity who appeared alongside George Bush in his second campaign for the presidency. From the New Hampshire primary on, Schwarzenegger appeared regularly as a Bush supporter, and his most crowd-pleasing line, uttered at the end of an attack on the current leading Bush opponent, was, of course, *'Hasta la vista*, baby'. The line next appeared in the Texas senatorial campaign held during the winter of 1992-1993 to fill the seat left vacant by the appointment of Lloyd Benson as Secretary of the Treasury.

---

[15] I owe this example to Barbara Babcock, who received the card in thanks for some kindness.

[16] Astonishingly, many Anglos believe that they can produce expressions of this type because they have been exposed to the Spanish language (this is true even of some quite sophisticated informants). Thus, in addition to directly indexing a speaker's sense of humour, such utterances may index that a speaker has some education and cosmopolitanism (but carries it lightly).

[17] I take the concepts of 'direct' and 'indirect' indexicality from Ochs (1990).

[18] Schwarzenegger is taught the *'Hasta la vista*, baby' tag as part of a larger repertoire of insults by John Connor, the tough little Los Angeles kid who is under the protection of the Terminator.

While both candidates used Schwarzenegger's tag, the Democratic aspirant, Robert Krueger, made an especially memorable picture, appearing in television commercials dressed in a sort of Zorro suit, with black cape and hat, uttering the famous line. It was very important for Krueger to suggest that he had a 'common touch', because it was well-known that he was in everyday life a college professor of English, specializing in Shakespeare, and, thereby, a snob and a sissy until proven otherwise. Interestingly, the line backfired; Krueger was apparently considered too much of a wimp to dare to use this famous 'tough guy' tag. Increasingly, he became a figure of fun (the commercials were even held up to ridicule on national television), and lost the election by a substantial margin to Kay Bailey Hutchinson. We must also consider the possibility that the large Hispanic population in Texas, a key component of the Democratic electorate there, was offended by these commercials and declined to support Krueger.

A second example of the strategy of pejoration was reported in the *Tucson Weekly* (8 December 8 1994; cited in García 1994:11). The organizer of an incipient effort to develop Proposition 187-style legislation in Arizona reported to the *Weekly* that he had had badges and T-shirts printed up for sale to support his campaign. These items bore the legend, "If you're an illegal, head south, Amigo". This usage obviously invokes the lower reaches of a semiotic range for 'amigo' in Mock Spanish that extends from mere jocularity to this case, where 'amigo' obviously means anything but 'friend'. The legend attempts to differentiate "illegals" who should "head south" from legal immigrants and citizens of Latin American background. This distinction is, however, completely undone by the fact that in order to 'get' the humour of the legend, audiences must have access to a general negative image of Spanish and its speakers that includes no such subtle discriminations.

Mock Spanish constructions using Spanish inflectional and derivational elements such as *-o, el*, and *-ista* frequently appear in public discourse. In an example heard on the McNeill-Lehrer *News Hour* in April 1993, a spokesman for President Clinton stated that the then-current draft of the administration's health care reform plan was "not an el cheapo". This usage, of course, requires access to an image of extreme trashy cheapness associated with Spanish. David Fitzsimmons, the political cartoonist for the *Arizona Daily Star* (who is regularly attacked by conservatives as biased towards the left), produced a cartoon attacking Ross Perot, showing him holding a sign that said, in part, that he was running for "el presidente" (*Arizona Daily Star* June 26 1993). The image of Perot thus constructed was, of course, one of a tinhorn dictator, dripping with undeserved gilt medals, an image derived from pejorative stereotypes of Latin American public officials. The liberal newspaper columnist Molly Ivins is a frequent user of Mock Spanish elements, which are a part of the construction of her persona as a Texan. All the cases below are from Ivins columns printed in the *Arizona Daily Star* during 1993. In a column on the Canadian elections, Ivins said, "The chief difference between Campbell and Chretien is that Campbell thinks the Numero Uno priority is to reduce the deficit, while Chretien wants to reduce the deficit without cutting the hell out of the national safety net." In a column on health care, Ivins wrote, "one way to cut a little closer to the heart of the matter is to raise two pertinent questions. One is: what should we be allowed to die of these days? And numero two-o: What is actually going to affect the behavior of individual patients and individual doctors in consultation?" In a column on Kansas senator Bob Dole, Ivins opened as follows, "With the Clintonistas on a peppy schedule of at least two foreign policy crises a week [...]".[19]

A third type of selection from a Mock Spanish repertoire was used by CBS anchorman Dan Rather, on election night, November 1992. Discussing the tight race in Texas, Rather elucidated for his listeners what was at stake as follows: "Texas is the Big Taco [...] If Bush doesn't take [certain Texas counties] there is No Way José he can make it". Here, the expression "Big Taco", which endows Rather's speech with 'involvement' and authenticity, comes from a family of borrowings of Spanish food terms such as 'the big enchilada', and 'the whole enchilada' that constitute exaggeration and emphasis by substituting for English elements 'thing' or 'one'. By adding the Spanish name 'José' to 'No way', this everyday

---

[19] Don Brenneis (1984) suggested that Ivins might have borrowed her Mock Spanish from her partner in crime on the *Dallas Times Herald* in the early 1980s, Joe Bob Briggs. Joe Bob Briggs was especially well known for his reviews of outrageous grade-B drive-in movies, in which he commented on the number of severed limbs, the size and number of exposed breasts, the amount of blood, the disgustingness of the monsters, the sound of the chain saws, and the like. He wrote these reviews in a 'redneck' voice, of which Mock Spanish was an important component. Joe Bob eventually lost his job due to public objections to these reviews, which were considered to be especially demeaning and insulting to women. His defenders argued that Joe Bob was an especially pungent satirist, and that women who objected to his work had no sense of humour (does this sound familiar?). The reason I mention this here is that I am not at all sure that Mock Spanish is used by real rednecks. I strongly suspect that Joe Bob learned it at the University of Texas; it has been well-documented in campus contexts since the late 1940s. It is interesting that Joe Bob considered it to be an appropriate register for the racist and sexist persona of the reviews.

English negative is endowed with special vernacular pungency. Here, the indirect indexicality that is prominent is of course that Spanish is a particularly 'vernacular' language, appropriate to a slangy style.

Readers might object that English speakers can use other languages in exactly these ways. This is, of course, partly true. For instance, Japanese *Sayonara* can be used in a sense that is almost exactly like Spanish *Adios*. However, other European languages cannot easily be substituted in these kinds of expressions. I invite the reader to try out an English epithet such as 'sucker' in combination with leave-taking expressions from familiar languages. German, like Japanese the language of a former enemy power, almost works: '*Auf wiedersehen*, sucker'. Taking up more recent international enmities, I can imagine the hero of a colourful spy novel dispatching a member of the KGB with the wisecrack '*Do svidaniya*, sucker', although I don't think this expression is popularly available in the way that '*Adios*, sucker' is. French and Italian really do not work, in spite of the familiarity of the expressions –* '*Ciao*, sucker', * '*Au revoir*, sucker' (well, perhaps in some future thriller constructed around the recent Haitian intervention, a villainous attaché might be knocked off to this sound effect by a heroic American agent). In summary, such usages seem to require access to contempt or enmity which, in the case of Spanish, is not traceable to any political threat, real or perceived, since 1898. Similar experiments can be conducted with lexical equivalents of the other expressions cited above, and I predict even less success.

All these are cases where Mock Spanish is part of a code-switch into a light register, in which the speaker is represented as a person with a sense of humour and the common touch, a truly egalitarian American who doesn't have fancy pretensions. This characteristic conceit of the middling style requires a metaphorical code-switch into the private social space, where people are thought to be at their most 'authentic'. Thus Mock Spanish can inject authenticity and 'common sense' into public discourse which might otherwise be too serious. Such talk blurs the boundaries between public and private discourse. It is fairly easy analytically to show that Mock Spanish is driven by a racist semiotic, and that it functions to reproduce negative views of Spanish-speaking people. Yet Mock Spanish is not racist in an obvious way: there are no epithets here. If the examples above were uttered in private, most people would consider it ridiculous to censure them. This resistance to censure leaks into the public space by way of the metaphorical code-switch, so it is extremely difficult to attack these usages even though they are obviously public and contestable along the interest–innocence continuum. Further, such an attack would require that the 'interest' involved be characterized: it is, of course, the interest of 'whiteness', a quality that is largely invisible and not conventionally defined as an 'interest'. Furthermore, to characterize such talk as 'racist' requires that one familiarize one's audience with the complexities of modern thought on racism, which is again remote from the understanding of a public that thinks of itself as 'anti-racist'.[20] Thus, such usages of Mock Spanish are generally defined as 'innocent'.

5. Conclusion

At the same time that Mock Spanish functions at the blurred boundaries between public and private talk, it also illustrates the permeable boundaries of language itself. Mock Spanish has moved into public discourse in the last decade, at the very same time that heightened concern about language boundaries, in the form of the Official English campaign, has grown in American life. Why, then, is there no objection to Mock Spanish by language purists? I believe that no objection occurs because Mock Spanish in fact strongly supports the essence of the purist campaign: that foreign languages, while they may be permitted in the home, should not be allowed in public discourse. As is well-known (Woolard 1989), Official English objections to foreign languages have been aimed especially at bilingual ballots and other forms of the public use of Spanish. The use of Mock Spanish constructs a particular place for the Spanish language in American public discourse: it can function *only* in light talk, in the 'code-switching' that protects an American speaking in public from being seen as too pompous and domineering. This function seems to be well established, and will make it increasingly difficult for any public uses of Spanish to be heard as 'serious'. It will, by definition, always be 'private', and thus will have in the public sphere no more than a poetic function. For this reason, Mock Spanish in fact advances the purposes of the Official English movement. Furthermore, to the degree that it is covertly racist, this will presumably be sensed with approval by those with racist agendas.

Finally, the use of Mock Spanish (as well as other subtly and not-so-subtly coded forms of racist discourse) in public talk functions importantly in 'constructing the public'. If an appreciation of the humour in Mock Spanish requires unreflective access to negative stereotypes of Latinos, then these sallies are clearly shaped for the appreciation of people who

---

[20] Claudia Brodsky Lacour (1992:139) has pointed out the paradox of racism, "whose pervasive existence depends on its tenacious nonadmission and complicitous nonrecognition".

define themselves as 'not Latino'. (I use this phrase rather than 'define themselves as "White"' because the public thus defined almost certainly includes African–Americans, although this fraction of the US population is of course the object of an unending repertoire of other exclusionary discursive strategies.) Mock Spanish thus is one of many devices through which the sphere of public discussion in the most widely diffused media in the United States becomes profoundly, invisibly, exclusionary against people of colour.

In closing, I wish to turn to a point raised recently by David Palumbo Liu (1994). Liu suggests, in an analysis of the media characterization of racist alignments in the recent Los Angeles riots, that Hispanics in some contexts can stand in as a surrogate for more dangerous and problematic African–Americans. Liu points out, for instance, that Latino participation in the riots was hardly mentioned in the mass media, which emphasized the polarization of the Black and Asian communities. However, after the riots Hispanics were apparently arrested and deported in great numbers. Liu suggests that the deportations projected on to Hispanics desires that were in fact aimed at African–Americans – who cannot, of course, be deported because they are, without doubt, recognized as citizens of the United States. It is interesting to consider a similar complementary distribution between Mock Spanish and African–American materials in the English of Anglos. African–American slang expressions of course move rapidly into the slang of White Americans. Often, this slang is reshaped into virtual unrecognizability, so that those who use it are unaware of its Black English origins.[21] However, a register that might be called 'Mock Black English' is an important component of the gross jokes that are told in the zones of privacy mentioned above, in light talk especially among men. Graphically offensive jokes are often told using reported speech in a broad 'Sambo' or 'Aunt Jemima' dialect. However, as far as I know, no whisper of this practice ever leaks into the public discourse. In fact, as long ago as the 1970s a cabinet officer Earl Butz, Secretary of Agriculture

---

[21]A particularly famous case involves the expression 'up tight', which in White English means overly concerned for propriety (the organ that is 'tight' is the rectum). The expression probably entered general American English in a song made popular in the 1960s by African-American singer Stevie Wonder, in which the line was "everything is up tight, all right, clear out of sight" (the organ involved was probably the penis). In recent years, with the enormous popularity of rap music and hip-hop culture among young people of all races, slang of known African-American origin is increasingly widespread among whites. However, I am unaware of a parodic register of African-American English that is comparable in range of usage and context among whites to Mock Spanish.

under both Nixon and Ford, was fired after reporters overheard him telling a grossly offensive 'Sambo' joke. To produce obvious parodies of
African–American speech of the type that are apparent in Mock Spanish
is simply too dangerous. However, Mock Spanish is apparently considered to be entirely harmless. We must consider the possibility that it is a
safe substitute for this more dangerous possibility for covert racist discourse, for the voice of Amos 'n Andy, of Minstrelsy. Interestingly, even
parodists like Joe Bob Briggs, who tries to be as outrageous as possible
(see note 19) do not dare to venture into this realm, although Briggs' cast
of characters does include at least two foolish and quarrelsome buddies
who have Hispanic surnames.

Mock Spanish is a very useful tool for exploring the ambiguities and
problems of the boundaries between the public and the private. It is easy
to spot it: its obvious morphology and lexicon function like a sort of ra-
dioactive tracer, which can be identified immediately when it shows up at
a new site. What I think we learn from looking at these materials as they
move back and forth across the public-private boundary is that the idea of
the 'public' and of 'public discourse' continues today as an ideology that
mystifies and confounds what is going on in the way of race, sex, and
class-based oppression in American life, just as it did in the Revolutionary era. The imbrication of 'light talk', 'plain talk', 'humour', and 'common
sense' have created an impenetrable tangle under which a great deal of
racist and sexist talk, both public and private, can be produced, and a
shield by which critique of these practices can be very effectively de-
flected. Through these practices of language the structures of 'citizenship'
by which people are licensed to participate in public life are produced –
and also raced, and gendered.

References

Briggs, Joe Bob (1987) *Joe Bob Briggs goes to the drive-in*, New York:
    Delacorte Press.
Calhoun, Craig (ed) (1992) *Habermas and the Public Sphere*, Cambridge,
    MA: MIT Press.
Cmiel, Kenneth (1990) *Democratic Eloquence*, New York: William Morrow.
Cramer, Richard Ben (1993) *What it Takes*, New York: Vintage Books.
Fraser, Nancy (1990) 'Rethinking the Public Sphere: A contribution to the
    critique of actually existing democracy', *Social Text* 2:56-80.
García, Rogelio (1994) '"Well I've Reason to Believe, We All have been De-
    ceived": California's Proposition 187 and racist discourse', MS: University
    of Arizona.

Goldberg, David Theo (1993) *Racist Culture*, Oxford: Blackwell.

Habermas, Jürgen ([1962]1991) *The Structural Transformation of the Public Sphere*, trans. Thomas Burger. Cambridge, MA: MIT Press.

Hill, Jane H. (1993a) 'Hasta la vista, baby: Anglo Spanish in the American Southwest', *Critique of Anthropology* 13:145-176.

------ (1993b) 'Is it Really "No Problemo"?', in Robin Queen and Rusty Barrett (eds) *SALSA I: Proceedings of the first annual symposium society, Austin. Texas Linguistic Forum* 33, 1-12.

Kochman, Thomas (1984) 'The Politics of Politeness: Social warrants in mainstream American public etiquette', in Deborah Schiffrin (ed) *Meaning, Form, and Use in Context: Georgetown University Round Table '84*, Georgetown University Press: Washington, DC, 200-209.

Lacour, Claudia Brodsky (1992) 'Doing Things with Words: "Racism" as speech act and the undoing of justice', in Toni Morrison (ed) *Race-ing Justice, En-gendering Power*, New York: Pantheon Books, 127-158.

Morrison, Toni (1992) *Playing in the Dark*, New York: Vintage Books.

Myers, Frederick and Donald Brenneis (1984) 'Introduction', in *Dangerous words*, New York: New York University Press, 1-29.

Ochs, Elinor (1990) 'Indexicality and Socialization', in James W. Stigler, Richard A. Shweder, and Gilbert Herdt (eds) *Cultural Psychology*, Cambridge: Cambridge University Press, 287-308.

Palumbo Liu, David (1994) 'LA, Asians, and Perverse Ventriloquisms: On the functions of Asian America in the recent American imaginary', *Public Culture* 6(2):365-381.

Robbins, Bruce (ed) (1993) *The Phantom Public Sphere*, Minneapolis: University of Minnesota Press.

van Dijk, Teun A. (1993) *Elite Discourse and Racism*, Newbury Park: Sage Publications.

Warner, Michael (1990) *The Letters of the Republic*, Cambridge, MA: Harvard University Press.

Woolard, Kathryn (1989) 'Sentences in the Language Prison: The rhetorical structuring of an American language policy debate', *American Ethnologist* 16:268-278.

7. State Speech for Peripheral Publics in Java

1. Introduction

Since the 1965 bloodbath which ended its failed experiment with constitutional democracy, Indonesia has been ruled by a highly centralized,
military-dominated government which has moved unilaterally to mod-
ernize the country's economic infrastructure and indoctrinate Indonesians
into the ways and sentiments of its own version of nationalism.[1] This
self-named New Order has quashed all opposition to its top-down implementation of policies which have as their goal, among others, the national
integration of rural communities such as those in south-central Java which
I discuss here. A self-legitimizing modernist ideology has licensed the
New Order's self-assumed right to oversee *pembangunan* ('development')
and *pembinaan* ('improvement') of the lot of Indonesia's vast, heterogeneous peasantry, and has underwritten as well the perceived superiority of
state officials. "All Indonesians I have ever met," one outspoken Indonesian intellectual has commented, "feel that they are the subordinates
(*bawahan*) of the government. Moreover there are very many of our officials in the regions or outlying areas who feel confident that they really
are the superiors (*atasan*) of the people".

The Republic of Indonesia (*Republik Indonesia*) is no *res publica*, and
harbours no such 'public' as has been described, debated, or imagined in
discussions following Jürgen Habermas' influential chronicle ([1962]1989)
of the rise of civil society. Indonesia's founders, largely a Dutch, educated
intelligentsia and suborned ethnic elite, took over a colonial administrative infrastructure along with its administrative language, Malay, suitably

---

[1] I am grateful to Cambridge University Press for permission to reprint material
presented in this article from Chapter 5 of my book, *Shifting Languages* (1998),
where I contextualize it more extensively. In many ways, the discussion presented
here was made a period piece by Suharto's fall from power in 1998. At present,
Indonesian politics are too fluid to allow even a guess about the enduring legacy
of his New Order regime, or its developmentalist ideology. But the sorts of public
events described here will continue to shape conceptions of Indonesian identity
and language, particularly at the nation's margins. For that reason they deserve
continuing close attention as peripheral but crucial dimensions of state-fostered
social change.

renamed Indonesian. The social and technological prerequisites for any sort of 'public sphere' hardly exist in Indonesia; the major weekly magazine in this country of roughly 190 million sold only 150,000 or so copies a week before being closed by the government in 1994; the nation's leading newspaper (over and against tabloid-style mass publications) sells about half a million copies a day. Marketing surveys show readers to be primarily university and high school graduates who live in urban areas and are employed as civil servants, managers, or other professionals.

The power of rigid, self-interested state oversight of public discourse is evident in the lack of explicit censorship laws and in statements such as that of the Minister of Information in 1989, for instance, that no opposition to government policy exists or should exist in the Indonesian press. (See Heryanto 1990.) When self-censorship has failed to prevent transgression of unstated limits on content and tone of reportage, the New Order has not hesitated to peremptorily close and sometimes eradicate newspapers and magazines. Such was the case in 1994, for instance, when three news magazines, including the most widely circulated mentioned above, were summarily put out of business.

Indonesia has developed out of a colonial empire into a state-dominated polity which fits better C. Wright Mills' characterization of mass society. This label resonates, for instance, with the New Order's own name for its longstanding 'floating mass' policy, which proscribes political activity in rural communities save during state-established, state-supervised election periods. The bulk of this citizenry forms a rural populace regarded by many elites as, to use a common, condescending phrase, *masih bodoh* ('still stupid'). Such backward villagers have been accorded a collective status as recipients rather than active participants in policy formulation or implementation, which are wholly within the New Order's purview. For these and other reasons it is easy to view the New Order as a kind of security apparatus oriented primarily to the political and economic interests of its elite and allies.

Whatever purchase such cynical, instrumentalist readings have on the practice and policy of the New Order elite, they offer little insight into the ideas and sentiments of 'ordinary citizens' engaged day-to-day with the many faces of modernity and nationalism. The dominant rhetoric of progress (*kemajuan*) and development (*pembangunan*) has real salience for many Indonesians' construal of, participation in, and resistance to, massive state-sponsored transformations of their lives, families, and communities. Peasants' engagements with superposed, centralizing policies are parts of complex responses to efforts to make them a peripheral, passive, yet self-perceivedly Indonesian public. As the state has progressively saturated villages and brought villagers under its political, economic, and educational aegis, it has likewise superposed the social identities and categories with which villagers are enabled and obliged to negotiate their relations with the state and each other in a new national polity.

I consider such massive change here through two transient but concrete points of contact between state and villagers, bits of events in which state officials addressed peripheral, public audiences. 'Public' serves here as a rubric for the events created and speech used when Javanese villagers are convened at state behest to listen to talk by state representatives about state concerns. Before, after, and (perhaps) during these events they are co-members of a local community, bound together by shared social biographies. But the goals, topics, and institutional logic of such 'public' events presuppose their temporary co-participation as a gathered fraction of their nation's citizenry. Even as passive participants, villagers then accede to an impersonal, superposed status which is mapped at least temporarily on to local community gatherings.

Officials publicly mediate these relations through genres of public talk, Javanese and Indonesian, which I discuss in this paper with recourse to transcripts of tiny bits of two such events. I consider ways in which Javanese speech genres serve to mitigate the state's institutional presence at such events, and simultaneously to create useful ambiguities in the 'publicness' of those gatherings. To explore the ethnic and national inflections of this double-sided engagement, I focus on speakers' capacities as mediators between an audience and the authority which they assume and implement. By contrasting Javanese or Indonesian modes of authoritative speakership, sponsorship, and audiencehood, I try to develop a sense of the genres of public speech which subserve public speakership, and reciprocally shape the collective roles of public audiences.

Javanese language commonly serves Indonesian officials, in Indonesian venues, to speak about Indonesian topics. This may on the face of things be surprising. Indonesian – devoid of ethnic inflection, strongly and transparently backed by the state, redolent of state ideology in public use – would seem institutionally normative for speech by state agents, at state-sponsored gatherings, about state business, to state citizens. But bilingual Javanese Indonesian officials commonly do Indonesia's public business in Javanese, as in the event from which is drawn the talk transcribed in text 1. Here the administrative head of a mountainous, eastern subdistrict of south-central Java deals with very Indonesian administrative and fiscal matters at an ostensibly Indonesian gathering called a *rapat desa* ('subdistrict meeting'). Several hundred residents and citizens of the district he supervises were gathered outside his office to listen to him speak through a loudspeaker at this event.

Text 1: Rapat desa/Village meeting[2]

Panjenenganipun párá bapak-bapak. Bilih	[1]	Honoured gentlemen
ing sakmangké kulá badhé ngaturaken		Now I will present the
wontenipun *keuangan desa* ing		*village fiscal* situation in
tahun anggaran séwu sangang atus		*budgetary year* one thousand nine hundred
wolungdásá gangsal, séwu wolung atus	[5]	eighty five, one thousand eight hundred,
séwu sangang atus wolung dásá nem		one thousand nine hundred eighty six,
ingkang kawiwitan wulan April tahun		which begins the month of April, year
wolungdásá gangsal dumugi ing wulan		eighty-five through the month of
Maret tahun wolungdásá nem.		March, the year of eighty-six.
Sadèrèngipun kulá ngaturaken wontenipun	[10]	Before I present
lapuran kula salebetipun setunggal tahun,		my *report* for the single year,
ing samangké mbok bilih anggènipun		at present perhaps [my]
ngaturaken sáhá ng*lapur*aken wontenipun		presentation and *reporting* of the
keuangan desa salebetipun setunggal tahun		*village fiscal* situation in the year
dhumateng párá bapak-bapak sedáyá, mbok	[15]	to all you gentlemen, perhaps
menawi wonten kekiranganipun. Kula		there will be shortcomings. I

---

[2] Javanese is given in Roman type; Indonesian in italics. Standard Indonesian orthography is used; consonant symbols have values close to their English equivalents, save that /ng/ represents a velar nasal. Vowels have roughly the following values: /i/ as in 'she', /u/ as in 'shoe', /e/ as in the first part of the diphthong in 'shade', /o/ as in the first part of the diphthong in 'shoal', /a/ as in 'shot'. Epenthetic glottal stops between vowels are not transcribed. With a few exceptions, Javanese words are transcribed with the same orthography: /dh/ represents a post-veolar dental stop, over and against dental /d/; /á/ represents a low, back, semi-rounded vowel somewhat like that in 'shore'; /é/, /è/, and /e/ contrast as do roughly the vowels in 'shade', 'shed', and the last syllable of 'sofa'.

nyuwun pangapunten awit bilih		beg forgiveness so that
sadèrèngipun kula *lapur*aken,		before I *report*, there are
wonten		[moneys]
ingkang kedah mlebet soal		which should be entered *village*
keuangan desa,		*finances*,
nanging dèrèng saged mlebet,	[20]	but can't yet enter, so
dados		
janipun sampun setor dhumateng		actually they're deposited to the
désa,		village,
nanging kabektá dèrèng cethá,		but [as they] are not yet clear,
pramilá ing		therefore at
samangké nyuwun pangapunten		present [I] beg forgiveness to
dhumateng		
párá bapak-bapak...		the gathered gentlemen...

Such usage provides convenient *prima facie* evidence of how little of the emerging relation between Indonesian and Javanese can be captured with bifurcate diglossic oppositions between high and low, formal and informal, or public and private languages (see Errington 1991 for a discussion of the relevant literature.) It shows, rather, the need to consider Javanese as an ensemble of speech styles, some of which can be performatively figured against an Indonesian institutional ground like this *rapat desa*: an event convened for governmental purposes, where the head administrator of a subdistrict discusses current fiscal matters.

Neither this brief segment nor the lengthy speech from which it is drawn contains much Indonesian verbiage beyond a few technical phrases – *keuangan desa* ('village finances') and *tahun anggaran* ('budgetary year') – for which no plausible Javanese equivalents exist. Otherwise the speech is replete with diacritics of the formal variety of the Javanese speech style often called *krámá* in the scholarly literature, and more often *básá* (or *básá alus*, lit. 'refined *básá*') by Javanese themselves. Such distinctively formal Javanese is normatively heard at ceremonies such as weddings, where it serves delegated, prototypically male masters of ceremonies to address gathered guests and announce events on behalf of a sponsoring host.

I call this style of Javanese 'exemplary' here to signal two ways in which I try to relocate this transcription in my description of its originary context. The first, taken up in the next section, has to do with traditional Javanese geosocial and linguistic hierarchies that can be invoked tacitly with such speech. The second involves relations between those who engage in 'public' speech and sanctioning persons or institutions whose authority they then manifest yet dissimulate. Together, these paired themes help suggest how ethnic and national modes of authority and speech genres might converge and diverge in Indonesian yet Javanese public venues.

2. Exemplary speech and speakers

By recalling the notion of 'exemplary centre', the phrase 'exemplary speech' helps thematize longstanding links between the social dialectal significances of the speech genre in Text 1 and geosocial hierarchies in precolonial Central Java. A common theme in literature on Southeast Asian statecraft (see, e.g. Anderson 1972; Geertz 1980; Tambiah 1976, 1985) is the place of exemplary centres as geopolitical and symbolic foci in precolonial kingdoms. So too the Central Javanese kingdoms of Jogjakarta and Surakarta, sustained and moulded under Dutch aegis through the beginning of the second world war, focused on kings, courts, and cities which defined geographic centres and pinnacles of political and cultural hierarchies.

Exemplary language was the most elegant of the well-known Javanese speech styles, paradigmatically associated with the courtly circles of those cities to which its use was largely restricted. Use of such speech could be highly polite in face-to-face interaction, and mark a speaker's formal or deferential relation to a speech partner. But because knowledge of this style could only be acquired in these closed elite circles, its use could also be salient as a linguistic diacritic of the speaker's high status. The longstanding association of elegant language with elite circles of exemplary centres enhanced the aura of refinement accruing to such speech, and its speakers. Exemplary usage could be perceived, then, as a quasi-natural attribute of elitehood, what Habermas has called "a status attribute" through which a noble personage "displayed himself [*sic*], presented himself as embodiment of some sort of 'higher' power" (Habermas [1962] 1989:7). Recognized (or misrecognized) not as evidence of training in linguistic technique but a perceptible index of imperceptible, intrinsically refined nature, exemplary Javanese was distinctive of what Bourdieu (1984) calls an "aristocracy of culture" and its speaker's character.

This association of exemplary language and geosocial class has long shaped geosocially variable understandings of the significances of exemplary usage such as that in Text 1. Though this refined style can still occasionally be heard in everyday conversation among city elites, it has been largely displaced by Indonesian or less polished styles of Javanese for many speakers and in many contexts (see Errington 1985). But in villages relatively distant from those cities, like that in which the speech in

Text 1 was recorded, exemplary Javanese has long served primarily as mode of address on public occasions to gathered groups. This circumstance correlates with the fact that active command of such exemplary Javanese in rural areas has long been the province and verbal mark of local elite representatives of the exemplary centre (see Errington 1998). Villagers then counted as members of audiences for address by socially privileged speakers, whose showing forth of exemplariness simultaneously legitimized the public event at which they spoke and their own spokespersonship. Such refined conduct could then be admired by a silent audience whose members recognized the distinctive worth of exemplary language but, by the same token, the unfittingness of any attempt on their own part to use it.

As doubly passive participants in the use of a language they neither speak nor are able to speak, villagers then accede to an asymmetric collective role which is not exchangeable for that of exemplary speaker. The exemplariness of this speech genre as a mode of 'public' speech is underwritten by a prenational, patrimonial ethnic hierarchy, which stands in sharp contrast to the legitimacy of standard Indonesian. Constructed and disseminated as standard rather than exemplary language, Indonesian is putatively omni-available, thanks to the state, and ostensibly uninflected for ethnicity or class because it is backed by an ideology (if not practice) of Indonesian democracy. In this respect, Indonesian's ostensible non-exclusivity as a vehicle of speech to a national public stands in tacit but clear contrast to traditionally exemplary Javanese speech and speakers.

3. Exemplary speakers and sponsors

This genre of Javanese can also be called 'exemplary' in relation to modes of sponsorship for acts of exemplary speech, and the perceived nature of those who license such acts and whose interests are then mediated in exemplary fashion. Exemplary speakers at traditional Javanese gatherings normatively spoke as intermediaries for sponsors whose tacit presence and authority were figured in ways resonant with broader understandings of power-laden relations between the sources and surrogates of power in exemplary centres.

A common theme in literature on Javanese statecraft (e.g. Anderson 1972) is power's efficacy, which emanates from exemplary centres and persons independently of their own overt action or direct involvement. A (normatively male) person's power to control his environment and other persons, by this logic, is evident mediately rather than through directly perceptible actions: the presence of power is deducible from its effects, including the actions of a powerful person's delegates. Centres of potency are, as it were, evident in their absence, prototypically, in the persons of kings who oversee and exercise their will invisibly and mediately from the detached seclusion of their palaces. Ward Keeler has described in similar terms the "dissembled control" (1987:163) which is exercised by sponsors of ritual events. Their potency is indirectly manifested not just by the coming together of individuals to form an audience, but also by the 'sponsor's voice': a spokesperson who simultaneously represents the interests and dissimulates the involvement of a sponsor. By dissembling their involvement, sponsors manifest a capacity to attract an audience which lends gravity to the sponsored event, but counts also as an effect and index of the sponsor's potency. This "dissimulation of exertion" (Keeler 1987:141) lends such events significance as forms of status display, which presuppose that the work of talk be delegated to an exemplary speaker, who acts as sponsor's surrogate to a gathered audience.

In this way, public, exemplary speech does not just set off the person of an exemplary speaker; it also underwrites that speaker's role as ventriloquator of interests and sentiments of a sponsor, a legitimizing entity whose silent authority a speaker manifests and mediates. Ostensibly powerful figures dissimulate their authority as what Goffman (1974) might call dissociated but not disinterested principals, and are complementarily represented by exemplary animators whom they sanction. Public exemplary speech can defer and refer to that authority, disclosing it by dissimulating its presence.

Exemplary Javanese talk such as that transcribed in Text 1 can be construed as imputing broadly similar forms of authority to the sponsor of this ostensibly Indonesian event, a silent, anonymous sponsor which is more powerful than its Javanese precursor: the Indonesian state. Potency's dissimulated, anonymous character in this respect permits the transposition of exemplary speech into a modern 'public' venue, and the adoption of a guise of traditional authority by a different, 'public' sponsor. Exemplary Javanese in Indonesian events helps in this way to blur differences between forms of authority and public speakership, allowing a minor bureaucrat to localize his privilege of public speech and the privileging power of the state he subserves.

Such a dual interpretation of official, public uses of exemplary Javanese can be specifically as well as broadly apposite. In the talk beginning at line 15 in Text 1, for instance, this duly appointed subdistrict official completes a preface to his review of the district's finances. He is at pains to note a lag in book-keeping which is beyond his control and prevents him from presenting a full and accurate account of the monthly figures. By dwelling on what is, in the larger scheme of things, a minor accounting problem, he shows himself to be a punctilious keeper of books and a worthy functionary in the administrative framework within which such matters have significance. But in exemplary Javanese, he is able to punctuate these prefatory remarks with the quintessentially Javanese act of 'begging forgiveness', uttering *nyuwun pangapunten* (line 23). This does not just signal regret at a state of official affairs; it involves an act and stance typically adopted by exemplary speakers at Javanese gatherings. This phrase is a virtually obligatory signal of speaker (and sponsor) sensitivity to the needs of gathered others, and to the possibility of his own shortcomings. At the same time, it dissimulates any hope of a 'perfect' performance that a speaker might in fact harbour.

Insofar as such an utterance invokes the feel of Javanese exemplary speech, speakership, and 'public' events, it can also invoke the absent, sponsoring power of the state which this official duly represents, and which underwrites the event at which his audience is duly assembled. This elegant phrasing simultaneously allows self-figuring as a conscientious yet exemplary representative of that potent sponsor. If exemplary qualities indirectly legitimize the official's privilege, they help legitimize the authority he mediates, not just overtly by an ideology of modernist nationalism, but covertly through a received logic of speakership, sponsorship, and authority.

4. Audiences, local and national

If exemplary Javanese speech genres can supplement rather than subvert state authority, then such public events can accomplish a noteworthy symbiosis between state interests and institutions on one hand, and local understandings of 'the public' among Javanese Indonesians on the other. Such events can assimilate Indonesian publicness into received understandings of hierarchy and conduct, and dissimulate Indonesian authority in local forms and terms. To these linked convergencies between speech and authority must be added a parallel doubleness or ambiguity in the nature of the 'publics' so addressed, that is, the nature of the co-presence assumed and created by its silent co-participants.

Co-present persons addressed with exemplary speech in traditional rural venues are largely bound together before, after, and during public events as kin, neighbours, and acquaintances; they are members of what Alfred Schutz calls "a community of space and time" (1967:163) which allows direct, mutual experience through more or less enduring, more or less dense networks of interaction. As such persons "grow older together" (ibid.:165) they are for each other what Schutz calls "consociates": persons with overlapping, resonating, sometimes conflicting lifeworlds. In this respect, public speech can represent a single, ceremonialized moment in an ongoing, collective social biography.

But the consociateship of such *gemeinschaft* differs greatly from the kinds of national imaginings which, as Anderson ([1983]1991) has argued, engender senses of community among anonymous co-citizens of nations. Such anonymous, typified others count as what Schutz would call "contemporaries" (ibid.:176), who occupy the national space delimited, controlled, and rendered homogenous by a state system like the New Order. The New Order has worked effectively to homogenize politics and culture among its hugely diverse ethnic groups by reconstituting ethnicity in an Indonesian space, and supplanting it with a version of what Anderson calls "official nationalism". By singling out, assembling, and juxtaposing particular diacritics of ethnic difference, the state has reframed 'Javaneseness' (among other official identities) in its own custodial terms and political interests.

This translocal framing of ethnicity differs from, yet engages with, understandings of togetherness among Javanese villagers who make up audiences for Indonesian officials. Exemplary Javanese speech can mute the felt relevance of abstract citizenship, as it mutes the relevance of the translocal national language. On one hand, topic, venue, and speaker's official status self-evidently signal the shared status of residents of an administrative district and citizens of the nation. 'Public' use of exemplary Javanese, on the other hand, resonates with the local, non-national sphere of social life, within which persons know co-present others not as co-citizens but consociates. In this respect, exemplary Javanese speech genres can help localize modern governmentality, and Javanize exogenous forms of authority.

5. Bureaucratic Javanese?

Exemplary Javanese, I have argued, affords a way of performatively figuring self-evidently personal exemplariness, and mitigating the official character of state oversight of villagers' lives. In silent, sanctioning absence lies the possibility of state power being temporarily and publicly figured in local Javanese terms, and of state legitimacy being embedded in a traditional logic of power relations. But this is no seamless grafting of ethnic on to national forms of speech in a reinvented style of New Order authority. Smooth or not, this social transition is grounded and given impetus by the New Order's distinct interests and dominant governmentality, for which Indonesian is the efficient, uniform, superordinate language. The public use of exemplary Javanese is in this respect tacitly circumscribed by the state's purposes; when those purposes do not lend themselves to dissimulation, state functionaries are obliged to represent the state more transparently. Differences in the authoritativeness of standard Indonesian and exemplary Javanese can then refract in stylistically and socially dissonant acts of public speech.

Occupants of niches in the bureaucracy now superposed on local communities are ultimately responsible to the state as the implementers of rules and decisions conveyed through its official hierarchies. Their dependence on this hierarchy, and subservience to their administrative superiors, may be clearest when they must function as local conduits for state information and directives. To act publicly in such transparently mediating capacities requires a mode of talk which is correspondingly transparent in respect of both content and genre of official information, which is written and (ostensibly) disseminated uniformly across national space. That medium is Indonesian.

Such duties can impinge, then, on local enactments of authority, and engender the kinds of generic and social tension which appear in Text 2. This is taken from a meeting in which the state comes into its most local contact with a very tiny segment of its peripheral, partially illiterate populace. This is a meeting of male heads of households of one of the state's smallest administrative units, the neighbourhood of forty or so households called the *rukun tetangga*, or *RT* (pronounced *er te*). The speaker is the official head of this unit, a kind of *primus inter pares* known and addressed as *Pak RT* (roughly, 'Father RT'). He meets every two weeks or so with members of this government-sponsored group called by the Indonesian acronym *Kelompencapir*. This is an acronym for *Kelompok pendengar, pembaca, dan pirsawan*, which can be glossed briefly as 'group of readers, listeners, and watchers', i.e. consumers of the (state-sponsored, state-supervised) mass media.

These are also convenient venues, by no coincidence, for doing local state business and mediating relations between subdistrict heads (like the *lurah* who provided Text 1) and neighbourhood groups. This *RT* normally addresses his audience in exemplary Javanese, but at this point in this meeting finds himself obliged to animate a directive issued by Indonesian authorities, in Indonesian words. His effort to effect a transition between his statuses, speaking roles, and relations to his audience is not entirely successful, and gives rise to generic tensions which are symptomatic of ambiguities and tensions implicit in the use of exemplary Javanese to a peripheral Indonesian public.

Pak RT has reached a point in the meeting – otherwise entirely in formal if not entirely exemplary Javanese – where he notifies his audience of new regulations which have come from the Ministry of the Interior concerning requirements for prospective local officials. That he presumes at least passive knowledge of Indonesian is clear from the fact that he reads but does not translate these regulations save for the word *underpol* (lines 16-17), which means something like 'accomplice' and is in fact extremely rare. But he is concerned to frame this considerable Indonesian verbiage (italicized in the text) within a sustained Javanese discourse, interpolating core Indonesian phrases and words into speech otherwise marked as generically Javanese by a variety of grammatical and syntactic markers. At lines 18-20, for instance, he reads directly regulation F – *tidak dicabut hak pilihnya berdasarkan keputusan pengadilan* – without a Javanese gloss, but does repeat the two key phrases (*hak pilih,* 'voting rights' and *tidak dicabut* 'not withdrawn') within an utterance otherwise marked as exemplary Javanese (by *Dados* 'so, thus' and *-ipun* 'genitive marker').

Text 2: Kelompencapir/The reading, listening, and watching group

Déné syarat-syaratipun mangké dados *ketua* sáhá *pengurus* èr té menika: setunggal,	[1]	As for the requirements to become *head* and *supervisor* of the neighbourhood: first,
nggih meniká ingkang *bertakwa terhadap* *Tuhan yang maha ésa*, nggih meniká		that is *devotion to* *God Almighty*, that is
setunggal. Bab *tugas kepengurusan,* setung-gal inggih meniká *bertaqwa terhadap* *Tuhan yang maha ésa.* Kaping kalih nggih	[5]	first. As for *duties of administration,* one is *devotion to God the* *Almighty.* Number two,
meniká, *setia* sáhá *taat kepada* *Pancasila* sáhá *undang-undang dasar empat*		that is, *faithful and observant of* *Pancasila* and *the constitution of forty-*

puluh
lima. Kaping tigá nggih meniká [10]
setia sáhá
taat kepada negara dan
pemerintah.
Sekawan nggih meniká
berkelakuan baik,
jujur, adil, cerdas dan berwibawa. Lajeng
E: *tidak pernah terlibat langsung*
atau
tidak langsung wontenipun [15]
pengaruh
gerakan *Gé* tiga puluh *S/PKI*, sáhá
*underpol*ipun, *underpol* meniká
bawahan-
nya *dari pada Pé Ka I.* Ef: *tidak*
dicabut
hak pilihnya berdasarkan
keputusan
pengadilan. Dados *hak pilihipun* [20]
tidak
dicabut. gé: nggih meniká *sehat*
jasmani
lan *rochan*inipun. Ha: *dapat*
membaca dan
menulis aksárá latin. I: *telah*
bertempat
tinggal tetap sekurang-kurangnya
nam
bulan dengan tidak terputus-putus. [25]
Menika
*syarat-syarat*ipun. Dados
bertempat wonten
mriki *sedikitnya enam bulan tidak*
terputus-
putus. Lajeng *yang dapat ditunjuk*
menjadi
pengurus rukun tetangga
*seluruh*ipun
warga sebagai yang dimaksud [30]

five. Third, that is
faithful and
loyal to nation and
government.
Four, that is *good*
conduct,
fair, just, clever and authoritative.
Then
E: *never involved directly*
or
indirectly in the *influence*
of the
*movement of G thirty S/*PKI or
their *underpol,* 'underpol' are
subordinates
of the PKI. F: *the right to vote*
has not
been taken away on the basis of a
court
verdict. So the *voting rights*
haven't been
taken. G: This is *healthy in body*
and the
mind. H: *can read*
and
write Latin letters. I: *have*
lived
permanently at least
six
months without interruption.
Those are
the *requirements.* So
residing here [means]
at least six months
continuously.
So *those who can be*
designated
neighbourhood heads all of
them
are *members as meant by, by*

maksud	*the intent of*
ayat satu dan dua adalah	*stipulations one and two are*
penduduk setempat warga	*local residents, citizens*
negara terdapat	*found*
terdaftar pada kartu keluarga.	*listed on the family register.*
Pokokipun	The main
meniká ingkeng saged dados	thing is, those who can
inggih meniká	are
penduduk asli, nggih meniká [35]	*native residents*, that is
penduduk	*residents*
ingkang sampun kagungan *Ka*	who have a *Ka*
Ka, Kartu	*Ka, family*
Keluarga kados kálá mbèn	*register*, like before.
meniká. Meniká	Those,
párá sedhèrèk *syarat-*	siblings, are the
*syarat*ipun. Mbok	*requirements*. Perhaps
menawi mbenjing mangké utawi	another day later or
mbenjing	in the future
badhé ng*leksana*kaken [40]	will be *carried* out *an*
pemilihan meniká	*election*, [candidates]
kedah *memenuhi syarat* menika,	must *meet* these *requirements*,
awit	because
meniká dipun, a,	these have been, uh, have been
dipun*sah*kan	*official*ized
saking *mentri dalam negeri.*	by the *Minister of the Interior.*

Pak RT ventriloquates official Indonesian words by imbricating them into the fabric of 'his own' Javanese speech, but in so doing creates a momentary stylistic awkwardness. This could be traced, along lines suggested by Bakhtin (1981), to the monologic nature of discursive authority: two such ostensibly authoritative modes of discourse are forced here into a heteroglot, dissonant juxtaposition. That dissonance indexes the broader lack of fit between the state's translocal business and the mutualistic expectations of locally gathered consociates. *Pak RT* here attempts to maintain a double relation to the text he is reading. As faithful mediator between state and citizens, he tries to mitigate social differences by juxtaposing their differentially appropriate genres. He works to domesticate the state's business by setting off a temporarily unmuted officialness from his otherwise exemplary talk as co-ethnic neighbour.

6. Conclusion

Such institutional, generic, performative tensions appear as tiny, transient wrinkles in the social fabric of Indonesian Javanese public talk, but they bespeak a broader, underlying accommodation between the malleable political culture of prenational Central Java and the Indonesian state's ideology and interests. This might be less convergence than transient reflex of rapid change from prenational Javanese polity to postcolonial nation-state, and so from what Habermas might call the absolutist public sphere of an exemplary centre to Mills' state-dominated mass society. Such an argument would have much in common with neotraditional readings of political and cultural change in Indonesia, and can be reinforced by the obvious, nontrivial observation that the Indonesian state apparatus is dominated by a new Javanese elite which has done much to assimilate a particular version of Javanese tradition into a new Indonesian high public culture.

To situate (transcripts of) tiny bits of talk against the backdrop of complex social transitions which they transiently serve, I have had recourse to a notion of 'public' not as sphere of neutral discourse by and among co-equal citizens, but in the more theatrical sense of audience, gathered for performances sponsored and performed by authoritative Javanese Indonesian speakers. I have tried to usc it as a rubric for construing the extension and implementation of state power at some of its peripheries. Talk to such peripheral publics may disguise or dissemble differences between modes of speakership, sponsoring authority, and co-presence among co-villagers who must partake of citizenship in the nation-state. New kinds of public, exemplary Javanese may help reproduce and modify hierarchical relations, and subserve a broader transition to Indonesian genres of public talk. And with these shifts, perhaps, will emerge genuinely new modes of public citizenship, modalities of public speakership, and, perhaps, of public political action.

References

Anderson, B.R.O'G. (1990) *Language and Power: Exploring political cultures in Indonesia*, Ithaca: Cornell University Press.

------ (1972) 'The Idea of Power in Javanese Culture', in C. Holt, B. Anderson and J. Siegel (eds) *Culture and Politics in Indonesia*, Ithaca: Cornell University Press, 1-69.

------ (1966) 'The Languages of Indonesian Politics', *Indonesia* 1:89-116. Reprinted in Anderson 1990.

Anderson, Benedict ([1983]1991) *Imagined Communities: Reflections on the origin and spread of nationalism*, London: Verso.

Bakhtin, M. (1981) *The Dialogic Imagination*, trans. Caryl Emerson and Michael Holquist. Austin: University of Texas Press.

Bourdieu, P. (1984) *Distinction: A social critique of the judgement of taste*, trans. R. Nice. Cambridge, MA: Harvard University Press.

Budiman, A. (ed) (1990) *State and Civil Society in Indonesia*, Clayton, Australia: Center of Southeast Asian Studies, Monash University.

Errington, J. (2000) 'Indonesian('s) Authority', in Paul Kroskrity (ed) *Regimes of Language: Ideologies, polities, and identities*, Santa Fe: School of American Research Press, 205-228.

------ (1998) *Shifting Languages: Interaction and identity in Javanese Indonesia*, Cambridge: Cambridge University Press.

------ (1992) 'On the Ideology of Indonesian Language Development', *Pragmatics* 2(3):417-427.

------ (1991) 'A Muddle for the Model: Diglossia and the case of Javanese', *Southwestern Journal of Linguistics: Special issue on diglossia* 10(1): 189-213.

------ (1988) 'Structure and Style in Javanese: A semiotic view of linguistic etiquette', *Conduct and Communication Series*, Philadelphia: University of Pennsylvania Press.

------ (1985) 'Language and Social Change in Java: Linguistic reflexes of social change in a traditional royal polity', *Monographs in International Studies: Southeast Asia Series* No. 65. Athens, OH: Ohio University Center for International Studies.

Geertz, C. (1980) *Negara*, Princeton: Princeton University Press.

Goffman, E. (1974) *Frame Analysis*, New York: Harper and Row.

Habermas, J. ([1962]1989) *The Structural Transformation of the Public Sphere*, trans. Thomas Burger. Cambridge, MA: MIT Press.

Heryanto, A. (1990) 'State Ideology and Civil Discourse', in A. Budiman (ed) *State and Civil Society in Indonesia*, Clayton, Australia: Center of Southeast Asian Studies, Monash University, 289-300.

Hoffman, J. (1979) 'A Foreign Investment: Indies Malay to 1901', *Indonesia* 27:65-92.

Keeler, W. (1987) *Javanese Shadow Plays, Javanese Selves*, Princeton, NJ: Princeton University Press.

Pemberton, J. (1989) 'The Appearance of Order: A politics of culture in colonial and postcolonial Java', Ph.D. dissertation, Cornell University.

Schutz, A. (1967) *The Phenomenology of the Social World*, Evanston, IL: Northwestern University Press.

Tambiah, S. (1985) 'The Galactic Polity', in *Culture, Thought, and Social Action*, Cambridge, MA: Harvard University Press.

------ (1976) *World Conqueror and World Renouncer*, Cambridge: Cambridge University Press.

8. Creating Evidence
Making Sense of Written Words in Bosavi[1]

BAMBI B. SCHIEFFELIN

1. Introduction

Since their earliest contact with Europeans, the Kaluli people, who live at
the foothills of Mt Bosavi in the Southern Highlands Province of Papua
New Guinea, have viewed books as powerful and authoritative sources of
information that white people use to shape and control the behaviour of
others. In a narrative told to Steven Feld and myself in 1990 about government contact in the early 1950s, an educated Kaluli man told us about
his father who had been selected by white patrol officers as the first local
counsellor. As he put it, "my father was given the black shirt with a red
stripe, the belt, knife, stick and *a book*, that book, people thought that if
you kill, the blood of a dead person will go inside in the book, and the
white man will know straight away and come and shoot you with a gun;
that fear, everywhere so, everyone got frightened when my father got this".

This book, which was kept by the counsellor as part of his responsi-
bilities and taken out only during infrequent government patrols made
by white officers, listed the names of villagers. While Kaluli people did
not share an understanding of why their names were written down by
government people, they did not miss the fact that this book and its meanings were created and owned by white people, who used it as an instrument
of control, authority, and information. These early census and record-
keeping activities, part of pacification efforts, were used to track and
document Kaluli people in order to discourage their periodic relocation
to new village sites, a practice that was their means of minimizing the

[1] I would like to thank the National Science Foundation and the Wenner-Gren
Foundation for Anthropological Research for funding fieldwork in 1984 and 1990.
Thanks also go to Steve Feld and Elinor Ochs for their always helpful comments.
Finally, I would like to thank Sue Gal and Kit Woolard for their cogent written
comments, as well as the other members of the Center for Transcultural Studies
Working Group on Language and the participants in the School for American
Research Seminar on Language Ideologies for asking tough questions.

This essay is dedicated to the late Kulu Fuale; his patience and assistance in
helping me understand the Kaluli language for over fifteen years was enriched by
his unique linguistic curiosity.

depletion of local resources. This was one of the earliest experiences for Kaluli people of what books could do, and what people did with books.

In the mid-1960s, two other changes occurred that would introduce additional ideas about books and literacy more generally. The first, which I would like to think was relatively benign though not inconsequential, was the arrival of anthropologists, first E. L. Schieffelin, followed by myself and Steven Feld, whose visitations of different durations would continue into the present. The second change, which has had far-reaching consequences for Kaluli social and ceremonial life, was the establishment of a fundamentalist mission and air strip which was managed by a Papuan National until Australian missionaries arrived in the early 1970s.[2]

This essay focuses on new communicative practices that emerged as a result of interactions between Kaluli people and two Australian missionaries from the Asia Pacific Christian Mission, a small undenominational fundamentalist Protestant group who arrived in the early 1970s. To do this, I draw on ethnographic and linguistic fieldwork begun in 1967 that has continued intermittently into the present. Tape-recorded, transcribed analyses of social interaction over time and across a wide range of situations and activities, in addition to participant observation and informal interviews form the foundation of this analysis (Schieffelin 2000, 1990, 1986). Additional ethnographic, sociolinguistic, and ethnomusicological analyses have also informed my assertions (Feld 1990, 1988; Feld and Schieffelin 1982; Schieffelin and Feld 1998; E. L. Schieffelin 1976).

As Kaluli people were introduced to new forms and sources of knowledge about their own and the outside world, their ideas about truth, knowledge, and authority were challenged and changed, affecting their communicative practices as well as their social structures. In such contact situations, new communicative practices express the interests of both the missionized and the missionizers. Kaluli people were active contributors to the linguistic and social reorganization of their own society, as evidenced in the emergence of several genres new to the area.

In such situations of social change, new language socialization activities often develop. Particularly relevant for this essay are literacy lessons and sermons, both of which constitute important activities for language socialization – socialization through the use of language and socialization to use language – which continues throughout the lifecycle (Ochs and Schieffelin 1984). From a Kaluli perspective, lessons and sermons share interpretive frames and participant structures as they originate from the

---

[2] For an overview of contact and the establishment of the mission, see Schieffelin and Crittenden 1991:262-268.

same source, the Christian mission. Combining spoken forms and written materials, both genres provide a new discursive space in which Kaluli people rethink their past, one consisting of particular social practices and beliefs – and distance themselves from it.

To accomplish this distancing, several techniques are deployed. In the literacy lesson and in the written text that it draws on, two terms *mo:lu*, *tamina* ('before,' 'a long time ago, before') are systematically opposed to *o:go:* ('today, now') to create narratives about how things used to be, in contrast to how things are and should be. Part of this contrast invokes the source of the difference: what "our fathers" believed is contrasted with what "this book shows us really well" and "new words which really tell us". New facts, such as those drawn from health lessons and bible stories are used to revise boundaries or create new ones. For example, Kaluli people are reminded both in the written text and in the oral presentations that "before we didn't know", "we didn't understand", in contrast to "we now know", "we hear it really well". In classroom interaction, students are asked to register their agreement with these claims.

The practices of the past and the present/future are also coded by their assignment to gender roles; women's beliefs and activities are connected with the past, what was done before the mission was established, while men's beliefs and actions are seen as forward-looking, progressive, taking up the new ideas. Not surprising is the evaluation associated with each of these positionings: women are negatively evaluated while men are viewed positively. These concepts are promoted in literacy materials and fortified through oral presentation and lessons by extensive linguistic means, including an innovation in the evidential system, which further underscores an increased remoteness of the not-very-distant past.

2. Literacy and social change

This essay draws on a body of ethnographic work that views literacy practices and activities as historically contingent, ideologically grounded, and culturally organized (Besnier 1995; Collins 1991; Duranti and Ochs 1986; Gewertz and Errington 1991; Guss 1986; Heath 1983; Kulick and Stroud 1990; McKenzie 1987; Street 1984; Street and Besnier 1994). This work demonstrates that societies 'take up' or organize literacy practices in culturally variable ways, depending on who is interested in literacy and how literacy is viewed. As with other genres and activities, those involving literacy practices are constituted through specific interactional roles, arrangements, and sequences that use particular forms of language to enact social relationships and negotiate social identities. In situations where literacy is introduced as part of Christian missionization, literacy activities are often shaped by competing epistemological and cultural frameworks. These frameworks are encoded in the ways in which information is presented, knowledge is talked about, and analogies are drawn; they are also apparent in the connections that can *not* be made. Forms of resistance to literacy practices reflect not only linguistic ideology, but also social and historical forces more broadly. Thus it is also useful to situate this work within current ethnohistorical accounts of competing language ideologies that have played a role in shaping colonial and missionary encounters (Cohn 1985; Comaroff and Comaroff 1991; Fabian 1986; Mignolo 1992; Rafael 1988).

3. Truth and evidence for it

Kaluli people, like many Papua New Guinean societies, are concerned with the source and truth of what they and others know. They have well-elaborated ideas of how truth is constituted, proven and linguistically marked. In the so-called old days, before missionaries, government patrols, and anthropologists, sources of knowledge and proofs of truth were relatively stable – what the fathers said was what was known and believed by mature members of society. There was little reason to doubt the truthfulness of what had always been said about the natural and supernatural worlds that Kaluli people inhabited. Through direct experience, the spoken word and face-to-face interaction, cultural knowledge was orally represented, and authority and responsibility could be argued, and often were.

Through the mid-1970s and into the 1980s, the missionaries introduced new facts about the world, ones they claimed to be either scientific or religious. These facts were soon represented through new words, genres, registers, and conventions for speaking. Literacy in the vernacular and Tok Pisin was introduced. The Bosavi mission primary school used English as the language of instruction, but Kaluli people did not know either English or Tok Pisin. The few who successfully completed six years of primary school were drafted immediately into mission service: some were trained as pastors, store assistants, or medical assistants. All became important players in the changing social order. With the exception of one individual whose narrative opened this essay, before the early 1980s no one had been educated beyond grade 6.

The fundamentalist missionaries worked hard to establish their authority and took the view that conversion should move rapidly. Their evaluations of local cultural practices were echoed in Kaluli conversations, arguments, and sermons. By 1984 Kaluli people had given up traditional ceremonies and many 'traditional' practices. With Christianity and its new material resources, the social organization of Kaluli society began to change: what had been a small-scale egalitarian society began to reshape itself into a loosely stratified society with new roles (jobs) such as pastor, deacon, aid post orderly, and trade store manager. Eventually, Christians and non-Christians took up residence in different parts of the village. Whatever power had been granted formerly to older men was now taken by those who had gained knowledge of how the mission, the mission store, and the missionary worked.

These social changes had linguistic consequences. Young men who acquired Tok Pisin extended their interactional range and could work as interpreters for the government patrol officers. The few young men who became literate in Tok Pisin and Kaluli, and were part of the mission effort, collaborated with the Australian missionary and translated texts from Tok Pisin (*Nupela Testamen*) or English (health booklets and literacy primers) into new varieties of the Kaluli language – varieties that were constructed by a powerful non-native speaker in conjunction with native speakers who wanted to acquire power. Of the four mutually intelligible dialects in the Bosavi area, one had been randomly selected earlier by a mission field linguist to be used for the orthography (Rule 1966) and many features of dialect variation exist in the literacy materials, in addition to many spelling inconsistencies and syntactic simplifications and errors.

As a result of these collaborations, a new medium was created – booklets printed in a new variety of the vernacular. Written with the authority of the mission, they introduced several new types of evidence into Kaluli life; the first is the written Kaluli word. Simple but dramatic narratives urged social change. The motif here, and in sermons, was consistent: the past versus the present/future, articulated through examples of Kaluli ways of life which were depicted as backward, wrong, and deriving from false beliefs. These were in contrast to European ways of doing things (from building houses, to health practices, to hairstyles) which were presented as new, right, and good. Simple line drawings by the missionaries served as illustrations. Narratives took place in recognizable local places, and characters had Kaluli names. To make these narratives more believable, the missionary illustrated the more advanced booklets with black-and-white photographs of local people engaged in the activity described in the narrative. So in reading the texts, Kaluli could see themselves imaged, participating in the new practices being promoted. These graphic and photographic images were used as and became evidentials, that is, another new source of evidence for authority and truth. Combined with print, they became a source of knowledge that could be seen, referred to, and reported on. Booklets introduced new information in new formats. They became the source of that information, and evidence for it. Those with access to these new sources of knowledge and truth, or those who could claim to understand them, became authorities themselves.

4. Evidentials

From a linguistic perspective as well as a social perspective, Kaluli people have always been concerned with evidence.[3] Their language provides them with a range of evidentials, morphological and lexical means used by speakers to formally mark the source or evidence for the basis of their assertions, their attitudes towards knowledge, and the responsibility assumed in making a claim.[4] Evidential particles, metalinguistic verbs (e.g. verbs of saying) and other sensory verbs indicating sources of knowledge (e.g. hearing, seeing), and reported speech are just some of the means by which speakers establish the truth of their assertions and take responsibility for them. For example, in Kaluli discourse, ranging from casual conversation to more formal arguments, speakers indicate through morphological or lexical means whether what they are saying derives from direct experience, visual, verbal or sonic information, speech reported to them or re-reported to them, common knowledge, or inference made from other secondary evidence.

---

[3] This seems to be the case for several groups on the Great Papuan Plateau. Ernst, for example, describes the importance of evidence among the Onabasulu, who are neighbours of the Kaluli, noting that, "the importance of 'seeing' or experiencing something in determining its 'reality' is ubiquitous" (Ernst 1991:203). He reports that the Onabasulu language as well as the nearby Etoro language, grammatically encodes distinctions between knowledge which is acquired by direct experience (hearing, seeing) in contrast to knowledge that is secondhand, a pattern similar to Kaluli.

[4] According to William Foley, "evidentials are restricted in Papuan languages to the Engan family and languages geographically contiguous to it in the Southern Highlands Province. It is clearly an areal feature" (Foley 1986:165).

Selected evidentials in Kaluli*

-lo:b	speaker's assertion is based on visible/visual evidence that can be shared by addressee. *Magu we mogago:lo:b* 'this banana is bad I see'; *Do:wo: ha:na:nigabo:lo:b* 'my father is about to go I see'
-o:m	speaker's assertion is based on deduction or inference from something sensed aurally or through other senses, but with out attribution of particular source. *To o:dowayo:m* 'there's talk around I'm hearing' *No: mun o:dowayo:m* 'there is the smell of cooked meat I'm smelling'
-ko	indicates direction in which an event being talked about is taking place.
-a:le	used in interrogative forms to indicate doubt regarding accuracy of information, can elicit confirmation from addressee. *Dimia:iba:le?* 'I wonder if he will give it?.' Also used when wondering aloud to indicate uncertainty and possibly seek an opinion from addressee, *Ha:na:no:wa:le? mo:ha:na:no:wa:le?* 'I wonder will I go? Will I not go?'
-le ~ -de	indicates certainty of assertions, really/truly/only. *Hedele* 'it's really true'; *Ho:nde* 'it's really water and not anything else'
-mala: ~ -bala:	negative after inference indicating disappointment. *Ne alima:no:mala:* 'I will not lie down' (seeing there is still more work to be done)
-malo: ~ -balo:	affirmative emphasis after question or when answer is opposite to what is expected. *Aoleya:le?* 'is it his real brother?' *aolemalo:!* 'it's truly his *real* brother!' but *aolemala:!* 'it's not his real brother!'[5]
-lo:do:	emphasis with disappointment/sadness. *Ha:na:no:lo:do:* 'alas you are going away'
*-lo:do: a:la:bo:	'we now know from this source, we did not know before' (used when referring to information from written sources)
*hia	extended use from the Tok Pisin 'here', visible/visual evidence, used to indicate meaning similar to *-lo:b*.

Evidence based on verbal sources use a range of forms, such as *-do:* 'immediate repeat of direct quoting of someone else'. For example, Speaker

---

[5] The form *–mala:* has two distinct meanings which are disambiguated by stress/pitch differences in the language. These are not indicated in the orthography.
* indicates recent innovation

A → B *we!* 'here!' Speaker C → B *wedo:!* 'here! (he/she said)'. The majority of evidentials for reporting speech, however, are formed with *a:la:ma/a:la: sama* 'say like that'. Context and pronouns clarify number and person. Such forms include:

a:la: siyo:	used for speaker self report or to report what another has said
a:la: sa:labeka:	'some one else recently said' (not used for lst person)
a:la: siyo:laleka	3rd hand reported speech
a:la: siyo:lo:bo:ka:	4th hand reported speech
a:la: sili sa:la:ingab	someone (sing/pl) is saying (duration)
a:la: sili sa:la:ingo:	someone (sing/pl) was saying (duration)
a:la: salan	generally said/one says (habitual)

Other sensory verbs are also used as evidentials, and the appropriate noun disambiguates or adds emphasis when needed. For example, *dabuma* 'hear', but it can also mean 'smell', *goloma* 'touch', *bo:ba* 'see', *asuluma* 'think, feel, know, understand, experience'.

Emphatic markers, both lexical and morphological are used extensively with evidentials. For example:

-ka:	emphasis when close to addressee - lst time or lst repeat
-a:	emphasis - 2nd repeat
-o	emphasis when calling out to addressee
mada	'really,' 'very'
hede	'true'
hedele	'really truly'
made hedele	'really very truly'

In contrast to the more narrow linguistic view of evidentials, which tends to focus on categories of truth (Jakobson 1957), a broader social inter-actional perspective displays their multifunctionality (Silverstein 1985). Bybee describes evidentials as "markers that indicate something about the source of the information in the proposition" (1985:184). Willett has pointed out that the notional boundaries of eviden-tiality are still unclear, but as a semantic domain, evidentials "participate in the expression of the speaker's attitude toward the situation his/her utterance describes" (1988: 52). Bendix suggests that it is not enough to analyze the epistemological categories of evidentials, but one must view them as important resources used by speakers to manipulate claims of responsibility and evidence in strategic interaction (1994:243). The social and historical context of the topic of talk, as well as the social relationship that holds between inter-locutors, can affect the choice of evidential marker, which, as Fox and Clifford (1991) point out, is sensitive to differences in claims to authority.

Emphatic markers, affect markers, and evidentials often co-occur in the same word or same utterance, and must be considered together. Analyses of evidentials in discourse highlight the importance speakers attach to establishing their authority with their audience, while acknowledging the dialogical nature of the production of meaning. Evidentials are used to convey affective and propositional meanings, and the same evidential markers may serve both functions. Haviland suggests "propositions [...] live in a moral universe, which includes not only what participants take as true, or what they agree to think, but also agreements about *how* to think and feel about what they agree upon" (1989:61). Persons not only exchange claims about the world, but their affective stances towards such claims. Givón (1982) has pointed out that speakers and hearers have an implicit contract to mark degrees of certainty in their propositions. Propositions that are to be taken for granted and viewed as unchallengeable by the hearer require no evidentiary justification by the speaker. Propositions that are asserted with relative confidence and are open to challenge by the hearer require evidentiary justification (ibid.:24). Furthermore, in situations of conflict, what may be contested is not the claim itself, but how someone knows it. Thus the use of an evidential is telling, and its choice is critical.

Drawing on linguistic examples, Chafe and Nichols suggest that an analysis of evidentials reveals a "natural epistemology" (1986:vii). I would like to suggest that when evidentials are examined in the context of their use in social interaction, such analysis reveals a cultural epistemology. Everyday talk offers excellent opportunities to examine how individuals persuade, argue, and make claims using evidentials. Activities of talk in situations of rapid social change often take up the topic of competing epistemologies, each differently valorized. Such cultural situations may result in linguistic innovations, expressed through evidentials as well as other linguistic means. I share a view with other linguistic anthropologists (e.g. Haviland 1989; Hill and Irvine 1993; Lucy 1993) that the encoding of knowledge, authority, and truth is a linguistic as well as a social phenomenon; the two must be viewed as interdependent.

5. The health lesson

My analysis of Kaluli literacy lessons, which introduce 'scientific facts', shows innovations in morphological forms expressing epistemic stance, as well as in rhetorical and event structures. These linguistic changes are a notable response to missionization and underscore Kaluli concern with the sources and nature of knowledge and truth.

The particular event I draw from is a transcribed audio-taped literacy lesson that used a booklet about malaria, a health problem in the area. The event took place in 1984 at the Bosavi mission school. It is part of a larger project I am conducting on Kaluli language use and social change that draws on materials collected since 1967. In this new speech event, as in other innovated genres, all levels of language have been affected – the phonology, morphology, lexicon, syntax, semantics, pragmatics, and of course, the cultural assumptions that organize speech activities. In spite of the fact that literacy instruction events draw on models of instruction imported from Western classrooms, there is clear evidence of local language ideology throughout. We will see how at a particular point in Kaluli history, written texts were granted authority as Kaluli people constructed linguistic means for entitling texts and making them authentic and authoritative sources of factual knowledge, even when there was no basis in fact for doing so.

The participants in this speech event are the instructor, Kulu Fuale (KF in the transcriptions), one of the few Kaluli Christians trained to teach vernacular literacy, and 24 teenaged male students in the 5th grade class. Kulu, who was fluent in Tok Pisin and spoke a little English, called this a health lesson. The lesson lasted 45 minutes; most of the time was spent focused on a booklet about malaria.

Two printed texts that have been translated into the vernacular are used in this event. The first, a booklet about malaria, is based on an English script, and is widely used by missionaries in Papua New Guinea. The Kaluli version was created and translated by Keith Briggs, the missionary in charge of the Bosavi station, collaboratively with Kulu Fuale. However, during the course of the lesson Kulu repeatedly asserts that "Briggs wrote it". Kaluli people do not take credit for the production of these materials. The remainder of the lesson drew on a second written text, a selection of verses from the New Testament translated from Tok Pisin into Kaluli by Kulu. Both are presented as containing truths previously unknown. This essay focuses on the first part of the health lesson.

I base my analysis on my transcription of the entire 45-minute audio-taped event, during which time Kulu reads from and talks about both written texts, writes on the board, talks about other topics, and elicits class responses. The transcription and the printed texts must be considered together because of two significant relationships: between the written texts and the oral text (word–word relationship), and between the oral presentation and the world that is represented, or misrepresented, through it. Selections from the transcript will be used to illustrate how evidence is marked in a variety of ways.

6. General participant and event structure

The introduction of Christian church services and adult literacy classes exposed the Kaluli people to a radically different presentational and participation structure. Previously, in most Kaluli speech situations, no single speaker controlled the floor, speakers self-selected and many voices, some quite loud, made simultaneous contributions to whatever topics were being entertained. In contrast, Christian speaking events can be characterized as those in which a single speaker controls the floor and, in addition, has all the relevant and correct information. There are no interruptions; group response is elicited, coordinated, and in unison, in response to questions that seek one answer. Question–Answer sequences that are used in local sermons are similar to those found throughout lessons. They are unlike any other discourse sequence I have recorded in over 150 hours of transcribed Kaluli speech. They resemble the Western-style classroom Question–Answer sequence with one correct answer, which is searched for until it is reached. Furthermore, Christian discussion is orderly and voices are never raised. Literacy lessons are similar in this regard. In addition, they share framing devices and the participant structure found in local sermons. This is not surprising given the strong influence of and connection between Christian activities and schooling, including vernacular literacy classes. For example, in this literacy lesson, Kulu begins the class with the directive that all will sing a song that uses a popular hymn melody to which he has set new words.[6]

KF] tambo
1   *everyone*

2   gisalowo: mo:la:bi
     will sing a song

3   (sings) ne o:ba: ganalabo: da:da:sen da:da:sen da:da:sen
     I hear hear hear birds singing

4   okay
     okay

---

[6] Inconsistencies in orthography are due to the preservation of the dialect features of speakers. Inconsistencies in the written texts are presented as they appear in the original materials. There are inconsistencies of spelling, as well as grammatical errors throughout the written literacy materials, and these sometimes cause difficulty in reading. There are discussions in the lesson of problems with the 'writing' (spelling), but they are beyond the scope of this paper. See Schieffelin (2000) for a detailed discussion of this aspect of Kaluli literacy and its relationship to orality.

5   one two (class sings song in unison)
         one two

6   mada o:m
         thank you

After singing the first line of the song, Kulu uses 'okay' (1.4) as a discourse boundary marker, and counts in English, 'one, two' so that the students will all sing together. This introduced style of singing departs from Kaluli song style, which has a very different aesthetic structure (Feld 1988). After the students sing, Kulu thanks them. The use of *mada o:m* ('thank you') which is viewed by Kaluli people as a mission-introduced concept and expression, also marks this as a Christian activity.

All the students have copies of the booklet on malaria and its prevention called *Hamule e walaf bo:lo*: ('Hamule got sick') and standing in the front of the class, holding the booklet, Kulu announces the topic (1.9) "what mosquitoes do" and directs everyone's attention to the book, the source of the information.

Kulu is holding the booklet

9   o:go: kiso:wa:lo: dimidabo: ko:lo: kiso:wa:lo: dimidabo: ko:lo: agelema:niki
         today, what the mosquitoes do, what the mosquitoes do, that's what we are
         reading about

10-11   we bo:ba, Hamule we
         look at this, Hamule here (re the booklet)

12   taminamiyo: kiso:wa:yo: a:la: dimidabo:**lo:do: a:la:bo:** niyo: mo:asulan
         ko:sega
         *before, what mosquitoes do **we now know** we did not know these things but*

13   mo:lu nili doima:yo: ko:sega o:go: **dinafa asulab buko: wema: walasalab**
         before, our fathers (erg), *but now we really know, this book* (erg) *shows/*
         instructs

14   a:la:fo: ko:lo: niliyo: **buko: wena ba:da:sa:ga:**
         therefore when we look in this book

15   tif s/c taminamiyo: niyo: mo:asulo: ko:sega no niyo: nulu alifo: alifo:labamiyo:
         kiso:wa:lo: nanog diabo: we aungabo:**lo:do: a:la:bo:**
         later s/c before we did not know, but when we are sleeping at night the work
         *mosquitoes do is like this **we now know***

16   **buko: wenamilo: to salab we da:da:sa:ga: asuluma:niki**
         listening to what the words in this book say makes us know/understand

---

The transcription preserves the breath grouping of the speaker, and the numbers used throughout indicate those breath groups. However, in some lines, (1.153), breath groups are indicated as in the original transcript using the transcription convention –. Also used is [s/c] for self-corrections by speakers. Selections from

Kulu (1.9) sets up a rhetorical framework of contrast that organizes much of the lesson: what was believed in the past as opposed to what is now known. In creating the contrast he uses an innovative evidential construction *-lo:do: a:la:bo:*. This form, used repeatedly throughout the text, (for example, 1.15) has the meaning 'known from this source/not known before,' and marks information that is new, true, and only known from the written word. This evidential does not appear in any traditional speech genres and nor is it used in other relatively recent forms of Kaluli discourse, such as translation situations involving Tok Pisin. It is an innovation by Kaluli speakers to mark new information and its new source. Kulu further elaborates this theme of contrasting the past (1.13 and also 1.15), 'what our fathers (knew) before' with the state of knowing in the present, 'but now we really know', and makes the source lexically explicit, *buko: wema: walasalab* 'this book shows/instructs'. Note that 'this book' is marked with an ergative/instrumental case marker, *it* is the agent (or instrument) which instructs and shows, *(wala sa:lab* 'show and speak') and it is by looking at the book (1.14) and listening to what the words in this book say (1.16), that understanding or knowledge is obtained. This mode of achieving understanding is different from the ways Kaluli usually learn, which is by listening to what many others say, arguing with them, watching them, and being instructed while participating (Schieffelin 1990). Source or evidence, however, is still made explicit, as is the sensory mode in which it is offered. The book has been granted an authoritative voice and becomes an authoritative source. This new evidential marker is only used in speaking. It never appears in written form. In fact, no evidential markers appear in secular written vernacular texts, a point I will return to.

In addition to this innovative evidential, which we will see more of below, other evidential forms are used to indicate different sources of information. In directing the attention of the class to the booklet, Kulu uses the evidential marker *-lo:b* 'visually evident' to guide students to the top of the page, the place that they are to begin reading the text aloud as a group (1.27-28). He counts 'one two' in English to get them into vocal synchrony in the same way as when he instructed the group to sing in the opening of the class (1.5).

---

the transcript are used to illustrate particular points, but the sequential numbers of the complete transcript are retained to make this analysis usable with other analyses of the same transcript. There are no interruptions or overlaps in this speech event. Boldface is used to indicate the phenomena of interest.

KF] waːla aːnoː oːboː**loːbo**ː? taminamiloː oːdeyoː agelaːbi one two
27 *what is it* (**obv**) *on the top* (of the page)? *read the firstpart, one two*

28 haːga aːnoː agelaːbi
    what's underneath, read

Students slowly read aloud, syllable by syllable, a short text in Kaluli about preventing sickness in Bosavi.

KF] okay
29   *okay*

Marking the end of the group reading with the boundary marker 'okay' (1.29) which is used in Christian speech events, Kulu asks a number of questions which do not relate to the reading that has just been done. Instead, they relate to the cover of the literacy booklet that he is holding up and displaying to the class. The cover is simple: the words 'Bosavi' and 'Malaria' are typed in small letters at the top of the page. In the centre of the page is a black-and-white drawing of a mosquito (side view), which is circled. Placed below the drawing and filling the bottom half of the page is the title written in large bolded capital letters, '*Hamule e walaf boːlo*': it is apparent from the response of the students that the referent about which Kulu is speaking is not at all clear.

30   aːnoː oːba?
            what is it?

student]   walaf
31   *sickness*

KF]   kalu wi oːba?
32   *what is the person's name?*

class]   Hamule
33

KF]   Hamule Hamule aːnoː
34   *Hamule it's Hamule*

35   e oːbaː walaf boːloː**loːbo**ː?
            from what did he get sick (**obv**)?

36   walafoː oːbaː walaf boːloː**loːbo**ː?
            sickness, from what did he get sick (**obv**) ?

37   walafoː oːb walaf boːloː**loːbo**ː?
            sickness, from what did he get sick(**obv**) ?

student]   malalia
38   *malaria*

KF]   waːla bukoː aːnoː boːba waːla waːlamiloː aːnoː boːba39 *look on the front of the book, on the front, look on the front* [drawing of mosquito]

student] 40	kiso: *mosquito*
KF] 41	a:no: wiyo: o:b salaba? (pointing to title) Hamule e walaf bo:lo: what does the name say? Hamule he got sick
42	a:no: piksa we o:bo:**lo:bo**:? *this picture, what is it* (**obv**)?
class] 43	kiso: *mosquito*

In lines 30-34 Kulu establishes that what he wants the group to focus on is the title of the book. Once that is established, he attempts to elicit a particular response to his question about the source of Hamule's sickness. His attempt to get the class to view the drawing of the mosquito above the title as visual evidence of the source is accomplished over several turns. Using the evidential marker *-lo:b*, Kulu asks the class three times (1.35-37) about Hamule's sickness, what caused it, what it was. What is visually obvious is the drawing of the mosquito and after receiving an answer to his third question, Kulu asks the class to look at the picture on the cover of the booklet (1.39) for the answer. His assumption is that the visual evidence is obvious. When only one student answers *kiso:* 'mosquito', Kulu explicitly refers to the picture (1. 42). Only then does he get the desired group response. Throughout his talk about the source of the sickness, malaria (1. 25-37, 42 and elsewhere), he uses the evidential form *-lo:b* to indicate that the information is *visually* available.[7]

In contrast to this pattern of evidential choice, when Kulu refers to information, or wants the class to focus on information that is in the written texts, he shifts to evidentials that mark verbal evidence. In other words, the print and the book are classified as speaking subjects. Printed words do not have the same evidential status as graphic representations or

---

[7] Throughout the lesson, students do not use evidentials in their answers. In fact, their clipped one-word responses here and throughout the lesson have no morphological marking at all. In conversation, an answer would be marked with the evidential *–lo:b* to indicate that the hearer shares the same evidentiary base with the speaker. The only form produced by a student that resembles an evidential occurs in response to a question Kulu asks about how many students are in the class. One student responds using a code-switched English and Tok Pisin utterance "twenty-two *hia*" 'twenty-two here'. This is the context in which *–lo:b* would be appropriate, but it is not used. I am currently examining the extent to which Tok Pisin *hia* is being used as an evidential in other types of Kaluli discourse.

something that is visually evident. In addition Kulu marks these speaking subjects with ergative case marking, and uses verbs of speaking such as *a:la:ma* 'say like that' and *sama* 'speak/say' to provide evidence for what is in the text, as well as to give authority to the text, verbal authority. He extends this authority to himself at the same time.

52   **mada** a:la:sa:ga: kalu nowo: walaf bo:lo:wamiyo: kalu nowo: walaf
        ba:labamiyo: o: walafdo: a:na diya:sa:ga: a:la:sa:ga: no ami dimian**ka: a:la:**
        salabka: wema:
        really after one man gets sick, another man gets sick, (the mosquito) *takes*
        from the sick one and then gives it (malaria) *to another man it really says like*
        that, this **(erg-book)**

53   walafdo: a:na diya:sa:ga: nowa dimian**ka: a:la: salab** walafdo: a:no: ho:bo:wo:
        wasuliya:sa:ga: nowa iliga:ifa:la:i **so:lo:lka:** e mulumudo: a hononamilo: walaf
        ege owami a:na wa:ta:sa:ga: kalu amiyo: o:lan**ka:**
        having taken from a sick one, it really gives to another it says, after mixing the
        blood of the sick one it sends (the sickness) *to many I'm really saying, in the*
        sickhouse over there, after drawing the sickness in the needle (stinger), (mos-
        quito) *really shoots* (injects) *a man*

Kulu uses *wema: a:la: salabka:* 'this one [the book, marked with the ergative casemarker] really says like that', (1.52) *buko: wema:* [...] *walasalab* 'this book instructs' (1.62), *a:la: salab* 'it says like that' (1.53) in addition to variants of these expressions to locate the source of his assertions about mosquitoes. In addition he frequently adds *so:lo:ka:* 'I'm really saying', combining a range of emphatics including *-ka:* and *-balo:* 'emphatic counter to expected' (1.60) and other lexical items including *mada* 'really', *hede* 'truly', with their own emphatics to substantiate his own authoritativeness.

60   ni welo: nan**balo:** ko:lo: sab**ka:** ho:bo:wo: ko:sega ho:bo:wo: nan**balo:**
        a:no: noma:lo:wo: nowa a: dia:fa:na:lila wo:gelabamiyo:
        they really drink from us that really live here, blood but they really drink
        blood, from one to another they keep on putting it in mixing it all up

61   o: walaf ko:li ko:lilo:wo: a:na fa:la:lowab**ka: a:la: salab**
        all different sickness really comes up from that mixing it says like that

62   a:la:fo: ko:lo: o: walaf mo: a:no: o:go: **buko: wema:** iliki nimo: **walasalab**
        a:no:
        therefore the sickness's beginning/cause now having this book **(erg)** *in-*
        structs us about that

63   mo:wo: mada dinafa do:do:l
        I really hear/understand the cause well

64   a:la:fo: ko:lo: ege buko: lidisi buko: wenami **wema:yo: mada nafa salab**
        therefore uh book, in this literacy book this **(erg)** *really says it well*

Kulu's extensive use of emphatic markers intensifies his assertions about the 'facts', their truthfulness, and how well they are stated. The literacy book not only instructs and really says it, but says it really well (1.64). These assertions are repeated throughout the lesson, and are not to be challenged.

Kulu not only presents the book as a speaking subject with its own voice, but talks about how Papua New Guineans only recently have seen them, and heard them speak.

57   Papua Nugini kalu we taminamiyo: **wengo:wo: mo:ba:ba:** ko:sega
        *PNG men **did't see one like this** (**book**) before but*

58   no mada o:g Hamule **buko: wema:yo: kobale walasalab** nimo:wo: kiso:wo:
        nulu ya:sa:ga: alifo:lab ami e nanog diyaki a:namiyo: kalu ho:bo:wo:
        wo:gelaka: **a:la: salab**
        *really today **this Hamule book** (**erg**) **instructs us well**, mosquitoes having come at night while we sleep they do their work there really mixing men's blood **it says like that***

Books become the source of understanding through hearing them speak. Kulu asserts, 'I hear/understand the reason [from the book]', (1.63) 'we are really hearing new words spoken' (1.71) and reminds the class to think about and remember what they are hearing that is new.

67   wena asula:sa:ga:yo: go:no: gelo: alilabamiyo: nuluwo: asula:bi kiso:wa:yo:
        wengo: nanog diabo:**lo:bo:no: a:la:bo:**
        *when you think about this, when you are sleeping at night remember mosquitoes do this ***we now know**, don't forget**

68   a:sa:ga: Papua Nugini us wenamiyo: taminamiyo: asula:leno:? gimo: a:dabu
        bo:do:lka: giliyo: sama asula:leno:? kiso:wa:yo: a:la: nanog diabami walafo:lo:
        kalu amiyo: a:la: kaluka:isale amiyo: a:la: balabo:**lo:b a:la:bo:**
        *in the PNG interior here did we know this before? I'm asking you all again, you all say it did we know this before? that it was the mosquitoes work that made men sick, men and women too ***we now know***

class]   mo:asula:len
69   *we didn't know*

KF]   mo:asula:len **hede salab**
70   *we didn't know, **that's truthfully said***

71   mo:asula:lenka: **a:la: salab** ko:lo: o: niliyo: **hedele ho:gi to salabo:lo:do:**
        a:la: asula:sa:ga: dinafa asuluma:niki
        *we didn't really know **it says like that**, we are **really hearing new words spoken** ***we now know** after thinking about them we will understand*

7. The visual and the verbal: captioned photographs

The literacy booklet that is used in this lesson is illustrated with black-and-white photographs of Kaluli people that are captioned in the Kaluli language. These present an interesting site in which to examine evidential choice, that is, how particular evidentials mark particular aspects of the information Kulu is querying. At different points in the lesson Kulu asks the class to look at these captioned pictures as the source of information in order to answer his questions. For example, one picture shows Kaluli adults and children sitting around and eating. The caption reads, *'Hamu-leyo: walaf bulufo: ko:lo: eso:lo: kalukaisale ma:no: dowo:ta:sa:ga: sagalaki mo:no:* ('When Hamule got well, men and women in his family cooked food and ate happily'.)

KF]	falelo: dowo: ko:lo: – o: ba falelabiki sagalab – a:no: wagaba? nodowa
153	hono so:wagaleno: sagala:li **o:siyo:** – mo:wo: ha:h? sagalo: ilido: dowab
	a:no: – walafo: dowo:**lo:b**o:?
	because he got well – because he is already well they are happy –
	what about it? on the other side there – the child is happy right there
	it said – *what's the reason? they are happy – is there sickness (**obv**)?*
	(from the picture)

student]	falele
154	*he got well*

KF]	falelo: ko:**lo:b** sagalab kelego: dima:daki a:la:fo:ko:lo: o:go: sagalab
	a:no:
155	o:bdo: miyo:wagaba?
	he got well (**obv**) *(from the picture) so they are doing happy things,*
	this happiness now, what brought it?

Kulu uses the same pattern of evidential marking in Question–Answer sequences where the focus of attention is captioned photographs. Here he carefully distinguishes between evidence which is visually evident (*–lo:b*) and that which is verbally evident (*o:siyo:*). For example, the caption says that men and women are happy and Kulu asks that the students produce the reason for that. This requires inferencing. When no response is forth-coming, he provides a possible answer, directing students to base their explanation on how people look in the photograph – *walafo: dowo:lo:bo:?* 'is there obviously sickness?' (1.153). When the student is able to provide the correct answer, Kulu reinforces it, using the evidential marker, which the student does not.

8. In and out of the text

While much of the information Kulu talks about is covered in the text, there are several places where Kulu's words radically depart from the text and from any general Kaluli notions about illness, or those derived from Western instructions. Despite his extensive use of evidentials and emphatics, and assertions of telling the truth (1.74) there is considerable leeway for inventiveness. Kulu's words are never challenged by the class.

73   igo:wo: na:sa:ga:yo:lo: ka:yo: ka:yo: diniya o:lo:so:fa ko:lo: na:sa:ga:yo:lo:
mada ge alifo:likiyo: mego:fo:lo: hononaka a:la: ko:la:liya: dia:ta ka
alifo:mela:i**ka:**
after eating wild pig too fish, fish cooked in a pot, having eaten those things,
really while you are sleeping, into your mouth which is open, gets put in there
when you are really sleeping

74   **mada hede so:lo:l**
I'm really telling the truth

75   a:la:fo: ami eyo: o: egeyo: ko:lo: **mada** ege ko:li hinigan ilayamilo: ta:sa:ga:lo:
a:namilo: gesinamilo: babido: a:no: no a:no: ko:lo: meyo:diliya: ya:ga: a:naka
asifa: yaka
then they (mosquitoes) *the wachamacallit, really the wachamacallit different*
dirt from the shit house stays there on their claws (legs) *sticking there and*
they (mosquitoes) *come around smelling, come and sit there in the mouth*

76   a:la:ta bes hononamiyo: nagalo:wo: a:na dimia:ni mogago: e gesinamilo:
babidiliya:ga:lo: yab a:no: ge alifo:laba **mo:ba:daka: a:la: salab**
then they give tooth aches in there, with bad stuff sticking on their claws they
come when you are sleeping you really don't see it, it says like that

Kulu is able to claim authority through asserting the existence of a text that in fact is non-existent. There is no text that talks about mosquitoes and tooth decay, nor is this an idea that is shared among Kaluli people. Kulu is listened to as a teacher and a Christian, and he becomes a conveyer and interpreter of new truth because he can read the words and mark them convincingly.

The literacy lesson closely resembles sermons with its essentially monologic style, combining reading plus speaking by a knowledgeable leader. The speaking takes place without the usual feedback that organizes all other speech events and creates cohesion. Throughout this event, Kulu proposes that the class trust the language to mean what it says, to take it as literal truth. Facts are made into objects that can be pointed to in the texts, referenced through particular language forms. The genre marks the activity as being one in which only truthfulness is asserted, as in sermons, but in the literacy lesson, particular evidentials help constitute a genre and an interpretive framework for learning. It is monologic, without an author present. Without an author there is no one with whom to argue – Kaluli people have yet to have a dialogue, or an argument, with a printed text.

In this lesson, the written text and photographs are used to construct a reality that can henceforth become a material base for changes in social and linguistic ideologies and practices. These texts and their readings establish a new discursive orientation to knowledge, truth, authority, and time itself. The written text explicitly denies that Bosavi people had reasons or beliefs before contact. It presents a view that people can have control over their health if they listen to the new words. In spite of this, many local concerns are articulated throughout the lesson – and one is the Kaluli concern with evidence. Printed text and photographs come to satisfy that interest, while providing representations for re-imagining local life as Kaluli people see themselves re-located in books. In contrast to earlier fears about what white people would know about them from a book, today Kaluli names written in books take on a new meaning. Through collaboration between Kaluli and missionaries, not only have Kaluli people been re-imagined as modern Christians, but their linguistic resources have been adapted to accommodate this new view of themselves and their world. In creating themselves as a public of modern Christians, they use visual evidence in addition to printed texts. Perhaps this is the beginning of an imagined community, a prerequisite, I suspect, for a public sphere.

References

Bendix, Edward (1994) 'The Grammaticalization of Responsibility and Evidence: Interactional manipulation of evidential categories in Newari', in J. Hill and J. Irvine (eds) *Responsibility and Evidence in Oral Discourse*, Cambridge: Cambridge University Press, 226-247.

Besnier, Niko (1995) *Literacy, Emotion, and Authority: Reading and writing on a Polynesian atoll*, New York: Cambridge University Press.

Bybee, Joan (1985) *Morphology: A study of the relation between meaning and form*, Amsterdam: Benjamins.

Chafe, Wallace and Joanna Nichols (eds) (1986) *Evidentiality: The coding of epistemology in language*, Norwood, NJ: Ablex.

Cohn, Bernard (1985) 'The Command of Language and the Language of Command', *Subaltern Studies* 4:276-329.

Collins, James (1991) 'Hegemonic Practice: Literacy and standard language in public education', in C. Mitchell and K. Wesler (eds) *Rewriting Literacy: Culture and the discourse of the other*, New York: Bergin and Garvey, 229-253.

Comaroff, John and Jean Comaroff (1991) *Of Revelation and Revolution: Christianity, colonialism and consciousness in South Africa*, Vol. I, Chicago: University of Chicago Press.

Duranti, Alessandro and Elinor Ochs (1986) 'Literacy Instruction in a Samoan village', in B.B. Schieffelin and P. Gilmore (eds) *The Acquisition of Literacy: Ethnographic perspectives*, Norwood, NJ: Ablex, 213-232.

Ernst, Thomas M. (1991) 'Empirical Attitudes Among the Onabasulu', in Andrew Pawley (ed) *Man and a Half: Essays in Pacific anthropology and ethnobiology in honor of Ralph Bulmer*, Auckland: The Polynesian Society, 199-207.

Fabian, Johannes (1986) *Language and Colonial Power*, Cambridge: Cambridge University Press.

Feld, Steven (1990) *Sound and Sentiment*, 2nd ed. Philadelphia: University of Pennsylvania Press.

------ 'Aesthetics as Iconicity of Style, or, "lift-up-over-sounding"': Getting into the Kaluli groove', *Yearbook for Traditional Music* 20:74-113.

Feld, Steven and Bambi Schieffelin (1982) 'Hard Words: A functional basis for Kaluli discourse', in D. Tannen (ed) *Georgetown University Roundtable on Languages and Linguistics 1981*, Washington, DC: Georgetown University Press, 351-371.

Foley, William (1986) *The Papuan Languages of New Guinea*, New York: Cambridge University Press.

Fox, Barbara and Joseph Clifford (1991) 'Evidentiality and Authority in English Conversation', MS.

Gewertz, Deborah and Frederick Errington (1991) *Twisted Histories, Altered Contexts*, Cambridge: Cambridge University Press.

Givón, Talmy (1982) 'Evidentiality and Epistemic Space', *Studies in Language* 6(1):23-49.

Guss, David (1986) 'Keeping It Oral: A Yekuana ethnology', *American Ethnologist* 13(3):413-429.

Haviland, John (1989) '"Sure, Sure": Evidence and affect', *Text* 9(1):27-68.

Heath, Shirley (1983) *Ways with Words*, Cambridge: Cambridge University Press.

Hill, Jane and Judith Irvine (eds) (1993) *Responsibility and Evidence in Oral Discourse*, Cambridge: Cambridge University Press.

Jakobson, Roman (1957) 'Shifters, Verbal Categories, and the Russian Verb', *Russian Language Project*, Dept of Slavic Languages and Literatures, Harvard University.

Kulick, Don and Christopher Stroud (1990) 'Christianity, Cargo and Ideas of Self', *Man* (n.s.) 25:70-88.

Lucy, John (ed) (1993) *Reflexive Language: Reported speech and metapragmatics*, Cambridge: Cambridge University Press.

McKenzie, D.F. (1987) 'The Sociology of a Text: Oral culture, literacy and print in early New Zealand', in P. Burke and R. Porter (eds) *The Social*

History of Language, Cambridge: Cambridge University Press, 161-197.

Mignolo, W.D. (1992) 'On the Colonization of Amerindian Languages and Memories: Renaissance theories of writing and the discontinuity of the classical tradition', *Comparative Studies in Society and History* 32:310-330.

Ochs, Elinor and Bambi B. Schieffelin (1984) 'Language Acquisition and Socialization: Three developmental stories and their implications', in R. Shweder and R. Levine (eds) *Culture Theory: Essays on mind, self and emotion*, Cambridge: Cambridge University Press, 276-320.

Rafael, Vincente (1988) *Contracting Colonialism: Translation and Christian conversion in Tagalog society under early Spanish rule*, Ithaca: Cornell University Press.

Rule, Murray (1966) 'Customs, Alphabet and Grammar of the Kaluli People of Bosavi, Papua', Mimeo, Unevangelised Fields Missions.

Schieffelin, Bambi B. (2000) 'Introducing Kaluli Literacy: A chronology of influences', in Paul Kroskrity (ed) *Regimes of Language: Ideologies, polities, and identities*, Santa Fe: School of American Research Press, 293-327.

------ (1990) *The Give and Take of Everyday Life: Language socialization of Kaluli children*, New York: Cambridge University Press.

------ (1986) 'The Acquisition of Kaluli', in Dan I. Slobin (ed.) *The Cross-Linguistic Study of Language Acquisition*, Vol. I, Hillesdale, NJ: Lawrence Erlbaum Associates, 525-593.

Schieffelin, Bambi B. and Steven Feld (1998) *Bosavi–English–Tok Pisin Dictionary*, Pacific Linguistics Series C–153, Canberra: Australian National University.

Schieffelin, Edward L. (1976) *The Sorrow of the Lonely and the Burning of the Dancers*, New York: St. Martins Press.

Schieffelin, Edward L. and Robert Crittenden (1991) *Like People You See in a Dream: First contact in six Papuan societies*, Stanford: Stanford University Press.

Silverstein, Michael (1985) 'The Functional Stratification of Language and Ontogenesis', in James V. Wertsch (ed) *Culture, Communication, and Cognition: Vygotskian perspectives*, New York: Cambridge University Press, 205-235.

Street, Brian (1984) *Literacy in Theory and Practice*, New York: Cambridge University Press.

Street, Brian and Niko Besnier (1994) 'Aspects of Literacy', in T. Ingold (ed) *Companion Encyclopaedia of Anthropology*, London: Routledge, 527-562.

Willett, Thomas (1988) 'A Cross-linguistic Survey of the Grammaticalization of Evidentiality', *Studies in Language* 12(1):51-97.

9. Outlaw Language
Creating Alternative Public Spheres in Basque Free Radio[1]

JACQUELINE URLA

1. Introduction

The rethinking of Habermas'([1962]1989) *The Structural Transformation of the Public Sphere* by Negt and Kluge (1993), and by among others feminist and social historians Nancy Fraser (1993), Joan Landes (1988), and Geoff Eley (1992), has argued persuasively that the bourgeois public sphere has from its inception been built upon powerful mechanisms of exclusion. The idealized image of a democratic theatre of free and equal participation in debate, they claim, has always been a fiction predicated on the mandatory silencing of entire social groups, vital social issues, and indeed, "of any difference that cannot be assimilated, rationalized, and subsumed" (Hansen 1993b:198). This is especially clear in the case of those citizens who do not or will not speak the language of civil society. The linguistic terrorism performed with a vengeance during the French Revolution and re-enacted in Official English initiatives in the United States more recently, reveal to us how deeply monolingualism has been ingrained in liberal conceptions of *Liberté, Égalité*, and *Fraternité*. But perhaps silencing may not be the best way to describe the fate of linguistic minorities or other marginalized groups. For, as Miriam Hansen (1993b) notes, what the more recent work on public spheres suggests is that 'the' public sphere has never been as uniform or as totalizing as it represents itself to be. Proliferating in the interstices of the bourgeois public – in the eighteenth-century salons, coffeehouses, book clubs, and working class and subaltern forms of popular culture – were numerous counterpublics that gave lie to the presumed homogeneity of the imaginary public. Spurred in part by ethnic nationalist movements of the nineteenth and twentieth

[1] I would like to thank the many members of Molotoff Irratia in Hermani and Paotxa in Usurbil who welcomed me to their stations and gave generously of their time. I owe a special debt to Jakoba Rekondo, who first brought free radio to my attention and has provided guidance, prodding, and support throughout this project. Thanks also to Jokin Eizagirre, Olatz Mikeleiz, Ana Altuna, and Javier Esparza for their help in Euskadi, and to Kathryn Woolard and Susan Gal for intellectual inspiration and editorial advice.

centuries, speakers and writers of 'barbarous' tongues and 'illegitimate patois' can be seen as part of this history of counterpublics, who avail themselves of any number of media – from novels to oral poetry, from song and regional presses to, more recently, various forms of electronic media – to give expression to other kinds of social experience and perspectives on who the public is, what its interests might be, and what its voice sounds like.

This article examines the contemporary formation of one such counterpublic in the small towns and cities of the southern Basque country. Here, in the tumultuous years after Franco's death, Basque radical nationalist youth attempted to make use of intentionally marginal or 'outlaw' publicity – street graffiti, 'zines, low-power free radio – as well as a lively rock music scene, to give voice to their minoritized language and their not-so-polite critiques of the state, consumer capitalism, police repression, and a host of other social concerns. The alternative media and expressive culture that radical youth generated can be seen as having created a public sphere in the sense of a discursive matrix within which social experience is articulated, negotiated, and contested (Hansen 1993a). As I hope to show, the sphere they created and the linguistic strategies they mobilized in it differ significantly from those typically associated with minority language revitalization and/or ethnic nationalist movements. In the latter social movements, the nation or linguistic community is most often imagined in the singular and the public sphere is envisioned primarily as a bourgeois reading and writing public. Furthermore, in the Basque nationalist movement, as in many other linguistic minority movements, strategies of linguistic revival tend to be oriented towards *normalization*, generally understood as placing the minority language on an 'equal footing' with other official languages so that its use, oral and written, is commonplace in all spheres of social life. This involves expanding literacy and gaining legitimacy within the terms of state hegemonic language hierarchies. To this end, ethnic minority intellectuals have formed their own language academies, and literary and scientific societies, and they mobilize the tools of linguistic analysis, orthographic reform, mapping, and even the census in order to document the truth of their language and to reform the language according to notions of what constitutes a 'modern' or 'rational' language (Urla 1993). The kind of practical exigencies and urgency minority linguists and planners feel to transform their language into what Bourdieu (1991) calls a '*langue autorisé*', to demonstrate its equivalence to other 'world' languages, has led them to a concern with boundary drawing, purifying, and standardizing more commonly associated with the language ideology of the dominant public sphere.

Scholars of minority language movements have tended to focus upon these normalizing processes, yet if we look to other arenas such as the marginalized publicity of radical youth, we find a very different picture. What follows is an exploration of the public sphere of radical free radio, its distinctive ideology of radical democratic communication, and how these are reflected in a variety of linguistic strategies. Existing on the margins of legality, ephemeral, and often nomadic in both a geographic and temporal sense, free radios provide a soundtrack for minority languages, values, and cultural expression by pirating the airwaves, appearing and disappearing on the FM dial. The public constructed by radical youth is perhaps better described as a partial public, a segment of a plural, rather than singular, counterpublic sphere (cf. Hansen 1993b:209). Secondly, it is decidedly oppositional, challenging both the Spanish state and the Basque regional government's control over the terms of public discourse and the exclusions that control entails. Thirdly, while one of the aims of free radio stations is to open new avenues for the circulation of Basque, programmers embrace a more hybrid, playful, and anti-normative set of language practices than do language activists in other areas of language revitalization. Looking beyond formal language politics, beyond the academies and literacy programmes, to the particular modes of address and other linguistic forms used in these kinds of experiments in local media, I suggest, reveals a more heterogeneous conception of publics and language than our studies of minority language movements might otherwise convey.

2. The mini FM boom

In a particularly poignant passage from *A Dying Colonialism*, Frantz Fanon (1965) paints a vivid portrait of the radio as an instrument of revolutionary consciousness. Crowded together in front of the radio dial, straining to hear through the static used by the French army to jam the transmissions, peasants, not-yet-Algerians, heard more than fragmentary accounts of battles, writes Fanon; tuning in to the *Voice of Algeria* they were witness to and participants in the rebirth of themselves as citizens of the new nation of Algerians.

Besides fuelling anti-colonialist sentiment in France, Fanon's text established a link between radio and insurgency that was to inspire many of the originators of the free radio movement that emerged a decade later in western Europe. Sometimes called illegal, rebel, or pirate radio, free radio began in Italy as an underground movement of the autonomous left in the wake of May '68 and spread quickly among a variety of oppositional groups, young people, and ethnic and linguistic minorities.[2] Anarchic and ephemeral by nature, free radio captured the attention of intellectuals on the left including Félix Guattari, who, inspired by the work of Fanon and Brecht (1964) saw in the free radio movement the makings of "a molecular revolution" capable of triggering a profound social transformation from below (Guattari 1984:253).[3]

Free radio came somewhat late to the Basque provinces of northern Spain. The first ones appeared in the early eighties and by 1987-1988, at the height of the movement, there were about 50 or so stations in operation.[4] The passage of new telecommunication legislation, known as the LOT, (*Ley de Ordenación de Telecomunicaciones*) in 1988 with the attendant tightening of controls over the airwaves, was a major factor contributing to the closure of many stations and the eventual decline of the movement. They are by no means all defunct; at a meeting of the free radios of the Basque Country held in January 1994, there were representatives from sixteen radios, a handful of which have been in existence for ten years and are now permanent fixtures in town life. Nevertheless, as of this writing, free radio as a social movement has passed into history. The production of Basque language community media continues to be a very vital activity in the southern Basque Country, but most of these new media projects do not embrace the oppositional and rebellious identity that was free radio.

---

[2] For general overviews of the alternative radio movement in Western Europe and how it compares to pirate and community radio projects, see Barbrook (1987); Bassets (1981); Lewis (1984); and McCain and Lowe (1990).

[3] 'Molecular' and 'molar' are terms Guattari uses to contrast different ways of organizing social movements. Molecular collectives are composed of independent autonomous individuals, while molar collectives are homogeneous and one-dimensional (Guattari 1984). One might also find these to be useful ways of contrasting publics.

[4] Sabino Ormazabal reports that a group of Basque nationalist youth had visited the infamous Radio Alice in Italy, where Guattari worked, and set up their own clandestine radio station in San Sebastián (Gipuzkoa) as early as 1978 (Ormazabal n.d.). Certainly in its origins, Basque free radio has been closely linked to the *abertzale* or nationalist left, though most now prefer to maintain independence from any political party. Other accounts place Euskal Herria's first free radio (that is, independent of any direct political affiliation) as being created in 1984. How the history of this movement is written depends in part on one's definition of free radio. For some, affiliation with any political party disqualifies the station as a free radio.

The appearance of free radios is related directly to the radical youth movement of the eighties. In the expansive years after the Basque Statute of Autonomy was passed in 1979, youth, disenchanted with party politics, began to form youth assemblies, *gazte asanbladak*, in many towns across the southern Basque provinces.[5] Drawing on the political philosophy of the autonomous leftist movement of Italy and France, youth assemblies meld a radical democratic assembly structure with an eclectic blend of nationalist, anarchist, left, and green politics. Anti-authoritarian and bound to no party discipline, their activities call attention to the problems of youth: problems of unemployment (hovering at the time between 50 per cent and 60 per cent among people under 25), alienation, lack of housing, compulsory military service, drugs, and repressive Catholic morality. In concert with youth elsewhere in Europe, Basque youth assemblies were very active in the *okupa* ('squatters') movement. They occupied abandoned buildings demanding the right to have a youth centre, or *gaztetxe*, where they could have meetings, socialize, listen to music, and organize concerts or other kinds of events outside the framework of political parties. In some cases, depending upon the political climate of the town hall, youth houses were established easily, and in others, as in the case of the *gaztetxe* of Bilbo, the squatters were engaged in a long, drawn-out, and violent battle with the police and conservative town council that was ultimately unsuccessful. Youth assemblies and youth houses drew upon and gained strength from social institutions already well-established in Basque social life. Local bars, for example, have long been critical public spaces facilitating a healthy tradition of Basque associational culture (cf. Kasmir 1996). Typically, radical youth will have one or two bars that they frequent on a daily basis. Most often run by individuals sympathetic to the nationalist left, these bars, not unlike gay bars in the United States, function as gathering places and community bulletin boards. The walls are plastered with pictures of political prisoners, posters announcing upcoming demonstrations, sign-up sheets for various activities. Here the owners will play the kind of music youth like to hear and generally tolerate them sitting for hours playing cards, hanging out without ordering much. In some respects, then, bars have served informally as spaces for youth to

---

[5] The Basque Autonomous Community, *Comunidad Autónoma Vasca*, is an administrative unit within the Spanish state created by the passage of the Statute of Autonomy of 1979. It comprises the three provinces of Alava, Gipuzkoa, and Vizcaya. The fourth Spanish Basque province, Navarre, was established under separate jurisdiction with its own Foral Government. Three other Basque provinces are located within the territory of the French state.

find one another and interact. But the idea behind the *gaztetxe* movement
was that something more than a hang-out was needed. As one nineteen-
year-old free radio programmer explained to me, she and other young
people like her needed an alternative to the bar, a place where individuals
could come to read, organize talks, and do something other than drink
alcohol with music blaring in your ears. Bars were good for meeting your
friends and organizing concerts, she felt, but they were ultimately in the
business of making money by selling drinks. They could not provide the
kind of environment for some of the things she was interested in such as
film screenings, talks on sexuality, holistic medicine, or creative writing.
This desire for alternative public space lay behind the creation of not only
free radios, but other spaces such as Likiniano, a bookstore/coffeehouse
in Bilbo:

> Likiniano is a cultural project of a group of young people located
> within the orbit of the antiauthoritarian and assemblarian left. The
> almost quixotic aim is to break with the stupefying commercial cul-
> ture they have accustomed us to accept. Likiniano is not a store. It is
> the result of a rethinking of what our centers of debate and traditional
> culture could be (Usurbiaga 1993:8).

Free radios, like the media experiments of autonomous collectives elsewhere in Europe, need to be understood as part of this larger effort by
youth to create spaces for alternative modes of communication and cultural life (Kogawa 1985). Many radios in fact were begun by youth
assemblies and operated out of the youth houses. There is considerable
overlap in the ethos and individuals who work and frequent the radios,
gaztetxes, squatters' communities, and radical bars. Free radios, for example, placed the schedule of programmes on the bulletin boards of the
bars youth went to, sold their badges and T-shirts there, and typically had
a *kutxa*, or collection box, for donations to the radio on the counter. Free
radios performed an interesting role *vis-à-vis* these alternative spaces, for
the radios were themselves sites of cultural production – a technology
which made it possible to take the ideals, communicative practices, aesthetic forms, and cultural values of radical youth, and broadcast them
beyond the spatial limits of any specific site.

In contrast to large well-financed regional Basque radio stations that
emerged after autonomy, free radios were unlicensed, low-cost, low-tech
initiatives with a broadcast range of no more than a few miles. Being low-
tech was not just a function of inadequate money; low-tech was a part of

free radio's political commitment to democratizing access to media, making it as cheap and easy as possible to set up and sustain. Similarly, having a narrow broadcast range corresponds to free radio's attempt to use radio to create an egalitarian communicative sphere. As Kogawa, an activist in the Japanese free radio movement explains, "the service area should be relatively small, because free radio does not *broadcast* (scatter) information but *communicates* (co-unites) messages to a concrete audience" (Kogawa 1985:117). Because they are local creations and locally controlled, each station bore the imprint and reflected the interests of those who created and ran it. Those people, and only those, who participated in the radio managed the station's daily affairs, finances, and determined what would go on air. The creators of each show had virtually complete control over its content. All policy decisions regarding content or language were made by the general assembly. For example, the use of sexist language in some of the programmes came up often as a problem in my discussions with women radio programmers. But instead of writing a language code or policy, it was their feeling that the best way to address this problem was to raise the issue at general assembly and to raise awareness among members about the way in which this kind of language use reinforced gender hierarchies. What united free radios was a fierce commitment to freedom of expression, economic independence, and democratic control by assembly. In this respect, free radios were quite different in practice and in their ideology from the British offshore pirate radio stations that were so important to the development of Afro–Caribbean music and cultural styles (Barbrook 1987; Gilroy 1987). In contrast to the pirates, which were largely commercial music stations, free radios were vehemently non-commercial and refused advertising of any sort. Distinctive of free radio ideology is the notion that freedom of expression requires freedom from any form of economic control. Most radios therefore preferred to raise money for operations directly from local residents through weekly or monthly raffles, or by running a bar, *txosna*, during the annual fiestas. This produces, of course, a very precarious hand-to-mouth existence. Many stations were able to supplement their income with subsidies squeezed from local town halls by doing the paperwork to constitute themselves formally as cultural associations running workshops in radio production. It was common knowledge that the stations broadcast without a licence, which is technically illegal. Tolerance for the radios seemed to vary widely: some were constantly being shut down and harassed by the police, while others operated much more freely and openly with financial support or at least tacit acceptance from local officials. Depending on the prevailing political winds, some free radios, such as the one I observed in Hernani, were very open about the station's location, leaving their doors unlocked and inviting anyone to come and participate, while others had to be more secretive, fearing the loss of their leases or possible closures prompted by angry neighbours, by landlords or police.

Free from state regulation on the one hand, and the tyranny of the 'Top 40' on the other, Basque free radios took on the identity of unruly *zirikatzaile* ('provocateurs'). This is reflected in the names adopted by radios, which range from the incendiary to the irreverent: for example, the radio station I observed the longest called itself 'Molotoff Radio', after the favoured weapon of urban guerrilla warfare; another calls itself *Zirika*, or 'Pesky Thorn', while others chose more nonsensical or humorous names such as 'Monkey Radio' or 'Kaka Flash'. In the words of Jakoba Rekondo, one of the newscasters in the free radio of Usurbil, "we didn't want to make just another normal radio with lots of music and so on. For that, you can listen to a commercial station and get better quality anyway. We saw our radio as a way of contributing to the movement, *la movida*".

For free radios, being part of the rebellious spirit of *la movida* that swept throughout post-Franco Spain meant first and foremost, in their words, 'giving voice to those without voice' and providing what they call 'counter-information'. In practical terms, this entailed opening the airwaves to all the *herriko taldeak*, that is, local cultural and grassroots organizations – feminists, ecologists, amnesty groups for Basque political prisoners, Basque language schools, mountaineering clubs, and literary groups – to take part in the radio. Free radios were, for example, an important medium of expression for one of the largest youth movements of the late eighties and nineties, the *insumisos*, that is, youth who are refusing to comply with the mandatory military service requirement. Free radios saw their function in large part as one of community bulletin boards, providing a public forum for otherwise marginalized political and cultural perspectives which previously have had to rely on demonstrations, graffiti, and posters in the street as their primary media of public expression.

Sustained by and firmly rooted in an array of oppositional social movements, sympathetic to, but independent of, the Basque nationalist left political parties, free radios constituted an alternative public sphere that challenged the exclusions of the liberal bourgeois media, both Spanish and Basque. Tension surrounding these exclusions was becoming more, not less, heightened in the autonomous Basque provinces after autonomy. There is no doubt that the transition to a democratic regime in Spain brought about a tremendous expansion of the media and a reduction in censorship codes. Radical, leftist, and nationalist organizations were legalized and a flood of newspapers, magazines, and other publications emerged on to the streets. Among the more notable developments was the creation of the public Basque Radio and Television Network, *Euskal Irrati Telebista* (EITB) which includes a regional Basque language radio and two television channels, one in Basque and one in Spanish, controlled by the Basque Autonomous Community's regional government. The regional government's Ministry of Culture also began to provide subsidies to non-governmental Basque language publications that would not otherwise be economically sustainable. By the early nineties, an increasingly acrimonious struggle had erupted between non-governmental sectors of society and their publications and the Basque government, at the time a coalition of the Spanish Socialist Party (PSOE) and centrist Basque Nationalist Party (PNV). The government controlled access to the new television and radio network and much-needed public monies.

At the centre of the struggle were two daily newspapers: *Egin*, representing the perspective of the radical nationalist left and many of the autonomous social movements, and *Egunkaria*, the first all-Basque language newspaper. Both papers were the subject of a boycott on the part of the Basque government, which refused to place any official announcements – which represent handsome sums of money – in either of these papers. That newspapers would be at the vortex of this struggle is not accidental. Dailies are, as Benedict Anderson (1991) has argued, emblematic of the imagined community. The retraction of the government's official announcements crippled the papers by taking away a major source of revenue. It also communicated that these newspapers, and the publics they represent – that of the radical nationalist left on the one hand (*Egin*), and the non-governmental Basque language movement on the other (*Egunkaria*) – violated the conservative government's terms of belonging in the sphere of rational political speech. Both papers addressed themselves to a nation and its imaginary readers that incorporated all seven of the Basque provinces in both Spain and France, refusing in this way to accept the Autonomous Community as the *de facto* Basque Country. But even more important were these papers' real or assumed sympathies to the increasingly demonized radical nationalist left. In the case of *Egin*, the affiliation with the radical nationalist political party *Herri Batasuna* was explicit. It was also accused of supporting the armed organization ETA, whose communiqués it used to publish. *Egin*'s politics made it the subject of countless raids, police surveillance, and harassment tactics. It was eventually shut down for good in 1998. *Egunkaria*'s political pedigree was more neutral. When it was created in 1990, the Basque government regarded it with great suspicion and tried to form its own daily newspaper.

Failing in this attempt, it accused *Egunkaria* of being controlled by radicals. Perseverance and skillful negotiations ultimately brought an end to government boycotts in 1995. The only daily to publish entirely in Basque, *Egunkaria* represents the voice of a middle-class liberal *euskaldun* ('Basque-speaking') public sphere in the making. As we can see, the conflicts with the newspapers have been resolved in differing ways, but the overall chilling effect of the boycotts mobilized many smaller local publications and media to protest at these and their own exclusions. Under the banner *Adierazpen Askatasuna* ('Freedom of Expression') and *Gu ere Herria Gara* ('We, too, are the People'), free radios joined writers, intellectuals, and artists throughout the southern Basque Country in protest against what they perceived to be an attempt to exert ideological control over public discourse.

The latter slogan, 'We, too, are the People', is a particularly clear indication of the ongoing contestation in the Basque Country over who will get to speak as a public citizen, and whose concerns or interests come to be regarded as matters of the commonweal. Free radios, together with other grassroots organizations, Basque language, and cultural revitalization groups, understood themselves to be serving the cultural interests of 'the people', the *herria*. *Herria* is a semantically dense and highly resonant term in Basque nationalist discourse, which, as a noun, can mean, 'the town', 'the people', or 'the nation', and, when used as an adjective, as in *herriko*, or *herrikoia*, may mean 'popular', 'public', and even 'patriotic' (Aulestia 1989). Free radios claimed to be the voice of 'the People', the *herria*, that was being left outside the imagined community of the middle-class Basque media. What was left out, in their view, was not only the perspective of oppositional groups, but also the perspective and participation of local communities in defining public knowledge.

At stake for free radios and other experiments in local or community-based Basque language media was something more than *access* to the public sphere. Especially important in the eyes of free radio activists was not just finding a public space to express themselves, but getting members of the community, especially teenagers, to become *producers* rather than simply *consumers* of public knowledge. If, under consumer capitalism, mass-mediated forms of publicity construct the public as viewers or spectators (Lee 1993; Kogawa 1985), free radio imagined the public as *participants*. In interviews I had with programmers, they would often describe the radio as trying to be an open mike, where anyone 'from the street', as they say, could come and express their opinion. The ideology of communication in free radios, according to Guattari (1981), is to maintain a system of direct feedback between the station and the community. This could happen in a number of ways; radios encouraged people to participate in creating the news by phoning in a piece of information and, in some cases, they would broadcast the call directly on the air. Listener phone-ins were encouraged during many programmes and especially when there were demonstrations or confrontations with the police, of which there were many during this period of heated *kale borroka* ('street fighting') between youth and the Basque police. The radio would try to get reports from participants on location. In contrast to the mainstream media, individuals were encouraged to speak publicly on free radio, and they did so not as designated representatives, experts, journalists, or official spokespersons. There was a kind of counter-authority attached to free radio's defiant non-professionalism. People who speak the reality of the street, who speak as the common man or common woman, were valorized and endowed with an authority that came precisely from their marginality to any institutional authority. For Guattari, such individuals are seen as possessing more authentic knowledge based on lived experience, and to contribute new perspectives and fresh truths via their direct, plain speech.[6] More than just an alternative news outlet, free radios wanted to imagine themselves almost like a Habermasian ideal sphere of open communication: a communal space where local residents and especially youth could speak *as citizens* and engage in defining public knowledge and public culture.

3. Irreverent speech

This brings us directly to the question of language ideology and practice. How were these ideological commitments expressed in the linguistic practices of free radio? The political ideology and organizational structure of free radios seems to have been fairly consistent from one station to

---

[6] This commitment to 'free speech', explains Guattari:

> Basically represents a danger to all traditional systems of social representation; it questions a certain conception of the delegate, of the deputy, the official spokesperson, the leader, the journalist [...] It is as if, in an immense permanent meeting – that stretched as large as the limits of hearing would permit – someone, anyone, even the most indecisive of the lot, the one with the most shaky voice, found himself with the means to take the floor whenever he wanted. From that moment, we can begin to hope that some new truths [and] the basis for new forms of expression will emerge (Guattari 1981:233-234).

the next. However, the variation in the sociolinguistic make-up of communities across the southern Basque Country makes generalization about language use impossible. Some stations based in predominantly Castilian-speaking towns – *Hala Bedi* in Gazteiz (Alava), *Eguzki* in Iruna (Navarre), or *Zintzilik* in Renteria (Gipuzkoa) – operated almost entirely in Castilian, while others based in areas with high numbers of Basque-speaking youth used much more Basque in their programming. The analysis which follows is based on observations of two radio stations in the province of Gipuzkoa: Molotoff, located in the town of Hernani, (population 20,000) and Paotxa, located in Usurbil, 7 kilometers away (population 5,000). Paotxa operated entirely in Basque, while Molotoff had approximately 80 per cent of its programming in Basque; the other programmes were identified as bilingual or Castilian.

Language policy is probably one of the most controversial issues among Basque free radios. During my research at Molotoff in the spring of 1994, the radio's general assembly had reached an impasse over whether the station should adopt a Basque-only language policy. Some members closely connected to the language activist organization, Basque in the Basqueland, had proposed this, arguing that the radio should not only support language revival politically, it should demonstrate this through committing to use only Basque at the station. Without a Basque-only policy, or a commitment to move in that direction, argued this contingent, the radio would be contributing to the continued marginalization of Euskara (Basque) within the station and in Hernani as a whole.

For other programmers, there should be no policy. The very idea of a policy, they argued, went against the ideology of the station which is to be open to all youth, regardless of their mother tongue. Furthermore, it was argued that a formal language policy went against the station's commitment to freedom of expression and autonomy from any kind of political doctrines, including that of language revivalists. Few stations, in fact, opted for a Basque-only broadcasting policy, and those that did tended to be in towns where Basque speakers were in the vast majority.

This being said, there was an undeniable sense of solidarity between free radios in the Basque Country and the language revival movement. This is signalled by the fact that virtually all the free radios adopted Basque language names (*Txantxangorri*, *Tximua*, *Eguzki*), even if many of their programmes were bilingual or in Spanish. This kind of emblematic Basque language use is found throughout the world of grassroots organizations and the radical or *abertzale* left. In these spaces, Basque functions as a sign of alterity and oppositionality to the Spanish state and its institutions.

At Molotoff, for example, there were several programmes in Castilian whose programmers do not know Basque. Yet a conscious decision was made to have all *kuñas* or programme call-signs, and station identification (such as 'You're listening to the voice of Molotoff Irratia') in Euskara. Commonly used in mainstream radio broadcasting, the introduction of these devices domesticates the anarchic pleasure Guattari celebrated in free radio's uncontrolled free-form broadcasting aesthetic by giving a sense of order and pacing within and between programmes. It is significant that while the general assembly of Molotoff argued intensely and could not agree to a language policy for all the programmes, the use of Euskara for call-signs and station identifications seemed to be uncontroversial. There was reticence to restrict in any way the freedom of programmers to do as they pleased within the context of their programmes; their voice should be their own. Call-signs, on the other hand, occupy a special status as the voice of the radio as a whole. Interjected at regular intervals into programmes, the use of Basque call-signs, together with station identifications, work as framing devices for the ensuing talk, establishing for the radio and its audience symbolic membership in a *euskaldun* ('Basque-speaking') public even if later, Castilian might be used in the programme or in joking and other off-the-record comments.

In keeping with their anti-institutional and oppositional politics, free radio broadcasters interject a great deal of slang and colloquialism that mark them as closer to what they see as 'the language of the street'. One of the more interesting places to look for this is in the pre-recorded opening and closing of programmes. At Usurbil's Paotxa radio, for example, in the opening to the community news programme, the two announcers, male and female, would begin the programme with *aizak, hi!* (for males) and *aizan, hi!* (for women), roughly translatable as 'hey you!'. Their greetings are in a highly informal register, *hitanoa*, that in Gipuzkoa is found most frequently among native speakers in rural areas for speech among siblings, same sex peer groups, and for addressing animals on the farm. *Hitanoa* indexes familiarity associated with intimate friends of equal status. Opposite sex siblings will use it with one another, but men and women, especially married couples, generally use the more formal, respectful register known as *zuka*.[7] *Hitanoa*, or *hika* as it is sometimes referred to, may also index lesser status; children, for example, may be addressed frequently as '*hi*' by adults, but the reverse would elicit a reprimand, especially if the

---

[7] *Zuka* was also described to me as being sweeter (*goxoa*) than *hitanoa*. It is the preferred form to use with infants, for example, while *hitanoa* may be used when the child gets older.

adult were not a member of the family. *Hitanoa* forms have been lost in
many, especially urban, areas, and are not generally known by non-native
Basque speakers. Interestingly, *hitanoa* has begun to enjoy something of
a revival among some politicized *euskaldun* writers, intellectuals, and youth
interested in maintaining this distinctive aspect of spoken Basque.

My observations in Usurbil indicate that radical *euskaldun* youth in
this community, particularly males, were using *hitanoa* in many of their
everyday interactions with each other and with women in their *cuadrilla*
or friendship circle. They also occasionally exhibited a marked use of
hitanoa with shopkeepers, teachers, the mayor, the priest, or other individuals who would normally be addressed more formally. Strategic use of
this register in these circumstances, I would argue, is one among several
ways that some radical *euskaldun* youth were expressing their rejection
of the traditional status hierarchies that have dominated Basque society
including much of nationalist political culture.[8] When Paotxa newscasters
used the salutations, *aizak, hi!* and *aizan, hi!* to introduce the local news,
they were establishing their own relationship as one of informal equality
and recursively projecting this quality on to the communicative sphere
of their listening public. The pronouns served to construct the imagined
community as one of 'horizontal comradeship' that was in keeping with
free radio's anti-hierarchical vision of radical democracy. This is ac-
centuated by the fact that, at Paotxa, like most free radios, announcers
almost never identified themselves by name: there was none of the cult
of personality of named DJs found on commercial and some pirate stations. Everyone is nameless and in some sense equivalent in status.
Extending the sphere of intimacy to the town as a whole, of course, might
just as easily be perceived not as an expression of solidarity, but as a
kind of rude speech. Such a reading probably wouldn't bother most radio

---

[8] Another example of the appropriation of *hitanoa* modes of address in radical
political culture is found in the use of '*Azan!*' as the name of a radical Basque
feminist organization. However, I should note that my claims to an affinity between *hitanoa* and radical *euskaldun* youth culture are still speculative and not
meant to suggest that this is its primary meaning at all times and in all contexts. In
considering what the use of *hitanoa* may connote in any particular setting, it must
be remembered that knowledge of *hitanoa* forms marks a certain degree of flu-
ency or native control of Basque, since it is not commonly taught in Basque
language classes and few non-native speakers ever learn this form of speech.
Further study of the uses of *hitanoa* among activists might help us to understand
how politicized Basques strategically use their knowledge of the pronominal system as ways of not only asserting egalitarianism, but also staking claims to greater
Basque authenticity.

programmers since they often deliberately pepper their broadcasts with humorous, rude, and sometimes scatological expressions. Either way, it sets free radio apart from mainstream broadcast etiquette and differentiates it markedly from the language revival movement's emphasis on creating a formal standard Basque – on making Basque a language of science, technology, and high culture.[9]

As part of their commitment to language revival, most free radio stations would broadcast Basque language classes. But the overall goal of the station's language use was not didactic. Language play seemed to be more valued than imparting normative or standard Basque. Parody and humour were valued traits in both programming and in language use. Here again, we see some of the best examples of this in the introductions and titles of programmes. For example, a programme on Molotoff Radio ironically called *Erderaz eta Kitto?* ('[Is] Spanish Enough?') was put on by the local Basque language activist group, Basque in the Basqueland, and generally featured debates, interviews, and announcements of various Basque language cultural events. Basque in the Basqueland is one of the more radical grassroots language revival organizations. The title they chose for the programme reverses a well-known slogan of the language movement, *Euskaraz eta Kitto* ('Basque is Enough'). The programme begins with the following pre-recorded dialogue in Castilian that continues this parodic tone (Basque words are shown in bold type):

| 1 woman | *Pues, chico, yo ya hago algo; le he puesto a la tienda el nombre de* **Garazi.** |
| | Hey, guy, I'm at least doing my part; I named my store *Garazi.* |

| 2 young man | *Yo al perro ya le digo* **etorri**, *y al niño* **ixo.** |
| | Now I say *etorri* (come) to my dog, and *ixo* (hush) to my baby. |

| 3 man, 'grunge' voice | *Ba, yo paso del euskara.* |
| | Bah, I'm through with Basque. |

| 4 young man | *Pero, si esa lengua ya no tiene futuro, no?* |
| | But, that language doesn't have a future, does it? |

| 5 all together | **'Erderaz eta Kitto"** *EZZZZZZ!'* |
| | Spanish only? Nooooooo! |

---

[9] It should be emphasized that use of *hitanoa* varies widely from community to community. Very little *hitanoa*, for example, was used at Molotoff Radio only 7 kilometers from Paotxa. Besides considering how this form constructs the listening public, we might also think about how free radio changes the way speakers

Especially interesting is the way the dialogue pokes fun at people – represented by the first two speakers – who support language revival, most likely consider themselves to be nationalist, *abertzale*, and believe they are doing their part for the language struggle by sprinkling a few Basque words into their Spanish. I would hear criticism of this token use of Basque from language activists in private talk, but I rarely saw it in the public discourse of the language movement. Media campaigns advocating language revival have generally tended to use a strategy of welcoming and encouraging people to use Basque in whatever form they can. Speakers 3 and 4 represent the *pasota*, someone who does not care about this or any other political struggle, and the pessimist, respectively. By juxtaposing the well-meaning but Spanish-speaking *abertzale* with the latter two who reject Basque altogether, the programmers of this show are in some way saying that good intentions are not enough; the first two speakers, they suggest, are, in the end, no different from the latter. Activists would frequently say that this token way of 'speaking Basque' is really no better than no Basque at all. Indeed, it might be worse, in that using a few Basque words to speak to children or to call a dog trivializes the goal activists have of creating a living Basque language and Basque-speaking culture.

One final example involves the parodic spellings of Spanish words. The most common form this takes is the use of Basque letters, *k* and *tx* (pronounced 'ch') in otherwise Castilian words. Both of these forms are found in Basque orthography, but not in Castilian. They appear in Spanish phrases, as in *ke txorrada* for *que chorrada* ('what a foolish or stupid thing') or *la martxa* for *la marcha* ('the rhythm, the movement'). I also found them appearing often in the titles of punk music programmes, for example *El Moko Ke Kamina* ('The Travelling Booger') and *Koktel de Mokos* ('Booger Cocktail'). These types of orthographic mixings and the kind of Beavis and Butthead humour they encode are found throughout radical Basque youth culture. My examples appear in free radio programme schedules, but they also occur in comics, graffiti, and in the lyrics and album covers of Basque music groups associated with the Basque radical rock movement (*rok radikal basko*), all of which are self-identified as oppositional. In the case of one programme title, *Mierkoles Merkatu* ('Wednesday Market'), the Castilian word for Wednesday, *miercoles*, spelled here with a '*k*' makes the phrase profoundly ambiguous – it might

---

view *hitanoa*. It is possible that using *hitanoa* in oppositional radio, making it a part of the hip transnational music and culture of radical youth, may also have an effect on the connotations of *hitanoa*, shaking loose its associations with rural life and giving this form of speech a new urban feel.

be colloquial Basque or local Castilian. Such usages play on misrecognition, blurred language boundaries, and a feigned illiteracy in Spanish that is rare in a public culture and language ideology that emphasize the mutual exclusivity of Castilian and Basque and sanction code-switching and other forms of mixing as contamination or degradation.

These examples of 'bad Spanish' are very much in keeping with free radio activists' rude language ideology. In their deliberate mis-spelling of Spanish words, radical youth were turning what was once a source of stigma for many native rural Basques – the inability to read and write standard Castilian – into a way of mocking Castilian. Recent work on 'Mock Spanish' by Jane Hill (1993 and this volume) offers an elegant analysis of how joking imitations do their symbolic work. Expanding on the work of Bakhtin and Spitzer, Hill argues that absurd or parodic imitations perform a dual function of both distancing speakers from the voice they are imitating, and denigrating the source of that voice, making the source, whether it be women, Hispanics, or working-class people, appear ridiculous or contemptible. Hill takes as her case the joking imitations of minority group speech forms by majority language speakers to show that linguistic play can have very serious metalinguistic messages. The linguistic practices of radical Basque youth give us an example of this same semiotic principle in reverse. The impossible spellings of Spanish by radical youth perform an ironic reversal in which the language of the dominant group, Castilian, is pragmatically lowered.[10] My sense is that within radical youth culture, these parodic hybrid spellings signal a kind of marginal or oppositional stance *vis-à-vis* normative Castilian dominance and by extension the state. These orthographic markers of rebellion allow youth to use Spanish while distancing themselves from the associations that language has with state hegemony in this particular region.

4. Alternative public spheres

In short, Basque free radios create an alternative form of public culture that differs significantly in its language ideology and modes of resistance from the institutionalized sectors of the Basque language movement. Free radios may have seen part of their mission as that of 'exporting' Basque to

---

[10] Keith Basso's (1979) study of joking imitations of 'the Whiteman' by Apache speakers is another good example of how subaltern groups may use parody to construct, at least temporarily, a symbolic order in which they are culturally superior to and different from dominant groups.

the wider community, transgressing the existing geography of the language, but they cared little for norms and diplomas. In contrast to the conservative codifying concerns of the academics and planners who dominate the language movement, or the bureaucrats of the Ministry of Culture and Tourism, free radio tolerated and at times embraced a mongrel and hybridized 'Basque' language and culture. Subversive humour, parody, rude speech, and occasional inventive code-mixing were valued skills and markers of participation in this alternative public sphere. But we should not exaggerate: Basque free radios were not as linguistically anarchic as Guattari might have liked them to be. Radical Basque youth did not go the way, for example, of Latino performance artists, rappers, and radio programmers in the US who deliberately seek to blur the boundaries with their artful uses of Spanglish (Fusco and Gomez-Peña 1994). Unlike diasporic minorities, it appears that oppositional Basque youth have an investment in retaining the boundary between Basque and Spanish even in their irreverent speech.

The fact that youth turned to radio as a medium of oppositional cultural expression speaks to the centrality of media as a terrain of cultural life and politics. Free radio, like other forms of alternative media, operated on the philosophy that one must take what is dominant in a culture to change it quickly. One of the changes youth were attempting was to put their language and ideas into motion. In doing so, free radio uses the media not to disperse information to people – the consumer model of mainstream broadcast media – but to draw them into local communicative networks. To borrow from Guattari, free radio's motion was centripetal, hoping to foster in those who listen a sense of involvement in local events and local culture (Guattari in Kogawa 1985). This is quite different from the strategy of language standardization, which offers up a single translocal language with which to communicate across towns. As a form of activism, the logic of free radio was bottom-up rather than top-down. It worked by poaching on the airwaves, rather than by direct confrontation. For Guattari, free radios were to be extensions of the conversations people have in the street, in the cafe, around the dinner-table. This is especially clear in the news reports called *informatiboa* or *albisteak*. At Paotxa radio, for example, programmers attempted to give priority to topics that they believed interested residents. In this way, free radio news would sometimes break open the formulaic quality and categories of news found in mainstream media. Even when radio announcers were repeating news reported in the papers, they were encouraged to annotate the reports with their own opinions and perspectives. At Paotxa, a section on town gossip

and rumours – who was getting married when, what they were going to
wear, whether they were going to have it videotaped, and so on – was
annexed to the 'news'. This was done very tongue-in-cheek of course,
but programmers claim that of all the shows, the gossip section was the
most popular. They also announced on the radio the recent deaths of town
residents. One of Paotxa's programmers explained this to me in the following way:

> the first thing our mothers do when they get the paper is read the
> death notices. They used to be posted on the wall of the church. We
> are just taking that custom and putting it on the radio. We are taking
> what people actually talk about in town, in the street, and making that
> our definition of news.

The public sphere of free radio was framed as emphatically local. But we
have to ask, what does 'local' mean in this context? If we look at the
programming as a whole, these 'local' expressions of Basque radical youth
culture draw upon and are enriched by a wide array of extra-national cultural images, narratives, and modes of representation. In the early nineties,
African–American culture and politics were everywhere to be found in
the form of rap music, Public Enemy clothing, Malcolm X insignia, and
'Fight the Power' slogans which were written on the programme tapes
members of Molotoff Radio gave to me. Radical youth appropriated these
images and slogans into symbols of Basque oppositionality, inserting them
into local narratives, debates, and modes of representation.[11] A quick scan
of public cultures today shows us that such complex cultural brews are
increasingly common in the urban neighborhoods of London, Paris, and
Berlin, forcing us to rethink and redefine not only "the spatial, territorial,
and geopolitical parameters of the public sphere", but also the counterpublics, such as free radio, that emerge in its orbit (Hansen 1993b). As
Hansen has pointed out:

> The restructuring and expansion of the communications industries on
> a transnational, global scale more than ever highlights the quotation
> marks around the terms of national culture and national identity. In-
> deed, the accelerated process of transnationalization makes it difficult

---

[11] The appropriation of African-American rap music and cultural style by European ethnic and linguistic minorities is not uncommon. For a fascinating parallel
case among Franco-Maghribi youth see Gross, McMurray, and Swedenburg
(1992).

to ground a concept of the public in any territorial entity, be it local, regional, or national (Hansen 1993b:183).

This is *not* to say, of course, that free radios are not tied to specific places and specific times – they are. Radios are linked to identifiable social networks of radical youth in urban and semi-urban areas; they come out of particular social settings, bars, and youth houses, and are linked to contestations for particular public spaces. In this sense, the alternative public sphere they create does have a location that we need to address in attempting to make sense of their linguistic strategies.[12] It *is* true to say, however, that these 'local' expressions of Basque radical youth culture are constituted through a kind of cultural bricolage that is facilitated by transnational flows of media, commodities, images, and people. This is nowhere more apparent than in the musical programming which juxtaposes folk with thrash, funkadelic with *txalaparta* (a wooden percussive instrument), tex mex with Basque accordion music. Through these juxtapositions, radical youth affirmed connections to resistance struggles and marginalized groups elsewhere in ways that challenge the bounded and unified representations of Basque language and identity found in nationalist treatises or the census map.

Precisely because they have a history of marginalization, minority language groups have had the burden of establishing their difference from and equivalence to dominant languages. As a result, in certain domains activists have shunned hybrid cultural and linguistic forms as threatening to the integrity of their language (Jaffe 1993). This is not the prevailing attitude for all spheres of minority language production. Free radio worked by a different logic, creating a space that was simultaneously syncretic, local, and transnational. Free radios opened up, however ephemerally, new spaces at the same time that they addressed the mechanisms of a linguistic domination that relegates the minority language to the sphere of private talk. They aimed to take the Basque language out of the private domain and on to the street, and to take, as they say, the reality of the street into the public domain. In retrospect, their efforts evoke Lizzie Borden's film *Born in Flames*, in which radio is seized as a means of taking another kind of delegitimized talk, in this case the talk of feminists, and putting it on to the streets. Radio is conceptualized in both cases as an instrument of back talk/talking back (hooks 1990). In many ways, the imaginary space

---

[12] I want to thank William Hanks for making this point in his comments on an earlier version of this paper.

of free radios was heterogeneous in contrast to the unitary space of nationalism. It was also profoundly urban in the sense that Salman Rushdie gives to this term in his *Satanic Verses*. For Rushdie, what distinguishes the urban experience is not skyscrapers or concrete streets, but the simultaneous co-presence of multiple realities. Free radios were urban not because they existed in cities; in some cases – for instance, in Usurbil, they existed in a small town of no more than 5,000 inhabitants. These low-powered, ephemeral stations, with their radical philosophy of democratic communication, can be thought of as urban in the sense that they tried, in however imperfect ways, to place the heterogeneity of Basque society on the airwaves. Tuning in to these low-tech electronic productions and their linguistic strategies can enrich our understanding of the ongoing politics of minority language struggles.

References

Anderson, Benedict ([1983]1991) *Imagined Communities: Reflections on the origin and spread of nationalism*, London: Verso.

Aulestia, Gorka (1989) *Basque–English Dictionary*, Reno, NV: University of Nevada Press.

Barbrook, Richard (1987) 'A New Way of Talking: Community radio in 1980s Britain', *Science as Culture* 1(1):81-129.

Bassets, Lluís (ed) (1981) *De las ondas rojas a las radios libres: Textos para la historia de la radio*, Barcelona: Editorial Gustavo Gili, S.A.

Basso, Keith (1979) *Portraits of 'The Whiteman': Linguistic play and cultural symbols among the western Apache*, Cambridge: Cambridge University Press.

Brecht, Bertolt (1964) 'The Radio as an Apparatus of Communication', in John Willett (ed) *Brecht on Theatre*, New York: Hill and Wang.

Bourdieu, Pierre (1991) *Language and Symbolic Power*, ed. John B. Thompson, trans. Gino Raymond and Matthew Adamson. Cambridge, MA: Harvard University Press.

Cheval, Jean-Jacques (1992) 'Local Radio and Regional Languages in Southwestern France', in H. Stephen Riggins (ed) *Ethnic Minority Media: An international perspective*, London: Sage, 165-197.

Eley, Geoff (1992) 'Nations, Publics, and Political Cultures: Placing Habermas in the nineteenth century', in Craig Calhoun (ed) *Habermas and the Public Sphere*, Cambridge, MA: MIT Press, 289-339.

Fanon, Frantz (1965) *Studies in a Dying Colonialism*, trans. Haakon Chevalier. New York: Monthly Review Press.

Fraser, Nancy (1993) 'Rethinking the Public Sphere: A contribution to the critique of actually existing democracy', in Bruce Robbins (ed) *The Phantom Public Sphere*, Minneapolis: University of Minnesota Press, 1-32.

Fusco, Coco and Guillermo Gómez-Peña (1994) 'New World Radio', in Daina Augaitis and Dan Lander (eds) *Radio Rethink: Art, sound and transmission*, Banff, Canada: Walter Phillips Gallery, 223-244.

Gilroy, Paul (1987) *There Ain't no Black in the Union Jack: The cultural politics of race and nation*, Chicago: University of Chicago Press.

Gross, Joan, David McMurray and Ted Swedenburg (1992) 'Rai, Rap and Ramadan Nights: Franco–Maghribi cultural identities', *Middle East Reports* (September–October) 22(5):11-16.

Guattari, Félix (1984) 'Millions and Millions of Potential Alices', in *Molecular Revolution*, trans. Rosemary Sheed. London: Penguin, 236-241.

------ (1981) 'Las radios libres populares', in Lluís Bassets (ed) *De las ondas rojas a las radios libres*, Barcelona: Editorial Gustavo Gili, 231-236.

Hansen, Miriam (1993a) 'Early Cinema, Late Cinema: Permutations of the public sphere', *Screen* 34(3):197-210.

------ (1993b) 'Unstable Mixtures, Dilated Spheres: Negt and Kluge's The public sphere and experience, twenty years later', *Public Culture* 5(2): 179-212.

Hill, Jane H. (1993) 'Hasta la Vista, Baby: Anglo Spanish in the American Southwest', *Critique of Anthropology* 13:145-176.

hooks, bell (1990) 'Talking Back', in R. Ferguson, M. Gever, T. Minh-ha, C. West (eds) *Out There: Marginalization and contemporary cultures*, Cambridge, MA: MIT Press, 337-340.

Jaffe, Alexandra (1993) 'Obligation, Error, and Authenticity: Competing cultural principles in the teaching of Corsican', *Journal of Linguistic Anthropology* 3(1):99-114.

Kasmir, Sharryn (1996) *The Myth of Mondragón: Cooperatives, politics, and working class life in a Basque town*, Albany, NY: State University of New York Press.

Kogawa, Tetsuo (1985) 'Free Radio in Japan', in Douglas Kahn and Diane Neumaier (eds) *Cultures in Contention*. Seattle, WA: The Real Comet Press, 116-121.

Landes, Joan (1988) *Women and the Public Sphere in the Age of the French Revolution*, Ithaca, NY: Cornell University Press.

Lee, Benjamin (1993) 'Going Public', *Public Culture* 5(2):165-178.

Lewis, Peter (1984) 'Community Radio: The Montreal conference and after', *Media, Culture, and Society* 6:137-150.

McCain, Thomas and G. Ferrel Lowe (1990) 'Localism in Western European Radio Broadcasting: Untangling the wireless', *Journal of Communication* (Winter) 40(1):86-101.

Negt, Oskar and Alexander Kluge (1993) *The Public Sphere and Experience*, trans. Peter Labanyi, Jamie Daniel and Assenka Oksiloff. Minneapolis: University of Minnesota Press.

Ormazabal, Sabino (n.d.) 'El movimiento juvenil vasco', MS.

Urla, Jacqueline (1993) 'Cultural Politics in an Age of Statistics: Numbers, nations and the making of Basque identity', *American Ethnologist* 20(4):818-843.

Usurbiaga, Jon Ander (1993) '"Likiniano", Café y Cultura Alternativa', *Egin* 15 January 1993. (*Gaztegin* supplement):8.

10. Circulating the People

BENJAMIN LEE

1. Introduction

Circulation is a central dimension of contemporary global processes, involving the velocity, scale, and form of movement of ideas, persons, commodities, and images, in ways that disturb virtually all existing cartographies of culture, place, and identity. Yet circulation is more than the movement of people, ideas, and commodities from one culture to another; it is also a cultural process with its own types of abstraction and constraint that are produced by the semiotic nature of the circulating forms. Contemporary global capital flows presuppose the intertranslatability of financial instruments and information technologies while at the same time demanding that 'local' economic activities be translated into cross-culturally comparable economic categories. These 'interfaces' of translation transcend national borders and languages (of which the Arabic, Japanese, English, and Chinese versions of Windows '98 are only one example) and are reminiscent of the more nationally based projects such as censuses that also required regimenting local social processes into statistically denumerable categories.

The creation of new types of abstraction, possibilities, and constraints via the circulation of specific cultural forms is not restricted to financial instruments or new technologies. Arjun Appadurai (1996) has suggested that in addition to the circulation of financial instruments and technologies (what he calls 'financescapes' and 'technoscapes'), global cultural flows consist of circulations of people (ethnoscapes), images (mediascapes), and ideas (especially politically based – ideoscapes), a classification that is not meant to be either exclusive or exhaustive. Each of these flows is subject to its own constraints and incentives, placing them in 'disjunctive' relationships with one another that are increasingly the subject and object of contemporary social imaginations. They are the 'building blocks' of what Appadurai, extending Benedict Anderson's ([1983]1991) work on nationalism, has termed 'imagined worlds' – "the multiple worlds that are constituted by the historically situated imaginations of persons and groups spread around the globe" (Appadurai 1996:33).

The key component in both Anderson's and Appadurai's analyses is the linkage of imagination with circulation. The circulating objects are the tools for the construction of new images, worldviews, and ideologies, whether it be the 'imagined communities' of nationalism or transnational diasporas. Anderson also suggests that the cultural dimensions of circulation are derived from the semiotic properties of the objects circulated. Novels and newspapers contain modes of narration that allow 'imagining the nation' as a new form of collective identity ('we, the people') moving through the 'empty, homogenous time' of a secularized modernity. The circulation of these print commodities produced new forms of subjectivity and identity that are the bases for the political cultures of modernity. The circulation of specific cultural forms creates the new forms of community with their hierarchies of evaluation, contrast, and difference. If we expand Appadurai's notion of global flows and scapes with Anderson's insight into what might be called the 'semiotic mediation' of circulation, what appear to be complex circulations among different cultures are the products of interactions among different 'cultures of circulation'.

2. Nationalism and circulation

Although a culture of circulation can be identified by the objects circulating through it, it is not reducible to them. Instead, circulation interacts with the semiotic form of the circulating objects to create the cultural dimensions of the circulatory process itself. A particularly interesting and important example of the 'performative creativity' of circulation is the construction of the ideoscape of nationalism. One of the most intriguing suggestions of Jürgen Habermas' ([1962]1989) work on the public sphere and Benedict Anderson's on nationalism is that notions of public opinion and popular sovereignty arise out of the circulation and discussion of novels, newspapers, and magazines in coffeehouses, salons, and reading societies throughout the bourgeois public spheres of the eighteenth and nineteenth centuries. These ideas first develop in Europe, circulate to the American colonies where they form the basis for the first constitutionalized peoplehood, that of the United States, flow through Latin America and subsequently spread back to Europe. In the nineteenth century, these notions of peoplehood became infused with post-Kantian romantic ideas of national identity and spread from European countries to their colonies, with a subsequent circulation of Leninist notions of peoplehood to Russia, China, and parts of the developing world. Contemporary ideoscapes build upon a globalized communications infrastructure that is producing forms of identity that coalesce around interests that transcend national boundaries, often challenging the authority of the state, as in the case of human rights, and women's and environmental movements.

Although the invention of 'the people' was a long, historical process, its roots lie in the new forms of subjectivity developing in the public spheres of Europe and its colonies during the eighteenth century. In his *Sources of the Self* (1989), Charles Taylor has traced the 'inward turn' of Western subjectivity in philosophy, literature, and the arts; many of the figures he mentions such as Locke, Rousseau, Kant, and Herder, are also the philosophical ancestors of modern notions of peoplehood. In *The Structural Transformation of the Public Sphere* ([1962]1989), Habermas argues that changing ideas of publicness and public opinion that are crucial for the development of new forms of political subjectivity first develop in the literary public sphere and its "institutionalization of privateness oriented to an audience" (Habermas [1962]1989:43). The juncture between philosophy and literature will also provide the 'transportable' forms necessary for Anderson's imagined communities of nationalism.

Both Taylor and Habermas argue for what might be called an 'objectification of subjectivity' in philosophy and literature. Although Taylor traces the philosophical origins of this tendency to Augustine and Descartes (who share versions of a '*cogito*' approach to subjectivity), it becomes the basis for social theory in the contractual models of Hobbes, Locke, and Rousseau. These modern forms of political subjectivity developed in the bourgeois public sphere where they provided a political ideology for the emerging bourgeois class in its struggles with the absolutist state. In Habermas' account, this public sphere also nurtured the development of new forms of 'expressive' subjectivity that were most clearly realized in the development of fictional narration. Changes in novelistic form and narration during the rise of the bourgeois public sphere interact with those in philosophy. The authority of omniscient narration interacts with new forms of narration (the epistolary and realistic novel) to produce the image of an objective narration of subjectivity. The crucial moment is when a new structuring consciousness emerges through the development of a print capitalism mediated by an institutionally structured, self-reflexive appropriation of the metalinguistic potentials of narration. Narration is constituted by a semiotic reflexivity of the event of narration and the narrated event, whose coordination reveals the locus of a new type of subjectivity, that of the narrator; narrative point of view provides the discursive basis for the imagined communities of modern nationalism.

According to Habermas, the bourgeois public sphere first emerges in England during the late seventeenth and early eighteenth centuries. Its ideas of the individual develop in the literary public sphere through a network of coffeehouses, newspapers, literary journals, and reading clubs. 'Rational critical debate' arises in the world of letters out of a dynamic of reading, narration, commentary, and criticism. The structuring ideals of this literary public 'field' would be used in political debates to criticize absolutist conceptions of public authority. The political task would be the creation of norms to protect and regulate civil society, and the key idea mediating the literary and political fields would be that of a rational public opinion in which what is right converges with what is just; law should be the expression of public opinion which itself is the expression of reason.

While Habermas' work on the public sphere points to the complex interplay between institutions, textualized forms of subjectivity, and metadiscourses about these forms, it is Benedict Anderson's work that begins to show how the form of specific printed texts helps construct a new form of social consciousness, that of the imagined community of the nation. 'Thinking the nation' required transportable and transposable forms in which this new type of consciousness could be both embedded and extracted. Anderson finds them in the novel and newspaper which introduce a new form of social subjectivity: they present multiple experiences as occurring simultaneously in the 'homogeneous, empty time' of modern secularism and thereby provide the forms for imagining a shared community of non-co-present citizens moving through the abstract, rationalized time of the modern nation.

Anderson emphasizes that modern, secular time contrasts with mediaeval conceptions in its notion of simultaneity. Earlier conceptions consisted of a hierarchy of temporal orders tied to notions such as the Great Chain of Being. In modern secular time, simultaneity is "transverse, cross-time, marked not by prefiguring and fulfillment, but by temporal coincidence, and measured by clock and calendar" (Anderson [1983] 1991:24). The plot structure of a novel allows the reader to follow the simultaneous actions of many characters as they unfold in the 'homogenous, empty time' of narration; the perspective of the omniscient reader creates an image of society that is "a precise analogue of the idea of a nation, which also is conceived as a solid community moving steadily down (or up) history" (ibid.:26).

Although neither author makes the link explicit, it would seem that notions such as public opinion and 'the people' are tropes created by the interplay among new forms of narration emerging in the eighteenth and nineteenth centuries; the voice of the people is ventriloquated by the voice of the narrator, and the 'homogenous, empty time' of modernity is that of narration itself. 'We, the people' is a modern form of political subjectivity that weaves together fundamental political conceptions such as popular sovereignty, representation, and public opinion into a new form of political legitimation and subjectivity, that of a constitutionalized peoplehood.

3. Performativity of nationhood

In the (1991) edition of *Imagined Communities*, Anderson suggests that one of the reasons for the poverty of philosophical thought about nationalism has been the tendency to think of it as an 'ideology' and place it alongside concepts such as liberalism and fascism. Instead, he suggests that it should be treated anthropologically, as a category closer to kinship or religion. Yet the performative dimensions of 'we, the people' also link it to philosophical and linguistic issues of citation, quotation, metalanguage, self-reference, and self-reflexivity that are among the most complex in philosophical and linguistic analysis. Indeed, much of the German idealist tradition that plays a crucial role in the development of modern nationalism could be considered a protracted reflection on how to analyze the performative qualities of the first person pronoun. Kant's transcendental subject presupposes a distinction between things-in-themselves and the unity of our experience of them as given in the 'I think' that accompanies all mental representations. Fichte would reject Kant's thing-in-itself for an all-embracing idealism in which the objects of experience were posited by the 'absolute subject', the 'I=I', and not independent of it. Hegel wrote his thesis on Fichte and Schelling, and the sections of the *Phenomenology of Mind* on consciousness are extended analyses of the indexical categories of 'I', 'this', 'here', 'now', and the section on self-consciousness ends with a discussion of "the *I* that is *we* and the *we* that is *I*" (Hegel 1949:227) that directly precedes the famous master–slave dialectic. Both the Greater and Lesser Logics contain long discussions of the properties of the pronoun 'I', that culminate in his discussions of the Concept: "'I'" is the pure Concept itself, which as Concept has come to existence" (quoted in Taylor 1975:298; see also Hegel 1949,1969). In the *Grundrisse* and volume I of *Capital*, Marx acknowledges his debt to Hegel's *Logic*; capital replaces the Concept and becomes modernity's self-valorizing subject.

Over the last decade, it has been discovered that many of these issues such as performativity, metalanguage, and narration are not unrelated. Instead, the grammatical structures of languages systematically encode the relations between the ongoing speech event and whatever is being talked about or referred to. For example, among the pronouns (a linguistically universal category), the so-called third person forms are never indexical and can refer to any kind of object ('he', 'she', 'it', 'they' replace or substitute for other referential forms). The first person, on the other hand, is not only indexical, but explicitly self-referential: *I* refers to the individual who utters the instance of discourse containing the linguistic instance *I*.

The same structure also applies to narration where we can distinguish between the indexical event of narration and the narrated-about events. Forms such as quotation, direct and indirect discourse, and free indirect style also distinguish between the so-called reporting event, and the source or reported speech event, and it is these very forms that make up the repertoire of narrative devices and are also at the heart of Bakhtin's metalinguistics.

From this perspective, both the first person pronouns and the classic performative constructions such as 'I hereby promise...' are examples of indexical self-reference in that they seem to create the individual or event they refer to. As Benveniste has pointed out, their uniqueness lies in their creative self-reference:

> This leads us to recognize in the performative a peculiar quality, that of being *self-referential,* of referring to a reality that it itself constitutes by the fact that it is actually uttered in conditions that make it an act. As a result of this it is both a linguistic manifestation, since it must be spoken, and a real fact, insofar as it is the performing of an act. The act is thus identical with the utterance of the act. The signified is identical to the referent. This is evidenced by the word 'hereby'. The utterance that takes itself as a referent is indeed self-referential. (Benveniste 1966:236; original emphasis)

To the extent that performatives are creatively self-referential, that is, that they create the act they seem to refer to, they create the maximal contrast between the creativity of linguistic reference and the contextual conditions that need to be presupposed to make such reference effective. The creative indexical properties of performatives bring about the conditions that make them true; their referential and predicational structures seem to classify the created token as an instance of the speech act named by the predicate.

As a result of these self-referential and self-reflexive properties, performatives contrast with their third person counterparts that are neither indexical nor self-referential. Thus 'he promises...' is simply a report and not the making of a promise. These issues intersect with narration not only because performatives are examples of linguistic self-reference (Bakhtin's 'speech about speech'), but also because the performative verbs of speaking (and their mental act and state counterparts) are used in direct and indirect discourse to create the narrative strategies of voicing characteristic of novelistic fiction and historiography. Looked at from a logical perspective, these verbs raise a host of logical issues, such as sense and referential opacity and transparency. From a narrative perspective, they raise issues of voicing, focalization, and the generic representation of subjectivity. These two lines intersect in the performative first person 'we' and the constative nominalization 'the people' and gives 'we, the people' its epistemological and narrative implications.

The difficulties in giving an adequate analysis of nationalism lie with the semiotic complexity of its structuring tropes. The voice of the people is a rhetorical figure derived from the voices of narration. Narration is itself structured by the interplay between narrating event and narrated-about event in which the performatives and other verbs of speaking, thinking, and feeling play a crucial role; they are the vehicles par excellence through which the author depicts the speech, thoughts, and feelings of her characters, what, paraphrasing Habermas, might be called an inward subjectivity directed towards an audience. At the same time, the circulation of different kinds of narrated texts creates the 'public' which those texts address. 'We, the people' names a new kind of print-mediated community produced by the semiotic nature of the texts that circulate through it. Each reading of a 'nationalist' text creates a token instance of a 'we' that subsumes the narrator/character/reader in a collective agency that creates itself in every act of reading. These token 'we's', when aggregated across acts of reading, become the basis for the imagined community of we-ness at the heart of nationalism; nationalism is a particular example of the semiotic constitution of community.

The dual structure of narration as narrating and narrated-about event creates two levels of collective identification: at the level of narrating event, between narrator/sender/author and reader/receiver/addressee, and in the narrated-about event, between the reader and the characters who are themselves speakers and addressees.[1] Anderson's imagined community of nationalism is created through narratives that embrace the narrated-about characters as referents, the author/narrator as the sender of the narrating event, and the readers as the narrated-to addressees. Through different narrative devices such as quotation, psycho-narration, and free indirect style, different degrees of identification can be created between the narrator and reader and the reader and the characters. Such identifications create a feeling of interchangeability between different participant roles in the event of narrating/reading and the narrated-about events and a continuity between the communities constituted by the narrating events and those described in the narrated-about events. One could occupy the positions of narrator, characters, and addressees. The narrating/reading

---

[1] See Silverstein (2000) for a more detailed and linguistically precise account.

event is also felt to be shared among a community of like-minded readers; thus every act of reading is potentially a micronational token act that instantiates a macronational ideology of community. Narrators, readers, characters, are all potentially interchangeable in this new form of self-creating collective agency in which direct access is created via narration – a discursively produced *I* that becomes *We* and *We* that becomes *I*. What we have in effect, is an expansion of performativity beyond that of the first person and utterances, to a fully-fledged model of the performative construction of interpretive communities, including the 'we, the people' of both nationalism and identity politics. 'We, the people' emerges as the performative refiguring of the large circulatory processes of which it is a constitutive element. At the same time, it creates and names the semiotic space through which these new forms of collective identity will circulate, in effect creating the conditions necessary for their own circulation, not unlike the way sentential performatives create some of the conditions necessary for their own fulfillment or uptake.

Anderson uses his analysis of novels and newspapers as a way of relocating the intellectual spaces in which nationalism should be analyzed. His example is the Filipino writer Jose Rizal's *Noli me Tangere* which describes the spread of the news of a dinner party to be hosted by a local dignitary. The narrator traces its dissemination across an imagined community that is itself an index of the readers' imagined community, none of whom the narrator can presume to know, but whose narrative style addresses them in tones of ironic intimacy:

> Towards the end of October, Don Santiago de los Santos, popularly known as Captain Tiago, was giving a dinner party. Although, contrary to his usual practice, he had announced it only that afternoon, it was already the subject of every conversation in Binondo, in other quarters of the city, and even in [the walled inner city of] Intramuros [...] The dinner was being given at a house on Analoague Street. Since we do not recall the street number, we shall describe it in such a way that it may still be recognized – that is, if earthquakes have not yet destroyed it. We do not believe that its owner will have had it torn down, since such work is usually left to God or to nature, which, besides, holds many contracts with our Government. (quoted in Anderson [1983]1991:26-27)

Anderson points out that many of the depicted actions take place without their agents being aware of each other, but they are all seen by the reader through the eye of the narrator as occurring within a homogeneous time in a common social space. It is this projection, shared among readers, that forms the basis for the imagined community of the nation-state. Anderson writes:

> [i]t should suffice to note that right from the start the image (wholly new to Filipino writing) of a dinner-party being discussed by hundreds of unnamed people who do not know each other, in quite different parts of Manila, in a particular month of a particular decade, immediately conjures up the imagined community. And in the phrase 'a house on Analoague Street' which 'we shall describe in such a way that it may still be recognized' the would-be recognizers are we-Filipino-readers. The casual progression of this house from the 'interior' time of the novel to the 'exterior' time of the [Manila] reader's everyday life gives a hypnotic confirmation of the solidity of a single community, embracing characters, author, and readers, moving onward through calendrical time. (Anderson [1983](1991):27)

Newspapers present a similar semiotic structure. The recorded events occur, for the most part, independently, held together only by 'calendrical coincidence' of daily publication. Yet the timing of each edition (morning, afternoon, or evening) creates a community of readers most of whom do not know each other but know that they all regularly re-enact a 'secular, historically clocked imagined community' of daily readership.

In reading a novel or newspaper, the readers enact the very experience of community at the heart of a nationalist imagination. The narrator's voice, whether it be that of a novel or the objective reportage of a newspaper (or the timeless narrators of philosophical texts), presents an objective representation of events, agents, and subjectivities that are a microcosm of the larger (national) society that embraces the imputed narrator and his readers. The circulation of novels and newspapers in a global print capitalism are the semiotic basis for 'imagining the national' and producing 'the people' who will be the subject of nationalist literatures, histories, and politics.

4. Nationalism and hegemony

Another way of interpreting Anderson's account is that in its insistence on the 'unisonance' of identities it reveals how narrative forms can be used to construct hegemonic ideologies. Since readers might not choose to accept the terms of narrative address or identify with the characters, there is in principle no reason why narrative forms would have to produce consensual identities, as much of the discussion of 'minor' literatures shows.

Instead, what Anderson has produced is an account of how narrative forms can be used to produce hegemonic national identities in which the very act of reading 'ritually' enacts the national social imaginary.

By inhabiting the point of view of the omniscient narrator, readers construct an 'objective' vision of society that they share with other readers. Yet this objective perspective also obscures crucial power relations: those between the omniscient narrator and the people narrated about, between the objectivizing narrative discourse and the depicted discourses and actions. The fundamental asymmetry between narrating event and narrated-about event at the heart of realistic fiction and reportage is also one of the constitutive moments in the reification of social relationships characteristic of modern capitalism. In an often overlooked passage in *The Structural Transformation of the Public Sphere*, Habermas makes explicit the connections between capitalism, public sphere imaginaries, and ideology:

> If ideologies are not only manifestations of the socially necessary consciousness in its essential falsity, if there is an aspect to them that can lay a claim to truth inasmuch as it transcends the status quo in utopian fashion, even if only for purposes of justification, then ideology exists at all only from this period on. Its origin would be the identification of "property owner" with "human being as such" in the role accruing to private people as members in the political public sphere of the bourgeois constitutional state, that is, in the identification of the public sphere in the political realm with that in the world of letters; and also in public opinion itself, in which the interest of the class, via critical public debate, could assume the appearance of the general interest, that is, in the identification of domination with its dissolution into pure reason. (Habermas [1962]1989:88)

The identifications of property owner with human being in general and the interests of a specific class with that of the general interest, are rhetorical moves at the heart of modern ideology. These synecdochic equations create the space for the expression of the social contradictions they mediate; the resulting disjunction between social reality and ideology is a constitutive part of bourgeois society. The ideological (and metonymic) construction of 'we, the people' links the private expressions of subjectivity ("human being as such") with their public counterparts (the imputed potential rationality of public opinion) and gives the resulting social totality an agentive subject. It is in the interstices of the crossing of public spheres (England and colonial America; Spain and its colonies) that the modern notion of peoplehood emerges. A global print capitalism circulates new forms of objective narration among an internationalized elite. These forms become the bases for constructing a new form of political subjectivity, that of 'we, the people', which presents itself as an 'objective' representation of the 'fact' of nationhood. The valorization of 'objectivity' not only reorganizes the relations among local discourses (perhaps by elevating a local register into the position of national language), but brings along with it the full semiotic armature of capitalism: statistical measures derived from censuses and surveys, new financial instruments, 'value-free' research, and so on. The trope of peoplehood transfers to an ideological level the crisis developing between the global cultural economy of colonialism and traditional forms of political legitimation; the resulting ideology of the equality of nations and peoples becomes a necessary component of an emerging *international* global economy.

The narrative mediation of nationalist subjectivity was also accompanied by a change in how communication was viewed. Earlier ideologies of printing saw print as extending face-to-face communication, simply increasing the circulation of information without any qualitative transformation of it. In the bourgeois public sphere, people began to see printing as foregrounding writing's potential for unlimited dissemination, thereby creating a print-mediated difference between public discourse and the world of letters that characterizes private correspondence. The crucial transformation occurs when communication is seen not just as a face-to-face relation between people, but rather as consisting of a potentially limitless print-mediated discourse. It is into this space that narrated texts are inserted and become the semiotic basis for new forms of subjectivity. A new vision of community is formed in which a reading public is held together by a potentially infinitely open-ended process of reading and criticism.

5. Subjectivity and legitimation

It is from this conception of communication as an abstract circulation created by the possibilities of narration that a new form of social subjectivity emerges that is at the heart of modernity. In the American and French revolutions the idea of 'we, the people' emerges, an idea that will spread quickly and become a founding presupposition of the order of nation-states. Of course, there were notions of collective 'we's' that predate the great revolutions of the eighteenth and nineteenth centuries. But the peculiarity of the modern notion of peoplehood lies not in its linkage to these more traditional forms but in its abstractness. With the American and French revolutions, we see the emergence of a new form of subjectivity, that of a constitutionalized peoplehood, which would be abstract enough to legitimate the modern constitutional state, yet concrete enough to subsume all private citizens. It is this dual structure of the modern notion of peoplehood that also marks its uniqueness as a cultural construct. It is a doubled form of performative subjectivity, which mediates between the simple aggregation of 'I's' and the collective 'we' of 'we, the people', and it is this dualism that lies at the heart of the notions of peoplehood used to legitimate the modern nation-state. The idea of a constitutionalized peoplehood then rapidly becomes a key component of modern nationalisms.

The notion of a constitutionalized peoplehood introduces a new level of semiotic complexity to the problems of political legitimacy. The notion of 'the people' must be abstract enough to legitimate the founding law of laws, i.e., the constitution, as well as particular enough to apply to every citizen, past, present, and future. In addition, Hannah Arendt (1963) has argued that unlike pre-modern societies that invoke tradition or non-secular superhuman agencies, the modern constitutional state is involved in a fundamental legitimation paradox: since a constitution establishes the basic parameters of political legitimacy, those who come together to form a constitution are themselves unconstitutional, i.e., politically illegitimate. The modern notion of 'we, the people' solves this problem by attributing foundational legitimacy to a non-political collective agency that creates itself through its own actions in secular time. Perhaps it is not surprising that the first modern constitutionalized peoplehood is signalled in two explicit performative constructions, at the end of the Declaration of Independence and the preamble to the US Constitution: from "We the representatives of the United States of America [...] do [...] solemnly publish and declare, that these united colonies are and of right ought to be free and independent states" to "we, the people of the United States, do ordain and establish this Constitution for the United States of America".

The radicalness of this conception of 'we-identity' lies in its revolutionary origins. Revolution combines the ideas of a unique beginning and freedom while also creating a new historical subject and agent. In both the American and French revolutions, the battle to create a sovereign people contains within it the overthrow of an older order of legitimacy, that based upon the divine right of kings. Yet to overthrow this source of legitimacy was to call into question that which had always been assumed: governments were legitimated by higher laws. If religion could not provide the source of legitimacy, what could? Even more specifically, what legitimates the constitution of a modern nation when traditional sources of authority have become effaced by a rising secularism? Hannah Arendt describes the situation as a vicious circle:

> those who get together to constitute a new government are themselves unconstitutional, that is, they have no authority to do what they have set out to achieve. The vicious circle in legislating is present not in ordinary lawmaking, but in laying down the fundamental law, the law of the land or the constitution which, from then on, is supposed to incarnate the 'higher law' from which all laws ultimately derive their authority. And with this problem, which appeared as the urgent need for some absolute, the men of the American Revolution found themselves no less confronted than their colleagues in France. The trouble was – to quote Rousseau once more – that to put the law above man and thus to establish the validity of man-made laws, *il faudrait des dieux*, 'one actually would need gods'. (Arendt 1963:84)

Arendt's invocation of both the American and French cases points to two different solutions to the performativity paradox of legitimation that she has outlined. Each involves the creation of a form of peoplehood, which depends upon a specific model of communication and is abstract enough to legitimate the law. In the American case, the legitimation crisis occurs when the Continental Congress declared on 15 May 1775 that the authority of the crown should be replaced by new state governments based on the authority of the people. The question immediately arose of the legality of such a decree since the law derived its legitimacy from the King and the Parliament and there was no precedent for legally claiming the authority of the people. The solution involved the creation of a notion of peoplehood derived from the abstract properties of print mediation. In Rousseau's model, a face-to-face assembly creates the social contract which brings about the general will; the legitimation crisis occurred in the creation of the laws by which the general will can preserve itself and endure. Although writing and print make it possible for society to continue, they merely transmit the general will whose abstract properties arise from the initial face-to-face contract; the legitimation crisis occurs in the creation of the founding law of laws, not in the creation of the people.

In Rousseau's *On the Social Contract* ([1762]1983) , the social compact between assembled individuals brings into existence the general will and the body politic. Legislation will give it "movement and will" (Rousseau [1762]1983:36) and allow society to reproduce itself over time. Since the laws of state are a product of the general will, their objects will be similarly abstract and general. Laws do not name any individuals or stipulate particular actions, but "consider[s] subjects as a body and action in the abstract" (ibid.:37).

Yet it is the very abstractness or non-indexical nature of the general will and the law that make setting the model in motion impossible. On the one hand, the "existence of the State is only ideal and conventional" (Rousseau quoted in DeMan 1979:272). On the other hand, law demands context specificity in order to function; it must apply to specific cases. The law is always future-oriented; its illocutionary mode is that of the promise, but a promise also presupposes a specific date when it is made – "laws are promissory notes in which the present of the promise is always a past with regard to its realization" (ibid.:273), and this temporal structure and movement is at the heart of the law. The practical realization of the model demands a concomitant specification of the general will:

> the law of today should not be an act of yesterday's general will but of today's; we have not committed ourselves to do what the people wanted but what they want. It follows that when the Law speaks in the name of the people, it is in the name of the people of today and not of the present. (Rousseau, quoted and translated by DeMan 1979:273)

Yet no such "people of today" can exist, because "the eternal present of the contract" precludes "any particular present (*idem*)". The general will lacks a voice which "can state [*énoncer*] the will of the people" (ibid.:274).

Indeed, there seems to be a fundamental performative paradox whose resolution would require a metaleptic reversal of cause and effect:

> For an emerging people to be capable of appreciating the fundamental rules of statecraft, the effect would have to become the cause. The social spirit which ought to be the work of that institution, would have to preside over the institution itself. And men would be, prior to the advent of laws, what they ought to become by means of laws. (Rousseau [1762]1983:40)

Men, in the state of nature, would not have experienced or had knowledge of the benefits that a state governed by laws would bring about and are governed primarily by self-interest. So where would the notion of the social good to be produced by legislation come from? What would motivate them to create binding laws? From their assembled state, it seems they could only make promises that would govern that particular assembly, but not any others; there would be no laws that would create a potentially

infinite temporal sequence in which present promises became the presupposed pasts for their future realizations. The general will requires the
creation of the law to preserve and reproduce itself. Rousseau's solution
is a lawgiver who has the "sight and voice that the people lack" (DeMan
1979:274), but who also is outside the system and free of the distorting
influence of particular interest: he who frames the law should not make it.
Even armed with such wisdom and foresight, the only way "the fathers of
nations" (the lawgivers) can set the model in motion is through deception –
"to credit gods with their own wisdom" (DeMan 1979:274):

> It is this sublime reason, which transcends the grasp of ordinary men,
> whose decisions the legislator puts in the mouths of the immortals in
> order to compel by divine authority those whom human prudence could
> not move. (Rousseau [1762]1983:41)

The appeal to a transcendent source of authority makes the source of inspiration at least as general as the general will and the law; at the same
time, it allows the lawgiver to give the people the knowledge they need to
create the law.

In the American case, the notion of peoplehood rests upon seeing the
nation as a print-mediated community. The critical transformation is when
communication is seen not just as a face-to-face relation between people
but rather as a potentially limitless print-mediated discourse. The performativity crisis is resolved through the relations between an oral model of
people creation in the Declaration of Independence and its subsequent
incorporation into the abstract peoplehood of the 'we, the people' of the
Constitution. The notion of the American people would face two directions: it would be a transcendent source of legitimacy yet be embodied in
every citizen. This would require the construction of a new ideology of
the political implications of print: the printed textuality of the Constitution allows it to emanate from no individual, collectivity, or state in
particular, and thus from the people in general. Its circulation among 'the
people' mitigated against the particularism of local interests, and thereby
solved one of the continuing problems of that period: how to balance local interest and the public good by creating a mediation between the two.
By building upon the translocal nature of the mediation, it created the
ground for a notion of disinterested public virtue.

The American solution avoids Rousseau's appeal to a transcendent
authority by creating an extra-legal source which is sufficiently abstract
and general to legitimize the law, and yet immanent within the legal process. This source will derive from the written qualities of the law and its

ability to create an 'imagined community' of readers and citizens based upon the abstract properties of print mediation. The constitutional convention and ratification process ensured that the source of this authority was extra-legal; it represents a higher will which legitimates particular acts of legislation, but can itself never be reduced to the normal legislative process. 'The people' are the embodiment of a general interest that transcends particular interests and is thus sufficiently abstract to legitimate the law of laws or a constitution. The metaleptic reversal of cause and effect is accomplished not through an act of deception as in Rousseau's case, but through a splitting of the performativity of the 'we, the people' into the Declaration's earlier performative moment (which still appealed to God and relies on an oral model of performativity – the first printed edition still contains Jefferson's diacritical marks) and the future self-interpretive process the Constitution creates (in the Supreme Court and the amendment process), in which the people will constantly re-interpret itself. Returning to Rousseau's gap between the abstractness of the general will and the performativity of the law, we can see that in the US case, the temporal trajectory that the performativity of promising establishes at the heart of the law is embodied in the Constitution in its amendment process and the Supreme Court. At the same time, the whole legislative process presupposes and continuously creates 'the people of today' immanent in every legislative act which 'the people' also legitimates.

The contemporary ideoscape of nationalism is produced by a segmentation of the global circulatory processes of print capitalism. In Anderson's account, the semiotic mediation of narration, especially in its realist forms in philosophy, fiction, and history, creates a transparency between the community of readers (represented by the participants of the narrating event, i.e., the narrator and reader), and the community of characters that are narrated about. The shared vernacular language and various forms of narrative address make possible a mutual identification of characters and audiences, giving a sense of a shared community moving through time. The performative construction of identity emerges at a particular historical juncture, at a point when older forms of religious legitimation are failing. The revolutionary origins of nationalism contribute to the demand for an autochthonous political subject, one that overturns previous forms of legitimation and thus seems born out of itself but can also serve as the founding subject for the nation. 'We, the people' emerges as such a performative subject, satisfying the dual demands of revolutionary subjecthood (the radical newness of the modern subject) while at the same time giving a name to the circulatory processes out of which it arises but also legitimates. 'We, the people' sutures the chiasmus between two forms of narrated community: that of the narrating event and that of the narrated-about characters, thereby linking text-internal references to the national to the larger community of which they are exemplars. In the American and French revolutionary cases, two different models of the relation between performative subject and circulation emerge: that of an abstract print mediation in the American case, and an extended face-to-face model in the French example.

The idea of a constitutionalized peoplehood is now a presupposition of the international order of nation-states. Circulated among an international elite held together by print capitalism, the double nature of peoplehood as abstract unity (a 'we' that can legitimate the law of laws) and individual manifestation (as citizen) provides national agents which move through 'the empty, homogeneous time' of modernity. To the extent that a constitutionalized peoplehood creates the dual category of people and citizen, the performativity paradox is internal to the modern nation. The renewed demands for an essentialized culture shared by a people emerges from the demand for values abstract enough to legitimate the state and yet broad enough to define every person as a citizen. Internal to such constructions is an aporia created by the disjunction between models of communication presupposed in legitimating the state and those generated by mass publicity and consumerism. Homi Bhabha (1990) and Paul DeMan (1979) have described the tension as between the self-generating subject of 'we, the people' moving in an abstract historical time, and the 'in-betweenness' of the production of 'we-ness' in present time. The political subject in its dual 'we-ness' as peoplehood and citizen emerges as the legitimating moment of the laws of laws, as the doubled solution to the performative paradox of modern nationhood; the paradox is resolved by an appeal to the peoplehood of the founding moment which binds every 'present we' in a past and future which is seen as its own. The ideology of peoplehood and the concept of national culture thus appear as each society's answer to its own founding and ongoing performative paradox; yet new communicative practices are constantly producing forms of 'we-ness' that challenge the abstract notions of peoplehood used to legitimate the modern nation-state.

References

Anderson, Benedict ([1983]1991) *Imagined Communities: Reflections on the origin and spread of nationalism*, London: Verso.
Appadurai, Arjun (1996) *Modernity at Large*, Minneapolis: University of Minnesota Press.

Arendt, Hannah (1963) *On Revolution*, London: Penguin Books.

Bakhtin, M.M. (1981) *The Dialogic Imagination*, ed. Michael Holquist, trans. Caryl Emerson and Michael Holquist. Austin: University of Texas Press.

Benveniste, Emile (1966) *Problems in General Linguistics*, Miami: University of Miami Press.

Bhabha, Homi (1990) 'DissemiNation: time, narrative, and the margins of the modern nation', in H. Bhabha (ed) *Nation and narration,* London: Routledge, 291-321.

DeMan, Paul (1979) *Allegories of Reading*, New Haven: Yale University Press.

Habermas, Jürgen ([1962]1989) *The Structural Transformation of the Public Sphere*, trans. Thomas Burger. Cambridge, MA: MIT Press.

Hegel, Georg W.F. (1969) *Science of Logic*, trans. A.V. Miller. London: George Allen & Unwin Ltd.

------ (1949) *Phenomenology of Mind*, trans. J.B. Baillie. London: George Allen & Unwin Ltd.

Rousseau, J.J. ([1762]1983) *On the Social Contract*, trans. D. Cress. Indianapolis: Hackett Press.

Silverstein, Michael (2000) 'Whorfianism and the Linguistic Imagination of Community', in Paul Kroskrity (ed) *Regimes of Language: Ideologies, polities, and identities*, Santa Fe: School of American Research Press.

Taylor, Charles (1989) *Sources of the Self*, Cambridge, MA: Harvard University Press.

------ (1975) *Hegel*, Cambridge: Cambridge University Press.

Notes on Contributors

RICHARD BAUMAN is Distinguished Professor of Communication and Culture, Anthropology, and Folklore at Indiana University, and Director of the IU Program in Performance Studies. His principal research interests include the poetics of performance, oral narrative, and language in religious practice. Among his publications are *Verbal Art as Performance* (1977), *Let your Words be Few: Symbolism of Speaking and Silence among 17th-Century Quakers* (1983), and *Story, Performance, and Event* (1986). Bauman has been Editor of the *Journal of American Folklore* and President of the Semiotic Society of America and the Society for Linguistic Anthropology.

JOSEPH ERRINGTON is Professor of Anthropology at Yale University. His chapter in this collection is drawn from his book *Shifting Language: Interaction and Identity in Javanese Indonesia* (1998). Among his other publications is *Structure and Style in Javanese: A Semiotic View of Linguistic Etiquette* (1988).

SUSAN GAL is Professor of Anthropology and Linguistics at the University of Chicago. She is the author of *Language Shift* (1979) and *The Politics of Gender after Socialism* (2000, with Gail Kligman). Her interests centre on language ideology, linguistic differentiation, and the political economy of language. She is currently working on the discursive aspects of political transformation in East Central Europe.

JANE H. HILL is Regents' Professor of Anthropology and Linguistics at the University of Arizona. Her interests are in Native American languages, language and political economy, and problems of representation broadly. She is author of *Speaking Mexicano* (1986, with Kenneth C. Hill), and she edited *Responsibility and Evidence in Oral Discourse* (1993, with Judith T. Irvine).

JUDITH T. IRVINE is Professor of Anthropology at the University of Michigan. Her interests lie in language ideology, the social and cultural dimensions of linguistic practices, and the history of languages and linguistics. She has conducted fieldwork among rural Wolof in Senegal and archival research on colonial African linguistics. Her publications include *Responsibility and Evidence in Oral Discourse* (1993, co-editor with Jane H. Hill) and *The Psychology of Culture*, (1993) a reconstruction and edition of a posthumous book by Edward Sapir.

BENJAMIN LEE is Professor of Anthropology at Rice University and Director of the Center for Transcultural Studies.

BAMBI B. SCHIEFFELIN is Professor of Anthropology at New York University. Her research areas include language ideology, language change, missionization, literacy, and language socialization. She has carried out ethnographic and linguistic fieldwork among Bosavi people since 1967 and is the author of *The Give and Take of Everyday Life: Language Socialization of Kaluli Children* (1990). She prepared the *Bosavi–English–Tok Pisin Dictionary* with Steven Feld and co-edited *Language Ideologies: Practice and Theory* (1998) with Kathryn A. Woolard and Paul Kroskrity. She is currently working on a monograph about the impact of missionization on language use and social life in Bosavi.

MICHAEL SILVERSTEIN is the Charles F. Grey Distinguished Service Professor in the Departments of Anthropology, Linguistics, and Psychology at the University of Chicago, where he has taught since 1970. With Greg Urban, he edited *Natural Histories of Discourse* (1996), a volume in a continuing series problematizing semiotics as the dialectical field of intersection of linguistic structure, discursive practice, and cultural ideologies. With several others who appear in this volume, he has contributed to *Language Ideologies: Practice and Theory* (1998) and to *Regimes of Language: Ideologies, Polities, and Identities* (ed. Paul Kroskrity, 2000).

JACQUELINE URLA is Associate Professor of Anthropology at the University of Massachusetts, Amherst. She has done ethnographic research on language revival and cultural politics in the Basque Country of Spain. She is completing a book entitled *Being Basque, Speaking Basque: Language Activism and Cultural Politics in the Post-Franco Era.*

KATHRYN A. WOOLARD is Professor of Anthropology at the University of California, San Diego. She is author *of Double Talk: Bilingualism and the Politics of Ethnicity in Catalonia* (1989), and co-editor of *Language Ideologies: Practice and Theory* (1998). Her current work is on language ideology in early modern Spain and its empire.

Index

academies 1, 142
access 150
address 153-154
affect markers 126
African languages 3, 10, 13-29
   classification 13-29
African linguistics 13-29
African-American(s) 100, 159
Afro-Caribbean 147
agglutinating languages 33, 36
Algeria 143
Algonkin 56
alterity 152
Altuna, Ana 141n
amateur(s) 3, 35
ambiguity 88, 92, 101, 105, 111, 114
American
   Constitution 178-179
   Declaration of Independence 8,
   175, 178
   English 91-92
   Republic 8, 84-85, 174-180
Anderson, Benedict 8, 33, 108, 109,
   112, 149, 164-165, 167, 168, 170,
   171-173, 179
Anderson, J. 70n
animator 110
anonymity 112
anthropology 47, 120
   Americanist 51n
Appadurai, Arjan 164-165
applied
   linguistics 81
   science 80
Arendt, Hannah 175-176
Army Language Program 79
Aryan (languages) 26n, 33
audience 7, 8, 105, 110, 117
   literary 60, 61
Augustine 166
Aulestia, Gorka 150

Austin, J.L. 72
authenticity 7, 55-56, 61, 92, 97, 98,
   128
   rhetoric of 47, 53
authority 5, 6, 10, 32, 76, 105, 108,
   109-111, 112, 119-127, 134, 137,
   166, 178
   anonymous 6-7
   of authenticity 7, 55
   cultural 40, 43
   as sociolinguistically created 5, 9
   discursive 116
   dissimulated 110, 113
   institutional 151
   political 2, 8, 9, 43
   professional 41, 43
   scientific 80-81
   social 4
authorship 49
autonomous left 143, 145

Babcock, Barbara 95
backstage 88
Bakhtin, Mikhail 8, 78n, 116, 169
Bantu languages 21, 24
Barbrook, Richard 144n, 147
Basic English 3, 69-82
Basque 10, 141-163
   sociolinguistics 152
Bassets, Lluís 144n
Basso, Keith 157n
Bauman, Richard 2, 3, 7, 8, 46-68,
   182
Békés, Vera 35
Bendix, Edward 126
Bentham, Jeremy 73, 78, 80
Benveniste, Emile 169
Beöthy, Zsolt 36
Berend, I. 38n
Besnier, Niko 121
Bhabha, Homi 180

Bieder, Robert 47n
bilingualism 39
Black English 100
Bleek, Wilhelm 19, 20-23, 24
Blommaert, Jan 2
Bloomfield, Leonard 73n, 74
Bloomsbury 72
Boas, Franz 51n
book
    the power of 119-120
    as speaking subject 134-135
Borden, Lizzie 160
Border Spanish 94n
borrowing 94
boundary-making 2
Bourdieu, Pierre 5, 108, 142
Brecht, Berthold 144
Bremer, Richard 47n
Brenneis, Donald 46n, 83, 97n
Briggs, Charles 8, 46-47
Briggs, Joe 94, 97n, 101
Briggs, Keith 128
Budenz, József 36, 37, 40
Burke, Kenneth 77-78
Bush, George 92, 95, 97
Butz, Earl 100
Bybee, Joan 126
Byrne, James 23

Calhoun, Craig 5, 843
Caló 94n
capitalism 5, 142, 150, 173-174, 179
Carroll, J.B. 74n
Cass, Lewis 48
Castillian *see* Spanish
categories 1, 86n
    philological 3
    scholarly 1-10
censure 89, 92-93, 98, 104
certainty 127
Chafe, Wallace 127
Chase, Stuart 79
Chicano 94
China 79

Chippewa *See* Ojibwe
Cholos 94n
Christianity 3, 59, 123, 137-138
Churchill, Winston 71, 78, 79
circulation 164-167, 170, 179
civil
    society 103, 141, 167
    speech 91
class (social) 38, 101, 108-109
class
    grammatical 21-25
    noun 21-26
classification
    of languages 13-29
    system 21
classroom 88, 121, 128
Clements, William 47
Clifford, Joseph 126
Cmiel, Kenneth 7n, 84, 91
code(s) 2
code-switch 98
code-switching 133n, 157
cognitive science 71n
Cohn, Bernard 122
Collins, James 121
colloquialism(s) 85, 91, 153
colonialism 13-29, 103, 122, 143
colonial
    discourse 30-31
    linguistics 13-29
    power 14
Comaroff, Jean 122
Comaroff, John 122
common sense 93, 98, 101
communication code 5
communicative action 7
competition 2, 6
concept
    cultural 3
Condillac 14
conflict 2
consensus 2
consociate(ship) 112
constructivism 3n

contextualization 4
  cue(s) 8
control 110, 119
correctness 1, 41
counter-authority 151
counterpublic 141-142, 159-160
Cramer, Richard 92n
Crittenden, Robert 120n
Crow, Thomas 60n
Crowley, Tony 4
cultural
  capital 3
culture 50-51
  aristocracy of 108
  industry 6, 83
  popular 141

Dard, Jean 15-16
Daston, L. 4
debate
  on language 3, 31-32, 40
decontextualization 8
Degérando, Joseph-Marie 10, 15
DeMan, Paul 177-180
democracy 85, 91, 103
  ideology of 109
  radical 145, 154
denotation 71, 73
Descartes 166
Destutt de Tracy 14, 16
dialect 1, 81, 100, 123, 129n
  social 108
diaspora 165
dictionaries 1
difference 14, 141, 160
differentiation 2
  racial 20
diglossia 107
direct discourse 61, 169
Dippie, Brian 61n
Disney, Walt 79
displacement 10
distancing 121, 157
distinction

racial 20
diversity 88
domination 14
Duranti, Alessandro 121
Dutch 103, 108

east/west discourse 31
eastern Europe 30-31
editorial practices 56-58, 61
education 32, 122
Egin 149
Egunkaria 149-150
d'Eichtal, Gustave 18-19
Eizagirre, Jokin 141n
Eley, Geoff 141
elite 71, 104, 108-109, 117
  racist discourse 84
elitehood 5, 108
elitism 93
emphatic markers 126, 134-135
empiricism 72n
England 6, 166
English 69-82, 99, 122, 128, 133n.
  See also Basic English, American
  English
enregisterment 71, 73
Enriquez, Xavier 87
entextualization 3, 81
epistemology
  competing 122, 127
  cultural 127
  natural 127
ergative 131, 133
Ernst, Thomas 124n
Errington, Frederick 121
Errington, Joseph 5, 6, 7, 8, 9, 70n,
  103-118, 182
Esparza, Javier 141n
ethnicity 112
ethnology 50-51, 60
etiquette 155
Etoro 125n
evidence 119-140
evidential particles 124

evidentials 123-127, 131-137
  multifunctional 126
evolution 19
exclusion 2, 6, 83, 84, 86n, 100,
  141, 148
  reproduction of 83
exemplary
  centre 108
  speech 107-118
expert
  notions 2
expertise
  linguistic 32-33, 80

Fabian, Johannes 122
Fábián, Pál 39
Fábri, Anna 39n
face-to-face interaction 7
family
  imagery 13-29, 35
  romance 13-29
Fanon, Frantz 143-144
feedback 137, 151
Feld, Steven 119-120, 130
feminism 6, 89, 160
Fichte, Johann 168
fieldwork
  authority of 53, 55
Finno-Ugric 34
Fitzsimmons, David 96
Fliegelman, Jay 7n
Florence, P. 69n
Foley, William 124n
folk categories 84
folklore 1, 2, 3, 46, 51n
  studies 8, 62
footing 8
formality 107
form-content differentiation 54, 56
Foucault, Michel 2
Fox, Barbara 126
framing 129
France 6, 10, 145
Franco-Maghribi 159

Fraser, Nancy 6, 17n, 84n, 89, 90n, 141
fraternity 14-19
free speech 151
freedom of expression 147, 152
Freeman, Edward 26n
Freeman, John 47n
French 5, 16, 98
French Revolution 14-19, 141, 174-
  175, 180
Freud, Sigmund 13
Fuale, Kulu 119n, 128-137
Fusco, Coco 158

Gal, Susan 1-12, 30-45, 46n, 119n,
  141n, 182
Galison, P. 4
García, Rogelio 86n, 87, 96
Gauzinee, Gitshee 53
Geertz, Clifford 70n, 108
gemeinschaft 112
gender 13-29, 88
  dichotomy 6
  grammatical 14, 16, 21-26, 59
  hierarchy 89, 147
  system 21, 26
genealogical relationship 2, 3, 13-
  29, 34
general semantics 71, 80
generation 18-19
genre 1, 8, 88, 120, 122, 128, 137
  designation 62
  speech 105-118
German 38, 39, 98
German philosophy 8-9
Germany 6
Gewertz, Deborah 121
Gilroy, Paul 147
Givón, Talmy 127
Goffman, Erving 7, 8, 110
Goldberg, David 86n
Gomez- Peña, Guillermo 158
Goodman, Ellen 86
gossip 159
governmentality 113

grammar 1, 74, 168
grammatical structure 13, 21
Greenberg, Joseph 24, 27
Grimm brothers 46-47
Grimm, Jakob 23, 46
Gross, Joan 159n
groupness 71n
Guattari, Félix 144, 150-151, 153, 158
Guérard, Albert 78n
Gumperz, John 8
Guss, David 121

Habermas, Jürgen 4-5, 9, 33, 83, 103, 108, 117, 141, 151, 165, 166, 170, 173
Hacking, Ian 9
Haeckel, Ernst 19, 20
Hallowell, A. 47
Hamitic
    languages 23-24
    myth 24
Hanák, Peter 38n
Hanks, William 7n, 9n, 30n, 46n, 160n
Hansen, Miriam 141, 142, 143, 159-160
Hausa 19
Haviland, John 127
Hawaiian 95
Heath, Shirley 121
Hegel, Georg 168
hegemony 172-174
Herder, Johann Gottfried 23, 30, 51n, 166
Herri Batasuna 149
herria 150
Heryanto, A. 104
heterogeneity 161
hierarchy
    ethnic 109
    evolutionary 19
    racial 14, 19-26
    reproduction of 7

sexual 14
    social 1, 23, 108, 154
Hill, Jane 6, 7, 8, 83-102, 127, 157, 182
hip-hop 100n, 159
Hispanics 100
historiography 169
Hobbes, Thomas 166
Hoeningswald, Henry 26
homogeneity 112, 141
homogeneous time 167, 171-172, 180
honorification 70n
hooks, bell 160
Humboldt, Willem von 23
humour 95, 96, 98, 99, 101, 155-156, 158
Hunfalvy, Pál 36, 37, 40
Hungary 30-45
    linguistic heterogeneity 32, 38
    nationalism 32, 34
Hungarian 31-45
    correct usage 40-44
    language debates 30-45
    national standard 41, 43
    origin of 34-37
    purism 40
Hunt, Lynn 13, 26
hybridity 157, 160

identification 170
identity
    collective 165, 171
    formation 2
    national 159-160, 165
    social 105
Idéologues 14, 16, 18
ideology 2, 59, 79-80, 83, 101, 147. *See also* language ideology
    of communication 150-151
    cultural 71
    political 166
    state 105
ideoscape 164, 165

imagined community 8, 10, 33, 138, 149, 150, 154, 164-168, 170
immigrant(s) 86-87, 96
impersonality 8, 9, 90n
Imre, Sándor 41n
indexicality 95, 98
Indian languages
   style 56
Indian policy 48, 59-60, 63
individual (the) 3, 71
individuality 88
Indo-European (languages) 14, 17
Indonesia(n) 8, 9, 102-117
inequality 1
inferencing 136
inferiority
   of the Indian mind 59
inflecting languages 33, 36
informality 91
information 133
intellectual(s) 76, 77, 103, 142, 144
Internation Auxiliary Language 74n, 75n
interpersonal communication 9
interpretation
   moral 62
   racial 20
   shared 2
interpreting 54, 123
interpretive framework 120, 138
intertextual gap 52-63
intertextuality 8
intertranslatability 164
involvement 97
Irvine, Judith 1, 2, 4, 10, 13-29, 31, 127, 182
isolating languages 33, 36
Italian 98
Italy 143, 145
Ivins, Molly 91, 97

Jackson, Jesse 90
Jaffe, Alexandra 160
Jakobson, Roman 126

Japanese 98
Java 103-118
Javanese 5, 9, 70n, 105-118
   exemplary 107-118
   formal 107
Jefferson, Thomas 179
Johnston, John 48, 53, 54, 63
joke(s) 91-92, 100-101, 157

Kalahari 18
Kaluli 9, 119-140
   orthography 123
   varieties 123
Kant, Immanuel 5, 166, 168
Kasmir, Sharryn 145
Keeler, Ward 110
Kluge, Alexander 141
Kochman, Thomas 91
Kogowa, Tetsuo 146, 147, 150, 158
Korzybski, Alfred 71, 80
Kosáry, D. 40n
Kossuth, Lajos 35
Kroskrity, Paul 2
Krueger, Robert 96
Kulick, Don 121

Lacour, Claudia 99n
La Grasserie, Raoul de 19, 21n, 23
Lakoff, George 81
Láncz, Irén 34, 40n, 41
Landes, Joan 5, 6, 17n, 141
language
   boundaries 99, 157, 158
   classification 13-29
   construction 1, 70, 83
   contact 42
   death 30
   as discourse 71
   family 2, 13-29
   genealogy 13-29
   ideology 1, 5, 84-85, 122, 128, 143, 151-157
   inorganic 17
   loss 30

national 41
natural 72-73
as natural entity 4
organic 17
policy 152
politics 143
purism 99, 142
reform 30, 38-40, 41, 81, 142
and religion 1n
simplification 69-82
standardization 8, 41-42, 142, 158
standard 1, 33, 43
structure 1-2
and thought 56-59, 71
types 33
langue autorisé 142
law 176-178, 179
Lee, Benjamin 6, 8, 10, 150, 164-181, 183
legitimation 6-7, 8, 32, 70, 109, 111, 167, 174-180
Lepsius, Richard 20-23
Levine, George 3n
Lewis, Peter 144n
lexical
conjugates 70, 73
primes 73
simplexes 73
lexicon 73, 101
Likiniano 146
linguistic
anthropology 2, 46, 62, 70, 83, 92n, 127
correctness 41-42
domination 160
hierarchy 107
homogenization 79
ideology 3, 122, 137
innovation 128, 131
imperialism 78n
minority 141-143
revitalization 30, 142, 143, 152-153, 155
strategies 10

terrorism 141
linguistics 30-45, 65
as natural science 33
literacy 16n, 49, 119-140, 142
practices 121-122
literary
deficiency 58
society 142
taste 49, 57, 61. *See also* refinement
literature 166
concept of 49-50, 52
Liu, David 100
loan words 94
Locher, Michael 69n
Locke, John 166
Lockhart, L.W. 73
Longfellow, Henry Wadsworth 57, 61n
Lowe, G. 144n
Lucy, John 127

McCain, Thomas 144n
McKenney, Thomas 53
McKenzie, D. 121
McMurray, David 159n
McNeil, W. 47
magyarization 32, 35
Malay 103
Marsden, Michael 47n
Marx, Karl 168
marxism 78n
mass society 104, 117
meaning 72, 80
emotive 72, 80
production of 126
referential 72, 80
media 148-149, 158
alternative 141-163
mass 6, 7-8, 32, 113, 180
mediation 52-63, 170, 178, 180
Meinhof, Carl 20, 23-25
Merton, Robert 71n
metacommentary 62
metadiscursive practices 46
metalanguage 168

metalinguistic 169
  messages 157
  operations 73n
  verbs 124
metonym 93
metaphor 26
Mexican-American 84, 93-101
Mignolo, W. 122
Mikeleiz, Olatz 141n
Mills, C. Wright 104, 117
minority 141-163
missionization 119-140
Mock Spanish 83-102
monolingualism 141
modernity 104, 165, 167
modernism 70, 81, 103-104, 111
Moffatt, Robert 18
monarch(y) 6
monogenesis 20
morphology 21, 26, 94, 101
Morris, Alice Vanderbilt 75n
Morrison, Tony 86
Müller, Friedrich 20
Müller, F. Max 4, 17, 19, 33-34, 36, 40, 43
Myers, Frederick 83
myth 24

Nagel, Thomas 4
narration 166, 168-172
  dual structure 170
narrative 46, 121, 123
  oral 46-68
  textuality 46
nation 8
nationalism 32, 103, 104, 111, 141-163, 164-181
  ethnic 32, 141-142
  official 112
  semiotics of 170, 174
nationhood 32
nation state 4
Native American 46-68
naturalness 4

Negt, Oskar 141
Németh, Béla 40n
neologism 41
New Order (Indonesia) 103-104, 112, 113
newspaper 5, 39, 104, 149-150, 165, 166, 167, 172
Nichols, Joanna 127
nominalization 170
normalization 142-143
novel, the 165, 166, 167
Nyelv'r 40-42

objectivity 4, 173-174
Ochs, Elinor 95n, 119n, 120, 121
off the record 88
Official English 99, 141
Ogden, C.K. 3, 9, 69-82
Ojibwe 3, 48-66
  gender in 59
  morphology 56
Olender, Maurice 1, 41n
Onabasulu 124n
oral literature 2, 7, 46-68
  concept of 50, 52
oral narrative 46-68
orientalism 31, 36, 43
Ormazabal, Sabino 144n
orthography 156-157
Orthological English 9, 69-82
Orthological Institute 70, 76, 79
orthology 70-71
other (the) 31
Outram, Dorinda 17n
Oxford English Dictionary 73

Paine, Thomas 93
Papua New Guinea 119-140
paraphrasis 73
participant structure 120, 128-135
pathology 72
pejoration 94, 95-96
pembangunan 103-104
pembinaan 103-104

Peña, Guillermo Gómez 94n
people (the) 150, 164-181
peoplehood 164-181
performativity 168-172
Perot, Ross 96
philology 4, 51n, 60
    comparative 14, 17
    Danish 17
    German 17, 19
philosophy 166
photograph(s) 123-124, 136, 138
phraseology 74
pidgin 69
Pinter, J. 31n, 37
political
    action 1, 4, 6
    discourse 13
polygamy 21
polygenesis 20
Powell, John 51n
power 1, 109-111
    interpersonal 7
    misrecognized 5
    state 102-117
    traditional 109-110, 112
predication 73
principal 110
print 5, 8, 9, 32, 33, 123-124, 133,
    138, 165, 167, 178-179
private (the) *See* public vs. private
projection 8
pronoun(s) 154
    first person 168, 170
property
    intellectual 49
Proposition 187 86-87, 94, 96
protolanguage 21n
proto-public 7-8
Psyche (journal) 76
public (the)
    as a category 4-5
    as a concept 9, 105, 111, 142-143
    creation of 49, 60n, 83, 89, 99, 104
    as disembodied 6

multiple 10
national 32, 105, 109
public discourse 6, 84, 86, 88, 90,
    98, 104, 105-118, 143
    as ideology 101
    impersonal 90n, 105
public knowledge 150
public opinion 83, 87, 91, 92n, 94,
    165, 166, 167
public vs. private 6, 82-101
public sphere 3, 5, 17n, 70, 71, 75,
    77, 80-81, 83-102, 104, 138, 141-
    142, 143, 165-167
    absolutist 117
    alternative 9-10, 141-163
    bourgeois 5-6, 83, 90n, 141, 165,
    166-167
    disintegration of 6, 7
public speakership 105, 110, 117
publicity 142
publicness 105, 111, 166
Pukánszky, Bela 30
Pusztay, János 35

Question-Answer sequence 129, 136
quotation 168, 169

race 14, 85-87
racism 83-102
    as ideology 86
radio broadcasting 10, 141-163
    free 141-163
Rafael, Vincente 122
Ránki, Gy. 38n
Rather, Dan 97
rationality 80, 81, 83, 87, 90n, 91
readership 32, 39, 61, 165
recontextualization 8, 32
refinement 49, 52, 56, 61, 91, 108
reflexivity 166
regionalism 91
register 61, 69-70, 73, 85, 93, 94n,
    98, 100, 153-154
Rekondo, Jakoba 141n, 148

relativism 3n
religion 175-176
reported speech 100, 124-125
representation 1-10, 37, 85, 86, 138, 167, 170, 172
   linguistic 1, 13-29
   graphic 133
   regime of 4
   textual 62
reproduction 84-85, 87n
republicanism 8, 33
resistance 122, 160
responsibility 122, 124, 126
revelation
   rhetoric of 53
revolution 144. *See also* French Revolution
Rhodes, Richard 68n
Richards, I.A. 3, 70-82
Rickford, John 2
Rizal, Jose 171
Robbins, Bruce 5, 83
Roger, Jacques-François 15-16
Rohatyn, Felix 86
role model 90
Roosevelt, Franklin 71, 78, 79
Rousseau, Jean-Jacques 166, 176-179
Royen, Gerlach 23
Royko, Mike 91
rude speech 154-155, 158
Rule, Murray 123
Rumsey, Alan 1
Rushdie, Salman 161
Russell, Bertrand 72
Russo, John 69n

Sapir, Edward 24, 56, 74
Satanic Verses, The 161
Saussure, Ferdinand de 74
Schelling 168
Schieffelin, Bambi 1, 9, 119-140, 183
Schieffelin, Edward 120
Schlegel, Friedrich 17
Schleicher, August 19, 40, 43

Schoolcraft, Henry Rowe 3, 46-68
Schott, Marge 90
Schutz, Alfred 111-112
Schwarzenegger, Arnold 95
scientific analysis 4
self-image 86
self-reference 168-169
self-reflexivity 168
Semitic (languages) 14, 17, 33
Semitism 19
Senegal 15-16
sermon(s) 120, 123
sex difference(s) 16
sexuality 3, 14, 21
sexism 85, 88-89, 92-93, 94, 147
Silverstein, Michael 1, 3, 9, 10, 46n, 49n, 69-82, 126, 170n, 183
Simony, Zsigmond 40
simultaneity 167
slang 85, 90n, 91, 98, 100, 153
social
   change 119-140, 144
   movement 144, 148
   sciences 2, 4-5, 7
   structures 120
   theory 166
socialization 120
Société des Observateurs de l'Homme 15
sociolinguistics 2, 7
   concepts in 2, 7
sociology of science 2
solidarity 85, 89, 154
Spanglish 94n
Spanish 96, 152-153, 155-157. *See also* Mock Spanish
speech
   community 1, 2, 7, 8
   event 132, 137, 168
Spitzer 157
spokesperson 110
state (the) 102-117, 141-143, 166, 176-177
   making 34

status 108, 110, 112, 114
  display 110
storytelling 53
Street, Brian 121
Stroud, Christopher 121
style 84, 88, 91-93, 130
  middling 84-85, 91, 98
  monologic 136-137
  speech 107, 108
subjectivity 8, 165, 166, 170, 173, 174-180
  objectification of 166
Sudanese (languages) 23-24
Swedenburg, Ted 159n
Swift, Jonathan 73
synonyms 73
Szarvas, Gábor 35, 40, 41
Szegedy-Maszák, Mihály 39n

tale
  concept of 57
talk radio 92
Tambiah, S. 108
taxemes 74-75n
Taylor, Charles 166
Taylor, Talbot 4, 41n
theory of '(linguistic) fictions' 73
Thompson, Stith 47
Tok Pisin 122-123, 128, 131, 133n
transgression 2
transitivity 74
translation 1, 42, 53-55, 114, 123, 164
truth 120, 122-124
truthfullness 135
Turanian (languages) 34-35, 36
Turkish 34-37

Ugric-Turkish debate 34-37, 40
United States 6, 71, 76-79, 83-102, 174-180
universality 74, 85, 86
upward mobility 37, 40, 43
Urbain, Ismail 18

Urla, Jacqueline 7, 10, 141-163, 183
Usurbiaga, Jon 146

Valentine, Lisa 59
Vámbéry, Ármin 36, 37, 40
van Dijk, Teun 84, 86
variability 1
verbal
  excess 55-56
  interaction 5
verbiage 114
Vienna Circle 72n
voice(s) 8
voicing 169-170
Volf, György 40
Volk 8, 33
Vygotsky, Lev 78n

Wallace, Mike 90
Warner, Michael 6, 8, 33, 85, 90n
Wells, H.G. 74n
whiteness 86, 99
Whitney, William Dwight 24
Whorf, Benjamin 74
Wierzbicka, Anna 81
Wilkins, John 74, 80
Willett, Thomas 126
Williams, Raymond 49n
Wittgenstein, Ludwig 71
Wolof 15-16
Wonder, Stevie 100n
Woolard, Kathryn 1-12, 32n, 46n, 99, 119n, 141n, 183

youth
  radical 142, 143

Zsigmond, Gábor 36
Zumwalt, Rosemary 47